D0502985

With

Charity

for

All

KEN STERN

With

Charity

for

All

Why Charities Are Failing and a Better Way to Give

Doubleday | *New York London Toronto Sydney Auckland*

www.doubleday.com

DOUBLEDAY and the portrayal of an anchor with a dolphin
are registered trademarks of Random House, Inc.

Book design by Michael Collica
Jacket photograph and design by Oliver Munday

Library of Congress Cataloging-in-Publication Data
Stern, Ken, [date]
With charity for all : Why charities are failing and a better way to give / by Ken Stern.—1st ed.
p. cm.
Includes bibliographical references and index.
1. Charities—United States. 2. Nonprofit organizations—United States—Evaluation.
3. Humanitarianism—United States. I. Title.
HV91.S649 2013
361.7'6320973—dc23
2012028803
ISBN 978-0-385-53471-0

MANUFACTURED IN THE UNITED STATES OF AMERICA

1 3 5 7 9 10 8 6 4 2

First Edition

For my son, Nate,
who will someday write books of his own

CONTENTS

With

Charity

for

All

INTRODUCTION

WHEN THE FRENCHMAN Pierre L'Enfant laid out his plans for the new District of Columbia in 1791, he designed Sixteenth Street to be one of the grand avenues of the new capital. Two hundred and twenty years later, his vision has been mostly realized. Sixteenth Street rises from the foot of the White House, runs north past luxury hotels, rows of embassies, the blank façade of the national headquarters of the Freemasons, through parks and the prosperous leafy neighborhoods of Washington's Gold Coast, up past Walter Reed Hospital, before reaching a tired ending among the down-market strip malls and mini-marts of Silver Spring, Maryland. At key points, it commands sweeping views not only of the White House but of the Washington Monument and the Jefferson Memorial beyond.

Living in the Mount Pleasant section of Washington, I frequent a stretch along this storied street. From my home, it's a fifteen-minute walk along Sixteenth Street to our local grocery store. Along the way, I pass some of the landmarks of the neighborhood: the All Souls Unitarian Church, the Little Flower Montessori School, the Scottish Rite Temple, a dormitory for Howard University students. In a span of about eight blocks, I pass no fewer than sixteen nonprofit organiza-

1

tions: five churches, four educational institutions, five social service organizations, one credit union, and one fraternal organization.

Most people would be hard-pressed to name sixteen charities, but in fact my little trip is not that unusual. Every day our lives are touched by the charitable sector. To the extent that we think about charities, we tend to associate them with services for the poor and the dispossessed. But the charitable sector is much more than that. It educates our young; it takes care of our old and infirm; it fields the teams that we cheer for on Saturdays and serves up spiritual sustenance on Sundays; it provides much of the intellectual and cultural nourishment for this country. The nonprofit community occupies some of the most sacred real estate in our public square and cushions some of our most important private and intimate moments. We entrust our children and our parents to it, and it is often the first and most important responder in times of crisis—whether those crises are personal in nature or global in reach.

There are approximately 1.1 million charities in this country—not local chapters, but unique, full-fledged organizations.[1] Stop and think about that number for a moment. It means tens of thousands of charities in every state, thousands in every county. And the number grows by more than fifty thousand every year, in good times and in bad. The charitable sector employs approximately thirteen million people. In addition, more than sixty-one million Americans volunteer for charities, adding about eight billion hours of effort to charitable causes—roughly the equivalent of another five million full-time employees. Charities take in over $1.5 trillion each year in revenues and have assets approaching $3 trillion.[2] Charitable activity accounts for 10 percent of the economic life of this country.[3] And this percentage is certain to grow as the challenges of our society multiply and government proves unable to respond in a meaningful way.

Almost all of us are engaged in the charitable sector in direct ways: as employees, as volunteers, as donors, or as customers and clients. And even those few not so involved are indirectly entangled as taxpayers and citizens. While considerable funding for charities comes from purely private sources, our governments—federal, state, and local—provide hundreds of billions of dollars in direct grants each year. A figure for total government support of the nonprofit sector is difficult to calculate, but most estimates put direct charitable revenues from government at roughly $500 billion a year.[4] These same governments also provide an enormous amount in indirect support by exempting charities from income and property taxes and providing deductions for charitable donations. Even in this age of multitrillion-dollar government budgets, that indirect support is significant. If we chose to eliminate or even cap just these exemptions, our public coffers would swell by tens of billions of dollars yearly—in line with the entire federal appropriation for housing and education.

The charitable sector is one of the anchors of American public life. Its vast scope makes any quick catalog of its functions incomplete, but it includes areas as diverse as education, global health services, shelter for the homeless, preservation of public and private land, athletics, arts and culture, and some of our most important scientific research. We support this broad array of services because absent a robust charitable economy, these functions would either cease or devolve to government—an unpalatable option in a time of rising public debt and dwindling faith in the efficacy of government. In effect, we have privatized these public functions in the belief that charities can perform these tasks better and with greater efficiency than government. The public—and private—investment in the social sector is one of the critical elements of the American social compact, yet it is one of the oddities of public life that each year we renew this investment without ever pausing to ask the same questions that we ask of every other public and private investment: What are we getting in return, is the investment structured correctly, is the money going to the right places? Remarkably, we don't think much about the nonprofit sector at all. Our attention to it is largely scandal-driven (think of the United Way and ACORN) and ephemeral, due to a web of factors including the cloaked nature of the public investment, the fact that the public rarely perceives the millions of disparate charitable businesses to be a unified industry, and the fact that the sector includes sacred institutions of American life such as churches and schools.

We live in a society that is obsessed with results—from businesses, from government, from sporting events. Markets are endlessly debated, scrutinized, reduced to reams of data. Governments rise and fall on issues of accountability and results. Managers are fired, players traded, teams dismantled if a squad falls short of the expectations of ownership or of fans. Yet in this results-obsessed country, the public rarely demands measures of how effective charities are in implementing their services and meeting their service goals. And, as we shall see throughout this book, when the public generally and funders more specifically do not press for results-oriented organizations—and indeed value qualities that are inversely related to effectiveness—charities respond accordingly. The implications are extensive, not just for the prudent use of resources, but for how we as a society tackle our most challenging problems and how we serve the poor, the infirm, the hungry, the homeless, and others who do not have full voice in our public life. This book's story of charitable ineffectiveness is not one of greed or incompetence—though there are chapters on that—but one of misguided incentives and failed market structures. And it begins with one of the most venerated names in American charity.

With Hurricane Katrina bearing down on New Orleans in August 2005, the American Red Cross geared up for action. For the Red Cross, born in the blood of the American Civil War and tested through countless disasters, this was its Super Bowl, the biggest challenge of the new century. Contingency plans were activated; shelters opened; tens of thousands of meals, bottles of water, and other necessary supplies pre-positioned; thousands of volunteers drafted. Relief trucks began to roll even before the storm hit. The action, coordinated from the Red Cross's emergency operations bunker in Washington, D.C., had all the hallmarks of military precision, not surprising given the Red Cross's propensity to hire retired military supply-chain experts. And the size of its effort has rarely been seen outside a military operation. In many ways, it was the largest peacetime call-up in American history, ultimately activating 250,000 employees and volunteers across a thousand miles of the southern United States.

The Red Cross's brethren at the International Committee of the Red Cross (ICRC) also sprang into action, dispatching about eighty of its best disaster-recovery experts to support this mobilization. Among them was Thomas Riess, a veteran logistician from Germany. What Riess, used to working with relatively few resources in third-world countries, found upon arriving at the Red Cross site in Mobile, Alabama, astonished him. The human resources and material aid were tremendous, but the system of quality control was in absolute tatters. Volunteers were assigned to tasks without adequate training or any attempt to match their skills to the work. Goods poured into the Mobile warehouse, but often without regard to need. Included in the supply flow were Uno card games, stale Danish pastries, buns marked "perishable" that had to be destroyed, and radios without batteries. Whatever came in was shipped out to the field, regardless of its usefulness to the relief effort. Riess reported a lack of centralized planning and communications and a lack of accountability and record keeping: goods coming into the warehouse were not registered or recorded; pilfering was common. His colleagues observed similar chaos. Mike Goodhand, head of logistics for the British Red Cross, described the American Red Cross efforts in Mississippi as "amateurish." He noted one case where a Red Cross vehicle manager admitted to him that he had no idea as to the whereabouts of his entire fleet of more than a hundred cars and trucks.

The disorganization Goodhand and Riess witnessed was replicated across the region. Shelters were under- or incorrectly supplied, goods rotted in warehouses, the wrong things went to the wrong places, cash disappeared, supplies walked away. Too many key management positions were occupied by volunteers who were ill prepared and ill equipped to handle the flood of challenges. Rental cars, generators, air mattresses, and computers disappeared. At one point, it was reported that fully half of the goods supplied to the Red Cross could not be traced to confirm that they made it to their intended destination. The Red Cross supply-chain and inventory control management systems cracked. In the end, the British Red Cross and the ICRC characterized the effort as a "dangerous combination of ignorance and arrogance."[5]

The Red Cross failures during Katrina unfortunately do not stand out in any way. Not only did these failures largely duplicate the Red Cross's shortcomings after 9/11, they mirror, on a much larger scale, the inefficiencies and ineffectiveness displayed by hundreds of other nonprofits seeking to respond to the disaster. Katrina was a gold rush for the nonprofit community; hundreds of organizations descended on the Gulf Coast, hoping to aid in the relief and rebuilding of the area and share in the billions of dollars washing through. But many of them lacked the capacity and expertise to contribute significantly to the recovery, and their uncoordinated efforts ultimately led to confusion, delay, and the thinning of finite resources. These problems were magnified by the policies of the IRS, which fast-tracked more than four hundred new Katrina-related charities in the wake of the storm, in some cases granting tax-exempt status within hours of receiving an application. Not surprisingly, the vast majority of those new charities, organized during a flood of good intentions, have since failed, disappeared, or been diverted to other purposes.

It was neither the government nor the nonprofit community that reacted most effectively to Katrina. It was the private sector. Private companies were on the ground with disaster relief efforts before the American Red Cross, FEMA, and even the U.S. military. Walmart proved especially effective during Katrina, moving tens of millions of dollars in emergency supplies into the area, creating fast-action distribution centers, and rapidly responding to local conditions and needs. Its advantages were numerous: it had the scale and staffing to quickly mobilize a two-hundred-person emergency response center that could coordinate efforts around the clock; the company had the expertise in supply-chain management to move the right goods to the right places, and it had unrivaled local knowledge from its operations in three thousand communities around the country. In many places, Walmart was the first on the ground with goods and services, and its reports from the field became critical to government responders. At the time, Sheriff Harry Lee of Jefferson Parish in suburban New Orleans said, "If [the] American government would have responded like Wal-Mart has responded, we wouldn't be in this crisis."[6] Later, reacting to both internal and external criticism, the Red Cross announced its intention to redesign its supply-chain management system, this time to be driven by the expertise of businesses like Walmart.

It's tempting to shrug off this story as unrepresentative, the product of one unlikely-to-be-rivaled event. Katrina was a flood of biblical proportions that exposed the failings of numerous institutions, both inside and outside the charitable sector. Unfortunately, the modern history of the Red Cross is marked by the same type of organizational breakdown (and post-event confession of failures) across many major disasters. Those breakdowns have not affected every part of the enterprise, however; its fund-raising ability, especially during crises, has been nothing short of spectacular. Within weeks of the 2010 Haiti earthquake, for example, the Red Cross raised more than $450 million in the United States and more than $1 billion in total across its worldwide network.

But the more difficult task for the Red Cross in Haiti has been spending. Two years after the Haiti earthquake, the Red Cross was still sitting on more than $150 million in unspent and unallocated donations, a surprisingly large amount given the acuteness of Haiti's needs and the fact that most of the distributed funds went to intermediate organizations such as the United Nations, Habitat for Humanity, and the International Organization for Migration.[7]

On the surface, it is hard to figure out why the Red Cross fails so consistently. It is among the most storied and best resourced charities in this country. The organization's staff is handpicked from the top levels of business, government, and the military, and though slow-footed and devoutly bureaucratic, it has avoided many of the pitfalls and scandals that have tripped up other charities. Rather, the roots of the Red Cross's failures during Katrina and other crises lie in its inability—a failing shared by virtually all charities—to make the necessary internal investments that are the hallmark of all good organizations, be they for-profit businesses, charities, or government agencies.

This inability was clearly illustrated in the days after 9/11.[8] As in Katrina, the Red Cross during 9/11 proved unable to respond quickly and effectively. Resources were not adequately deployed, and blood and relief supplies were not moved quickly enough from place to place. In an acute embarrassment to the organization, the Red Cross proved unable to support the Pentagon victims, even though the scene of the attack was only about two miles from Red Cross head-quarters and its emergency response center. Bernadine Healy, then president of the Red Cross, was aghast to find on September 12 that no volunteers or supplies had gone to the Pentagon—no specialized teams, no emergency response vehicles, not even cots or food for the firefighters. Yet despite the organizational limitations of the Red Cross, as during Katrina, money poured in via the Liberty Fund, set up by the Red Cross to aid the victims. All in all, more than $543 million was donated to the fund, a remarkable outpouring of support by the American public and an amount that quickly far outstripped what the Red Cross could reasonably spend on the relief needs of what was ultimately a finite pool of victims of the attack. Recognizing that the Red Cross's failures during 9/11 reflected poor infrastructure, inadequate telecommunications, and insufficient supply-chain management, Healy made the understandable judgment to help the next victims by using excess funds from the Liberty Fund to build the capacity of the Red Cross to respond to large-scale disasters, and to increase the available blood supply from its then-depleted levels—so that in a future crisis, the Red Cross would not duplicate its failings.

When that decision became public, however, a huge outcry ensued, with many in the public, the media, and Congress insisting that all the Liberty Fund money had to be spent on the 9/11 victims, regardless of the actual need. At the inevitable public hearing, members of Congress shouted down Healy when she tried to explain the decision, and within days she resigned amid speculation about possible fraud prosecutions. The point was not lost on her successors, who hastily reversed course, announcing that Liberty Fund dollars would be spent only on victims of 9/11 and appointing the former senator George Mitchell to oversee the process and calm the waters.

The widespread fury was both predictable and misguided. Healy's goal of investing in infrastructure in order to avoid a repeat of the 9/11 failures was entirely understandable, but the dismay over the spending plans reflects a bedrock and simplistic assumption that has long shackled the charitable world: that money spent on direct services is the only worthy use of charitable funds, while money invested in organizational effectiveness is to be kept as close to zero as possible. It is an equation widely accepted by the donating public, by the press, by charity watchdogs, by government regulators, and by most charities themselves. To keep overhead costs down, charities forgo necessary investments with devastating and sometimes deadly results. When Katrina came four years after the 9/11 hearings, the results were entirely predictable: telecommunications failed, inventory and supply-chain management fell apart, the same antiquated systems bent and broke under the stress of the crisis. Equally predictably, many of the same pundits and members of Congress who decried the liberation of the Liberty Fund excoriated the Red Cross for its Katrina failings, never acknowledging or perhaps even recognizing that the failure to invest in 2001 had direct implications for the breakdowns in 2005.

The overhead imperative is so deeply ingrained in the charitable world that it is hardly ever questioned, even though the causal link between overhead spending and organizational effectiveness is probably the inverse of what most people assume. Organizations that invest effectively and fully in infrastructure, technology, training, strategic planning, building new programs and initiatives that mature over time, research, and self-evaluation will almost certainly bring the most value to their communities of interest. Yet the demands of the donating public ensure that the number of such organizations is kept to a minimum. When even the highest-revenue charity in the country is bound together by rubber bands and duct tape, it is a sign of profound misunderstanding of how to build effective charities.

The struggles at the Red Cross are representative of, yet probably understate, the challenges within the charitable sector as a whole. Compared with virtually every other American charity, the Red Cross is well resourced, strategically focused, and outcome oriented. Most American charities, by contrast, struggle with lack of resources, muddled strategies, operational challenges, and lack of clarity around impact; even the most doe-eyed defender of charitable institutions would hesitate to dispute these facts. But it is only now becoming clear how much charities are being weighed down by market forces—of which the low-overhead imperative is just one—and how few can demonstrate measurable success.

The difficulty of identifying effective charities is well captured in the creation story of a New York–based charity evaluation organization called GiveWell. In the summer of 2006, eight friends working in the financial services industry decided to pool their efforts and make a common commitment for their end-of-year charitable giving. All of them were single, in their twenties, and doing very well financially for having relatively little professional experience. They worked for a publicity-shy hedge fund called Bridgewater Associates, a company little known outside the clubby financial world but one of astonishing reach and wealth. Bridgewater, now reputed to be the world's largest hedge fund, manages about $160 billion in assets—a number roughly equivalent to the combined gross domestic product of Kuwait and Bulgaria. The group of friends, informally headed by two recent Ivy League graduates, Elie Hassenfeld and Holden Karnofsky, agreed to research and share information on different charities. Given the mind-numbing number of charities, they decided to focus on one industry per person (Karnofsky chose New York educational charities; Hassenfeld picked water charities in Africa) and limit themselves to charities awarded three or four stars by Charity Navigator, a reputable rating agency. They thought it would be easy; this was, after all, what they did every day for a living—research, analyze, and recommend the best investment opportunities.

Throughout the late summer and fall, the group met regularly in a conference room at Bridgewater to discuss their findings; in between sessions they searched the Web for data and called and asked for information from a vast number of charities. They discovered that the Charity Navigator rankings were unhelpful, as they were based largely on ratios of overhead to programmatic spending that they quickly realized had no correlation to organizational effectiveness and impact. They also found out that even if they wanted to rely on these ratings, it was unwise to do so because Charity Navigator depended on self-reports from the charities, which could easily, and frequently did, game the ratings. They read annual reports and IRS filings. They were mailed glossy brochures full of vivid pictures and stirring anecdotes. UNICEF even sent an oral rehydration package as proof of its good work—along with a donor card. None of the materials, from dozens of organizations, hinted at what they were trying to find out: Do the charitable programs effectively solve the targeted social problems? Their frustration wasn't for lack of trying, on the part of either the Bridgewater 8 or the staff of some of the charities they contacted. When pressed for more information from the Bridgewater group, the charities often furnished their own confidential internal reports and data—the inadequacy of which led the group at Bridgewater to understand that the charities themselves did not know whether they were helping or hurting a given situation. In a small number of cases their inquiries were met with hostility tinged with paranoia. As part of his inquiry, for instance, Karnofsky contacted Smile Train, a prominent charity that sponsors cleft palate surgery for third-world children. He was looking for basic information on effectiveness: In what parts of the world was Smile Train operating? How many of the Smile Train children come from financially disadvantaged families? Was Smile Train able to track the children after surgery to assess the impact of the operation? Smile Train staff refused to provide any of the answers, eventually telling Karnofsky that he would have to pursue the questions directly with the organization's president. Eventually, he received a call from the Smile Train CEO, who told him that no donors had ever sought this information before and openly accused him of spying for Operation Smile, a rival medical charity. Needless to say, Karnofsky never received any of the requested information. After six months of inquiry, the Bridgewater group found itself no closer to identifying effective charities than when they had started. In the end, they threw up their hands and made the best guess possible with their year-end charitable gifts, an unfulfilling outcome perhaps but one that closely tracks the thought process behind billions of dollars in giving each year.

The exercise, frustrating as it may have been, was a revelation to the Bridgewater group; they concluded that there had to be a better way of evaluating charities and helping donors find effective outlets for their contributions. In the summer of 2007, Karnofsky and Hassenfeld left Bridgewater to set up GiveWell, an organization dedicated to identifying demonstrably effective charities where donor money could be put to good use. Their approach was based upon the methodologies they had learned at Bridgewater: in-depth, research-driven evaluations supported by facts and data, not formulas and marketing brochures. By its nature, it is slow and handcrafted work that cannot be mass-produced, certainly not by a team that originally comprised only two people. Hassenfeld and Karnofsky determined to focus their work on a few charitable segments where they figured there would be reliable data (HIV, malaria prevention, water, and education, to name a few) and only on top-tier charities willing to provide access to relevant data.

Over the past five years, GiveWell, by now expanded to seven employees, has produced over five hundred investment grade reports, both on entire charitable sectors and on individual charities. After all this work, it has identified only eight organizations that can fully demonstrate material and effective impact and efficiently use additional funds. This is not to say that each one of the other 98.5 percent of charities is a failed organization, but it is to say that none of these charities can concretely demonstrate that they can effectively deliver promised results. In 2009, the GiveWell group decided to rate only charities that met a minimal standard of transparency—that the charity published on its Web site some meaningful self-evaluation. There was no requirement that the self-evaluation be positive, simply that the charity offer some proof of its commitment to making results publicly accessible. Only fifteen out of more than four hundred charities reviewed passed over this low bar—even though the organizations they targeted for review were culled from lists of the most respected and prominent charities in America. When Hassenfeld and Karnofsky dug deeper, they met resistance from startling quarters. Many nationally prominent charities simply refused to share relevant data with them. The Harlem Children's Zone and the Carter Center—organizations with outsized reputations for being effective, businesslike, and data-driven—both stonewalled the GiveWell team. Heifer International and the Millennium Villages Project required confidentiality and then still provided no pervasive research. This projects a deeply unsettling image of many of the stars of the charitable world—Geoffrey Canada (Harlem Children's Zone), Jimmy Carter (Habitat for Humanity), and Jeffrey Sachs (Millennium Villages Project)—as unable or unwilling to show whether their organizations are effective. It is hard to know what is worse, that Karnofsky and Hassenfeld can only find a handful of highly effective charities after years of intensive effort or that the organizations that failed their test are among the best that the charitable world has to offer.

The GiveWell staffers are not muckrakers. It is not their purpose to expose the failed, the muddled, the hopelessly un-strategic; rather, it is their goal to drive donations to the most measurably effective charities and create incentives for other charities to adopt similar standards of evaluation. In this, they have a long way to go. As we shall see, the market incentives of the nonprofit world push charities toward happy anecdote and inspiring narrative rather than toward careful planning, research, and evidence-based investments, to crippling effect.

I experienced some of these skewed incentives in my own work in the charitable sector. I joined National Public Radio (NPR) as chief operating officer in 1999 and became its chief executive officer in 2006. During my nine years running the company, NPR more than doubled its audience, despite the general national decline in radio listening, and more than tripled its revenues. We launched numerous successful digital initiatives, ranging from NPR's satellite radio channels to the award-winning NPR Music site. From the outside and by all reasonable measures, NPR was a high-performing organization, one doing almost uniquely well in a difficult media environment. On the inside, however, I found myself endlessly embroiled in diplomatic logjams with the NPR board and the public radio stations that controlled the board.

Public radio was in the midst of a media revolution, a transformation almost as profound as that brought on by the printing press. I knew that NPR needed to change just to survive. I wanted to see results demonstrating how NPR was reshaping itself to be more competitive in the digital age, results that were not merely anecdotal but specific and measurable: the reach of NPR to tens of millions of people, the growth of online and digital services, the impact of new programming to reach more diverse audiences, the financial health of the organization. We implemented a strategy to broaden NPR's reach beyond radio to the Internet, mobile phones, satellite radio—to meet and serve the audience wherever it was going to be—and to expand the historic definition of NPR's audience by creating new programming for younger audiences and audiences of color. In many ways, this clashed with the historic view held by many public radio stations that NPR should be an organization that served public radio stations first, with other activities viewed as either irrelevant or threatening. The NPR board was sympathetic to that view. The board was made up of donors and public broadcasting system politicians—station managers elected by their peers. They were not indifferent to measures of the organization's health, but they valued system peace over anything else. The results didn't matter as much for them.

This book is not my story. This is a story about how the charitable sector has lost its way. The NPR board, as it turns out, was far more in tune with the culture of the nonprofit world than I was. As a country, we direct enormous resources to and place substantial social responsibilities on the charitable sector, yet the vast majority of nonprofits can't demonstrate any commensurate return on this investment. The glossy fund-raising brochures, the moving videos, and the carefully crafted inspirational anecdotes often mask problems that range from inefficiency and ineffectiveness to outright fraud and waste. There is little credible evidence that many charitable organizations produce lasting social value. Study after study tells the opposite story: of organizations that fail to achieve meaningful impact yet press on with their strategies and services despite significant, at times overwhelming, evidence that they don't work. These failures are often well known within the nonprofit community but are not more generally discussed because the studies either are buried or tend to be so organization- and issue-specific that broader sector-wide conclusions are easy to avoid.

It's no joy to write these words, no fun to suggest that hundreds of thousands of people may be toiling in vain, but it is critical to ask how this can be, how the well-intentioned efforts of so many can result in so little concrete progress toward common social goals. The answer starts with the absence of market mechanisms that reward good work and punish failure. Those mechanisms are missing because the funders, the true customers of charitable organizations, are generally indifferent to results, for a number of reasons we shall explore. And even when donors do care, there is little available to guide them in their funding decisions. Few charities even try to measure their results in a meaningful way, and neither government regulators nor online charity monitors provide useful alternatives.

This could have been a bleak book. My early research was not promising. I found story after story of organizational and service failure, of charities that refused to evaluate their programs or, worse, swept unfavorable results under the rug. But over time, another story began to emerge, of a nascent movement to rethink how the charitable sector works, to build market mechanisms to reward effective charities and discourage the ineffective ones, and to create tools that will allow people to turn themselves from donors to investors. It is a small movement, operating in the millions at the edges of a trillion-dollar industry, but it's a sign of what the charitable sector can become. This book begins with the story of charitable failure, a narrative of systematic shortcomings, but it ends with a glimpse of those who are beginning to reshape the charitable world and show us what it can be.

ONE

Big Promises, Small Outcomes

Ineffectiveness in the Charitable Sector

B y casual measures, Ryan Hreljac is like any other twenty-one-year-old Canadian. He loves hockey and virtually any sport that requires a ball, stick, or some form of legalized contact, is obsessed with video games, and enjoys *The Simpsons* perhaps a bit too much. If you observed him in the classrooms of the University of King's College in Halifax, or saw him on the streets of his hometown of Kemptville, Ontario, he would probably escape your notice, with the possible exception of his six-foot, six-inch frame, which has made him a passable basketball player, at least by Canadian standards.

But Ryan is no ordinary young man, a fact that began to emerge when he was just six. At an age when sharing Thomas trains with a sibling might be considered a surpassing act of social virtue, Ryan launched a personal crusade to provide safe drinking water to communities around the world. It was all triggered by his first-grade teacher, Mrs. Prest, who told her impressionable charges about the needs of poor people in Africa and how little it would take to help: a penny for a pencil, a dollar for a day's supply of food for an entire family, and $70 to build a safe water supply for a school or small village.

That evening, as he tells it, Ryan lobbied his parents to let him do odd jobs around the house so he might raise the money necessary to build a well. Perhaps the Hreljacs doubted the effectiveness of a six-year-old's housekeeping efforts, because it took a few days of incessant pleading before they agreed to the proposition. But once empowered, Ryan washed windows and vacuumed his way to his goal, reaching $70 after what must have seemed an eternity to a six-year-old but was only four months in adult time. His mother proudly took him to the offices of WaterCan, a charity that builds wells in third-world countries, to present the money, but they were in for a rude surprise. Mrs. Prest, as it turned out, had things wrong. A no doubt mortified WaterCan executive had to tell young Ryan that $70 would only pay for a hand pump, not the well itself. He was short about $1,930 of the $2,000 that it would take to finance a new well in Africa.

By all rights, that should have been that; at his prior earnings rate of about $17.50 a month, it would take Ryan ten years (roughly a lifetime and a half from his perspective) to raise the entire sum. But the unwelcome news did not daunt Ryan. He took on new chores and unknowingly began to act as a nonprofit executive, waging a vigorous fund-raising campaign among friends, family, and neighbors and leveraging the Canadian government's standing offer of matching funds. It took months of effort, but Ryan, through astonishing focus and hard work and no doubt more than a little bit of youthful charm, collected the necessary funds. In January 1999, after Ryan had turned seven, the Canadian Physicians for Aid and Relief drilled his well, fittingly enough, next to a primary school in northern Uganda.

Ryan did not stop there. He continued to raise money for safe water, and in 2001, at the advanced age of ten, he formalized his efforts into a charity called Ryan's Well Foundation. Since then, Ryan's Well has raised over $2 million and funded over 630 water projects in sixteen countries on three continents. By its own calculations, the charity has brought safe water and sanitation services to more than 700,000 people. Even as he progressed through school, Ryan became a public ambassador for the cause of improved sanitation and safe drinking water, traveling extensively not only in furtherance of specific projects but also to educate the public on the critical and urgent need for safe water supplies.

When Mrs. Prest lectured her young charges about the need to improve drinking water supplies in Africa, she hit upon perhaps the world's biggest and most persistent public health challenge. Almost 900 million people worldwide lack access to safe drinking water, and even supposedly safe sources are often subject to contamination and supply degradation. Two and a half billion people lack access to basic sanitation for the adequate disposal of human waste. Over two million tons of untreated refuse—an unthinkable tidal wave amounting to four billion pounds of garbage, sewage, and industrial and human waste—are dumped *every day* into water supplies around the globe. The consequences of contaminated water are painful and wide-ranging. Waterborne illnesses include cholera, typhoid, guinea worms, hepatitis, and diarrhea. Children in the third world, it is estimated, have on average about a thousand parasites in their bodies. The health tolls of this parasitic invasion are staggering. Roughly speaking, more than four million cases of serious diarrhea are reported each year, leading to about two million deaths—virtually all of them among children—surpassing even war as the principal cause of man-made and preventable death.[1] Somewhere in the third world, four children have died from diarrhea in the minute or so it has taken to read this paragraph.

It is a little surprising that the world's water supply is so precarious. The problem is not know-how—the Romans maintained a usable public water supply two thousand years ago[2]—nor is it a lack of understanding of the consequences of adulterated water, though our understanding of that is of far more recent vintage. In the first half of the nineteenth century, the prevailing view in educated circles was that miasma—impure air caused by open sewage, decomposing vegetation, and rotting corpses—was the source of cholera and other terrible diseases that from time to time decapitated the growing urban centers of Europe. It was a compelling theory, given the observed patterns of outbreaks and the vast amounts of noxious and polluted air roiling these cities, but it had the misfortune of being flat wrong. To be fair to the scientific classes of modern Europe, the best minds of science were not terribly occupied with the issue, since cholera, while clearly horrible, was understood to be a poor man's disease. The indifference of the medical class changed quickly when the great 1832 London epidemic made clear that cholera was actually nondiscriminatory, felling the upper classes, the medical community, and the working classes with an indifferent equality. In response, the public health authorities in London began a relentless campaign to mitigate foul air. Still, virulent outbreaks plagued major Western population centers through much of the nineteenth century. In one particularly nasty pocket epidemic in 1854 in Soho, more than five hundred people died over ten days in one small neighborhood, making it one of the worst occurrences of sudden mortality in recorded history.

The miasma theory led to numerous false starts in the fight against cholera, but ironically it did produce the greatest public works project of the nineteenth century, a project that ultimately revolutionized public health in England and around the world. In the summer of 1858, London suffered a searing heat wave: temperatures crawled into the nineties and refused to leave. The heat was accompanied by a relentless drought, and waste, typically washed away by the rain, piled up across the city. The Thames became so foul and noxious that people could not bear to be near it. "The Great Stink," as it became known, made London virtually uninhabitable, and Parliament fled the city. Within weeks, the city fathers declared their intention to completely rebuild the London sewage system, which had been designed to drain off rainwater, not to handle vast amounts of solid waste. The rebuilding of the sewage system was a feat of civil engineering on an extraordinary scale. Under a relentlessly busy metropolis, the City of London set out to build twelve hundred miles of tunnels to carry off every bit of waste for more than three million people. The system had to accommodate expected developments such as population growth, urban sprawl, and expansion of the London Underground and be sufficiently capacious to accommodate what the former secretary of defense Donald Rumsfeld would one day refer to as the "known unknowns"—the knowledge that there inevitably will be unknown future developments, which in this case turned out to be gas and electrical lines that would power one of the most important and vibrant cities in the world. All this had to be accomplished on the modest budget of £3 million. The project required 318 million bricks and necessitated the redistribution of more than 3.5 million cubic yards of earth. It was a spectacular success. The sewage works built during the 1860s still drain the city more than a century and a half later. And when the German doctor Robert Koch discovered the cholera microbe in 1883 and revealed that it inhabited water supplies, London was already enviably positioned to ensure clean water supplies to its population.[3] In the wake of Koch's discoveries, most of the great developed cities invested significantly in sewage disposal and clean water facilities. By the twentieth century, contaminant-free water was increasingly an expectation of modern life.

Unfortunately, for much of the world, where running water and sewage systems are not available, this expectation is increasingly an illusory one. The press of human demand, the depletion of natural aquifers, and unregulated dumping of industrial and agricultural waste will only get worse as the earth's population grows from six billion to nine billion over the next fifty years. As if the health effects were not crippling enough, the problems of inadequate water and sanitation have repercussions in other areas, such as education, women's rights, and the environment. Each day, millions of people, almost always women and children, undertake the laborious and sometimes dangerous task of fetching water from distant sites in forty-pound jerricans. The time-consuming task of retrieving and boiling water effectively shackles the bearers to the water cans, meaning that opportunities for education, work, or advancement are narrowed or sacrificed.

The charitable community has energetically responded to this water crisis. Dozens and dozens of charities have been launched to provide safe drinking water in crisis zones. Not just Ryan's Well, but

Water for People, Water Missions International, WaterAid, Lifewater International, Living Water International, Water.org, and WaterCan. The list stretches on, a trademark lawyer's joy but a marketer's despair. All these charities have been organized around the simple plan of drilling new wells in population centers and giving communities, often for the first time, direct and immediate access to clean drinking water.

In part, the explosion in water charities reflects the urgency of a genuine public health crisis. But the charitable sector is also reacting to the seeming simplicity of the solution. The technology has long existed to provide water even in the world's most challenged communities. With a little bit of elbow grease, a modest amount of money, and perhaps just a little sacrifice, it seems as if the problem can be quickly solved. As described by the Advent Conspiracy (an international effort to reframe Christmas from getting to giving) and repeated endlessly around the Web: "[Ten dollars] will give a child clean water for life. That's not an estimate. It's a fact. And here's another fact. Solving this problem once and for all will cost about $10 billion. Not bad considering Americans spent $450 billion on Christmas last year."[4] Or put in very immediate terms, as the charities sometimes do, the cost of once and forever solving a problem that fells two million children each year is equivalent to three weeks' worth of American war spending in Iraq and Afghanistan.[5]

As a result of these promises, hundreds of millions, maybe even billions, of dollars have been poured into the fight for clean water, and many of the players claim victories, big and small. Even the smallest charities claim to have solved water problems for huge swaths of Africa, Asia, and Central America. Lifewater brags of bringing clean water to 2 million people, WaterAid has solved the problem for more than 7.5 million, and Water.org contents itself with the notion of sustaining "millions" of people with clean water. When these efforts are taken together, along with those of much larger governmental groups, the picture of an effective international movement begins to emerge. Add up the claims and the global community should be well on the way to meeting the UN goal of reducing the at-risk population by half by 2015.

Indeed, the stories of success offered by these charities can be deeply moving. Water Missions International, a Christian-inspired water and sanitation engineering charity operating in about nine third-world countries, tells this story about one of its projects:

> A community in Kenya called Wachakaheri "Tangi Nyeusi" meaning Black tank serves the marginalized Samburu and Turkana tribes. The site had an old diesel pump that had not been functioning for over seven years. Community members used to walk for 8km to fetch water that was unsafe. 410 Bridge [a U.S.-based Christian charity that works extensively in Kenya] funded the installation of a solar power system and renovation of the Tank.
>
> When WMI team arrived, the area looked deserted and we could hardly believe that a population of 4,000 people lived in this area. Some community members were just gazing and mocking us for wasting our time on an unfeasible project. On the fifth day, when we hooked on the solar powered system and water started flowing, the man who had been watching us was overwhelmed. With joy and disbelief, he climbed on top of the black tank and started shouting at the top of his voice. Within no time we saw a stream of women and children flocking in with containers, the 4,000 population became a reality! We could not believe the number of people. After fetching water, they took us to their huts commonly known as "Manyatta" and it was a joy to fellowship with them, now a church stands on that site.[6]

It's a compelling image: a man standing on top of the tank exulting at the arrival of freshwater in his village for the first time in the better part of a decade; the community streaming forth to share in his joy and a moment that promises to transform their lives in innumerable ways, big and small. It would take an iron heart to see that and not feel hope for the future of that community.

It is hard, however, to reconcile that picture with a global water situation that is not improving but in fact rapidly worsening. Some of that is due to factors outside the control of any charity: population explosion, rapid urbanization, governmental inefficiency, and corruption, to name just a few. But beyond the global trends, the data show that the particular efforts of the nonprofit community have largely failed, despite the claims to the contrary. Studies of most public water programs—whether a standpost project, a borehole project, or a public well project—show little or no impact on public health.[7] Despite the compelling story lines, the water charity community, in the aggregate, has been singularly ineffective in relieving the problems of waterborne diseases.

The difficult truth is that while the charities promote stories of villagers celebrating a gushing well tapped minutes before, the "real image," writes Edward Breslin, the CEO of Water for People, "should be the one that plays itself out every day all over the world of the woman walking slowly past a broken handpump, bucket at her side or on her head, on her way to (or from) that scoop hole or dirty puddle that she once hoped would never again be part of her life."[8] Drilling a clean well is far easier than maintaining one. Infrastructure maintenance has typically lagged in third-world countries, particularly in rural areas. The World Bank has estimated that about one-third of all water infrastructure projects in South Asia have been abandoned due to lack of maintenance.[9] Many water charities propose a community-based maintenance model, but fully 50 percent of the boreholes dug in eastern Africa and maintained in this model have fallen into disrepair. Drilling the hole is simply a first step in a process that requires training, tools, parts, and the supply lines to support them. The water charities lack the resources, the expertise, and indeed the intention to deal with what is actually a complex, long-term problem.

What's more, drinking water is one source of infectious microbes but by no means the primary source. Fecal matter and other pollutants can congregate not just in water but in food, on hands, and in fields. Sanitation, food quality, and hygiene are all important variables in the public health fight. Indeed, water is less important in this equation as a drinking source than as a cleansing agent, permitting cleaning of hands, clothes, and food supplies. The evidence is substantial that bringing a water source into the home improves public health because it allows for frequent cleaning of children's hands. Providing a public water point does not.[10] Even a new, more accessible public water point does not lead to greater use of water, more frequent washing, or better hygiene habits. Thus, a supply of clean water by itself does not solve the public health challenge.

This uncomfortable story of the failure of water drilling in the long and short terms is not found in the glossy literature or on the Web sites of the water organizations. Indeed, the entire business model of these charities is built around ignoring these problems. Money is usually raised for the drilling of wells, not for the more expensive and far less glamorous task of monitoring and infrastructure maintenance, or for the more complicated public health challenges that persist even when a public water point is available. It's relatively easy to engage people with stories of children delighting in the first burst of water from a new well; it's far harder to get donors excited when the primary visual is of a sanitary engineer checking or rethreading a pump long in operation. When Ryan Hreljac presented his hard-earned $2,000 to WaterCan in 1999, he brought every dollar necessary to dig that well in Uganda and not a single penny to ensure that the pump remained in operation over time. The heartwarming story from Water Missions International obscures but does not completely hide the fact that a well was already in place, a well that had sat idle for seven years. The evidence of the maintenance crisis—tens of thousands of abandoned wells across the developing world—is well known within the development community but largely unreported to the general public. The real story is displaced by one of exaggerated victory—all to ensure the flow of contributions for the underserved and needy, even when those contributions don't provide meaningful long-term help to them.

Much of the charitable industry is driven by just such marketing requirements, by the need to tell affecting stories rather than prove real, long-term results. Charities, like every other business, respond to market forces, which in their case means focusing on what generates donations. In a revealing article in the December 2009 issue of *Outside* magazine, Nicholas Kristof, the crusading columnist for *The New York Times,* argued that the charitable sector needs to be more aggressive in promoting stories like Ryan's vignette. Forget "logical arguments," forget descriptions of large-scale needs, forget careful impact studies, he wrote; what generates contributions, the bread and butter of charities, are stories of individual empowerment, of individual hope, and the promise that the donors can make a difference in someone's life.[11] Kristof is almost certainly right about what drives donor dollars, as we will explore later in the book, but his argument neglects the negative effect that this has on program development. When the WaterAid America site promises that $25 is enough to provide one person with "water, sanitation and hygiene programs," it signals that it will be putting all of its efforts into drilling holes, not creating long-term, provable, and measurable solutions to the water crisis. Twenty-five dollars will not do that.

Surprisingly, the most pointed critique of the water charity industry has come from within its own leadership. In 2010, Breslin, the CEO of Water for People quoted above, posted on his Web site a lengthy and detailed report accusing the water charity industry of everything from ineffectiveness to outright fraud. In his open letter, Breslin argued that the resources exist to solve the clean water and sanitation crisis, but that water charities have largely failed to make a dent because their resources have been focused on drilling new holes, not on ensuring the long-term effectiveness of existing investments. "The images that dominate the sector—pictures of children happily gulping water from a new tap or the counter-image of women collecting water from dirty puddles—do not tell the whole story . . . Africa,

Asia and Latin America have become wastelands for broken water and sanitation infrastructure. Go to schools throughout the developing countries and you will often find a broken handpump around the corner, or a disused latrine that filled years ago. Sector agencies intuitively know this but the general public is shielded from these hard truths as perceptions of failure could threaten 'the cause' of reaching the underserved."[12] The water crisis, according to Breslin, is one not of inadequate resources but of misallocation of resources, lack of accountability, and a perverse incentive system that obscures the real results in the name of keeping the tap open—not the water tap, but the dollar flows from donors.[13] In one case in Malawi involving Water for People, he notes that "reports have been exaggerated to keep funds flowing, with claims of diarrheal reduction that are absolutely unsubstantiated but remain unquestioned by financial donors." Breslin's world is haunted with misleading marketing, failing projects, and buried results.

PlayPumps International is one such failed project. PlayPumps are essentially merry-go-round water pumps, powered by the joy of children. As the children play on the merry-go-round, pumps connected to the apparatus drive water up into a large storage tank, the sides of which are covered with a combination of paid advertising and public service announcements. The concept thus kneads together several enticing ingredients: the provision of a clean and easily accessible water supply, the building of community playgrounds for children, prominent messaging on matters of public importance, and a business model cleverly built on local advertising. It's a charity marketer's dream. The concept was first described in 1990 but did not become fashionable for almost a decade. But once it did, it went through the roof. First Lady Laura Bush announced a major grant for PlayPumps at the Clinton Global Initiative in 2006, and contributions and awards flowed to the PlayPumps company from the U.S. government and the Case Foundation, among others, as part of a plan to install four thousand PlayPumps in Africa by 2010. It is hard to exaggerate the significance of this type of platform for a small organization like PlayPumps. The Clinton Global Initiative is a huge stage, and having the First Lady trumpet the promise of this technology to boot is like winning a Grammy and an Oscar on the same night. Thousands of the devices were installed across Africa within a few years, often replacing perfectly adequate hand pumps, before a young engineer from Engineers Without Borders Canada pointed out in a series of embarrassing blog posts that the emperor had no clothes:[14] the pumps were expensive, broke frequently, and could not be repaired at the local level; the business model never worked, because there was no advertising economy in rural villages; and, worst of all, kids did not use the merry-go-rounds very often, apparently favoring soccer and other more locally familiar activities. Lacking kid power, the pumps could only be powered by local women laboriously pushing the heavy wheel around and around. Rather than creating an effective mash-up of water supply and play, the PlayPumps displaced functioning water sources with a cumbersome, difficult to use, and hard to maintain albatross. The blog posts stopped the program in its tracks, and the Case Foundation issued a mea culpa report,[15] but not before thousands of PlayPumps had been installed across sub-Saharan Africa at the cost of tens of millions of dollars and much social disruption. All of this could have been easily averted by research and field testing, an approach that is all too rare in the charitable world.

Edward Breslin's analysis and the PlayPumps debacle should have been a wake-up call for the charity water industry, but they seem to have achieved little other than perhaps making Breslin a lonely figure at industry conferences. There have been no serious debates, no outcry from donors, no observable change in business practices or programmatic approaches from the industry. Breslin's message does not resonate, because all the marketplace signals go the other way. Positive reinforcement comes to these organizations from all directions. For example, virtually every charity referenced in this section is a four-star charity, the highest rating offered by Charity Navigator, the most widely followed of the charity watchdog organizations.

These ratings reflect traditional measures such as administrative ratios and compensation policies, neither of which bear any demonstrable relationship to actual impact on target populations, and yet they are widely accepted as the most valuable independent standards of charitable success. Positive market signals also come from donors who by and large are not that different from the six-year-old Ryan Hreljac; they are drawn to the exuberant image of water flowing for the first time, not to the less captivating, though no less important, picture of tightening bolts, oiling joints, and replacing corroded parts. With these unchanging incentives, it is natural that the charities continue to focus on drilling holes. All institutions are creatures of economic forces, and the incentives for water charities, and indeed for the entire charitable sector, encourage easy wins, short-term solutions, and, unfortunately, minimal or indeterminate impact.

Ryan Hreljac is a metaphor for charitable success—and charitable failure. Inspired and inspiring, he has dedicated his still young life to one of the most important issues of our time, a global public health crisis that also has implications for gender equality, economic opportunity, and social justice. The world needs more Ryan Hreljacs, but it also needs organizations that rigorously pursue effective solutions to problems. The difficulty of generating scalable solutions to a problem of enormous complexity can frustrate the best of intentions, and it would be both unfair and cynical to say that Ryan's lifelong efforts have been for naught. Cynicism is better left for our next story of charitable failure.

Big-city police chiefs, for all their power and resources, are largely an anonymous breed, trotted out from time to time to decry the latest urban mayhem and declare the intent of the police to bring perpetrators to swift justice. They tend to be bureaucrats, skilled in city politics, reassuringly bland before the cameras. Not Daryl Gates. For fourteen years as chief of the Los Angeles police, Gates cultivated an image as a hard-charging, straight-shooting leader whose skills were honed as a beat cop rather than as a city hall politician. He was a relentless innovator. He fathered the SWAT (special weapons and tactics) program to handle particularly volatile and dangerous armed confrontations and developed a model citywide communications system that substantially reduced police response time.[16] And he authored an aggressive, military style of policing to combat a rising level of gang and drug violence. His torturously named CRASH (Community Resources Against Street Hoodlums) units hammered gangs with intensive door-to-door sweeps, and his penchant for dramatic tactics was captured in the use of armored assault vehicles tipped with steel battering rams. President George H. W. Bush called him "an all-American hero."

But his aggressive approach courted controversy, which plagued the LAPD throughout his tenure. His CRASH teams—later immortalized in the movie *Colors,* starring Sean Penn and Robert Duvall, and in the federal courts by the Rampart Division scandal—were both successful in taking numerous gang members off the streets and notorious due to widespread complaints of false arrests and excessive use of force and for creating general hostility between the then mostly white LAPD officers and their largely black and Latino targets. The tense and deteriorating relationship between Gates and the black community reached a low point with the Rodney King incident in 1991, when a high-speed police chase ended in a vicious facedown beating that left King with a broken cheekbone, eleven broken bones at the base of the skull, and a broken leg. The level of hostility between the black community and Gates personally was captured by two very different public personalities: Ice Cube, who rapped, "Don't let me catch Daryl Gates in traffic / I gotta have it to peel his cap backwards"; and the former secretary of state Warren Christopher, whose investigative commission in 1991 blamed the excessive force used by the LAPD on a lack of top leadership and management controls.

Gates, while universally described as courtly and pleasant in person, also had a penchant for incendiary rhetoric. After his officers were criticized for using a carotid choke hold that caused injury and sometimes death, Gates commented, "We may be finding in some blacks [that] when it is applied, the veins or arteries do not open up as fast as . . . on normal people." In 1990, Gates told a Senate Judiciary Committee hearing that "casual drug users ought to be taken out and shot."[17] His views on drug issues were colored by both personal and professional experiences. Gates's rise to the top of the LAPD more or less coincided with the intensification of the nationwide war on drugs, and he was an implacable, take-no-prisoners warrior in the fight; some of his most vitriolic rhetoric and most violent police operations occurred in this context. The fact that Gates's son struggled for years with drug addiction served as a sad, painful backdrop to his professional life.

Ironically, it was in the war on drugs—the arena where he earned his reputation as a tough, grinding battlefield commander—that Gates devised his most durable, perhaps his most important, and certainly his most community-oriented and pacific strategy. In 1983, in partnership with the Rotary Club of Los Angeles, he took the fight against illegal drugs to a new, unexpected front, the elementary school classroom. His weapon, a new nonprofit called Drug Abuse Resistance Education (D.A.R.E.), was an innovation in solving the drug problem from the demand side. It envisioned a curriculum for students as young as fifth graders about the dangers of drugs, both illegal drugs and legal ones such as tobacco and alcohol. The D.A.R.E. model is highly structured, involving ten to twenty weekly hour-long sessions featuring lectures, class discussion, and role-playing. The goal of the program is to educate students about the dangers of drugs, build good decision-making and peer pressure resistance skills, and boost students' self-esteem. Critical to the concept of the program is that all the teachers of the D.A.R.E. curriculum are police officers who have received at least eighty hours of specialized training in child development, classroom management, elementary school teaching, and communications skills. Thus D.A.R.E., in addition to creating a strong classroom experience, sought to forge an understanding between children and the police force. Ironically, Gates, who had stood strong as the old guard against the innovations of community policing, had birthed a unique relationship between the police and the youngest members of his public.

The timing of D.A.R.E. could not have been better. In addition to having the built-in institutional support of the third-largest and perhaps most storied police force in America—a force made iconic by *Dragnet* and *Adam-12* and lampooned by O. J. Simpson of all people in *The Naked Gun: From the Files of Police Squad!*—D.A.R.E. hit all the right political notes during the Reagan and the first Bush administrations' war on drugs. It had the proper mix of political theology—a strong stand against the evils of drugs, action at the local level—and it leavened to some degree other more punitive programs that were the foundations of the enforcement effort. Significant federal funding followed, and D.A.R.E. grew at extraordinary rates. By the end of the 1990s, it had become by far the largest drug education program in the country, penetrating 75 percent of American school districts. At its apex, D.A.R.E. annually reached thirty-five million children in the United States alone and was present in fifty-four countries around the world. While those numbers are slightly lower today, it remains by far the most expansive and prominent American drug prevention organization.

By most measures, D.A.R.E. is a great example of the power of the charitable sector, an organization that has built a novel and needed program and scaled itself dramatically to reach its vast target audience. D.A.R.E. has leveraged substantial cooperation and funding from individuals, nonprofits, and government to create a wide and strong base of support. Its Web site and literature are filled with warm anecdotes from police officers, parents, and students testifying to the success of the program. It is widely known and largely admired, so much so that President Obama has, as did presidents before him, annually declared a National D.A.R.E. Day in early April. There is only one minor blemish to this picture: virtually every piece of quantitative evidence demonstrates that the D.A.R.E. program doesn't actually work.

With its astonishingly rapid spread around the country and its connection to the broader and politically charged war on drugs, D.A.R.E. not surprisingly drew substantial scholarly scrutiny. D.A.R.E. in fact did not spring fully developed from the fertile mind of Daryl Gates; it was based upon the intriguing, but largely untested, social influence theory of a well-known psychologist named William Hansen. Hansen's model was built around the concept of resistance-skills training, giving youth the skills to reject negative social pressures. While D.A.R.E. had these respectable theoretical roots, it was unheard of for an educational program to be so extensively implemented without trial runs and careful testing. Many in the educational research community were understandably suspicious that D.A.R.E.'s growth owed more to political convenience and the personal influence of Gates than to good and careful educational policy, and they set out to test its effectiveness.

In the early 1990s, researchers began to release the first studies on the impact of D.A.R.E., and the results were not promising. In 1991, a Kentucky study for the National Institute on Drug Abuse found "no statistically significant differences" between the drug habits of youth who went through the program and youth who did not. In 1993, a Research Triangle Institute report declared that D.A.R.E. has "a limited to essentially non-existent effect" on drug use, and a Canadian government study found "no significant effect on the use of . . . marijuana, acid, heroin, crack, glue and P.C.P."[18] Most of the reporting, which generated substantial debate about D.A.R.E., was challenged by the program's advocates as preliminary in nature or lacking in the long-term statistically valid tracking that could form the foundation for a firm evaluation of the program.[19] That was not available until 1998.

"Assessing the Effects of School-Based Drug Education: A Six-Year Multilevel Analysis of Project D.A.R.E." was—and still is—the most comprehensive study of D.A.R.E.[20] The study was much anticipated by D.A.R.E. proponents since the lead investigator, Dennis Rosenbaum, the head of the Department of Criminal Justice at the University of Illinois at Chicago, was a longtime advocate for the program and because it was such a comprehensive undertaking. Over six years, researchers followed different groups of students, some of whom were randomly assigned into D.A.R.E. programs and some of whom were randomly placed into control groups. Six years is a long time to wait for a report, so one can imagine the excitement and perhaps trepidation with which it was anticipated. It is only a little harder to imagine the profound disappointment when the report landed with a big negative thud: overall, the study found that D.A.R.E. had no material effect on participants, certainly not in the long term. In just one or two subcategories, the study found D.A.R.E. to have some modest positive short-term effects, but the positive effects disappeared completely by the critical high school years. The researchers even found a small "boomerang" effect on suburban students; that is, suburban students who went through the D.A.R.E. program were *more* likely to gravitate toward drugs than their control group peers. The researchers offered a number of theories for this unexpected and unintended consequence, with the most plausible scenario emerging that suburban children were less knowledgeable about drug use and drug paraphernalia going into the program and therefore could be unintentionally recruited into drug use by the information provided by the D.A.R.E. officers. In this view, a drug prevention education program became a drug use education program, with very unappealing implications. The Rosenbaum report was followed by other, smaller studies with similar results, but it effectively capped the scientific community's view of D.A.R.E. Even William Hansen, the theoretical father of the program, concluded that the program "should be entirely scrapped and redeveloped anew."[21] In 2005, the surgeon general took the unusual step of categorizing the D.A.R.E. program as "Does Not Work," a rare designation that it holds to this day.[22]

The judgment on D.A.R.E.'s effectiveness is one of very significant economic consequence. The budget of the D.A.R.E. charity itself, derived from a combination of government, foundation, and individual donations, is very modest, ranging in the area of $6 million and covering about two dozen employees. But virtually all of the program's expenses are hidden below the surface, like a budgetary iceberg. The real costs of the program are the thousands of police officers who form the field staff of D.A.R.E. Their salaries and benefits are maintained in city, county, and state budgets and are covered by local taxes, federal grants, and local corporate and individual donations. D.A.R.E. itself has tried to estimate these expenses and has usually put the number at about $200 million per year, but independent studies have put it much, much higher. Many communities have full-time D.A.R.E. coordinators on their police payrolls, and many D.A.R.E.-trained officers work full-time or close to full-time on their D.A.R.E. duties. In 2001, a study looked at community data and provided a national estimate of seven thousand to eight thousand full-time equivalent officers nationwide, just about enough to fully staff Daryl Gates's L.A. Police Department.[23] Based on these costs, plus associated training, support, and administrative costs, the study's authors estimated the annual cost of D.A.R.E. to be between $1 billion and $1.3 billion—a lot of money by any standard and far too much money to spend on a program that does not work.

Beyond the cost, the scope of D.A.R.E. is of consequence because it maintains an effective stranglehold on school drug prevention curricula. School systems, for obvious reasons, offer at most one drug prevention program to students, and D.A.R.E., as the best-known and most PR-savvy program by far, occupies that space. Once they have invited police officers into their schools, school boards and superintendents are loath to kick them out, though some big cities such as Seattle, Houston, and Milwaukee have done so over the years, usually on budgetary, not effectiveness, grounds. The D.A.R.E. monopoly means that other drug prevention programs such as Project ALERT and LifeSkills Training, programs with much stronger evidentiary bases, are locked out of the school system.[24]

This boxing-out syndrome is by no means limited to the drug prevention field. The nonprofit field is extraordinarily stagnant, even though tens of thousands of new charities are created each year and billions of dollars of grants and donations annually flow to American charities. In a market economy, the process of creative destruction cuts the slow moving and the clumsy from the pack, making room for and incentivizing the growth of new, more agile players. The *Fortune* Top 50 list of 1970 is a testament to this weeding process. It is a retirement row of companies like American Can, LTV, and Bethlehem Steel that have failed or been gobbled up by more aggressive and effective competitors. Their disappearance has helped open space for new giants like Microsoft, Intel, Apple, Oracle, Walmart, and Google, all of which have transformed American society and none of which existed two generations ago.[25] We would all be driving Chryslers and Pontiacs and making calls on our Ma Bell landlines, and I would be typing this on a heavy and expensive IBM desktop or Selectric typewriter if the for-profit marketplace did not allow for enormous change brought by innovation, competition, and choice. On the charitable side, however, the largest nonprofits of forty years ago are, almost without exception, the largest charities of today; the Salvation Army, the United Way, Catholic Charities, the YMCA, and the American Cancer Society all cling to their positions at the top of the charts. This stagnation is remarkable given the vast changes to society and the economy, the roughly one million new charities that have been launched over this period, and the tidal wave of new social needs, new research and ideas, and new ways to deliver information and services that have arisen since the days of the Great Society. There are many and overlapping causes for this inertia, some of which are neatly captured in D.A.R.E.'s response to the scientific evidence mounting against it.

As the trickle of evidence in the early 1990s turned into a river of proof by decade's end, D.A.R.E. plotted out an aggressive counter-campaign, one more evocative of a political contest than a scientific debate over the efficacy of a social service program. To the press and to its political and financial supporters, D.A.R.E. intimated that its critics, by and large well-credentialed and rather dull social scientists, were part of a pro-drug conspiracy against D.A.R.E. They pressured news organizations, scientists, and policy makers with threats of litigation and with heavy-handed references to their links to powerful political figures. And they bobbed and weaved on the relevance of the tests, suggesting that every study was necessarily outdated since D.A.R.E., according to its own reckoning, is constantly updating and improving its curricula, thus rendering all previous studies irrelevant.

D.A.R.E.'s most effective tack evolved from its faith in anecdotal evidence. Glenn Levant, the executive director of D.A.R.E. during the 1990s and a former deputy chief of the LAPD, rejected all of the studies with the airy dismissal that "scientists will tell you that bumble bees can't fly, but we know they can." It's easy to make fun of Levant's rejection of all modern science, but the statement is more representative of an important view within the charitable sector than people would care to admit. The strongest defense of D.A.R.E. programs throughout this period came from parents, students, teachers, and police officers. They believed their direct observations and experiences validated the program, from the kids who love the curriculum's coloring books, fluorescent pens, and Daren-the-Lion dolls to the principal of P.S. 20 in New York City who relies on his own intuitive sense of D.A.R.E.'s success: "The bottom line is that it creates relationships between children, students and parents that you rarely find anywhere. My opinion is that the national data does not tell the story of the great effects on children."[26] For most charities, the story from the front lines is the most important measure of success, one that typically confirms the importance of the work and reassures stakeholders. Empirical and research studies are to be avoided as expensive, distracting, and potentially dangerous. In some ways, the charitable world exhibits an almost medieval aversion to scientific scrutiny and accountability. Most charities avoid careful, randomized testing of their outcomes: they see little gain and much risk in testing that might reveal flaws in their approaches. When they do such studies, it is typically at the behest of a funder who has tied grants to such evaluations. And, as we shall see throughout this book, even when those tests show failure, charities often resist the findings in favor of their own affirming narratives.

This faith in anecdote is more than sentimental; it reflects economic and personal self-interest. At the height of the attacks on D.A.R.E. in the late 1990s, one researcher, Michael Roona, noted that the studies were certainly "scaring the hell out of [D.A.R.E.]. DARE America is like any other multimillion-dollar corporation; they're very concerned about competition in the marketplace. They were the IBM of drug-prevention programs for a long time."[27] The IBM analogy is striking yet ultimately inapt. True, like D.A.R.E., IBM faced fundamental challenges to its core business; in IBM's case, the challenges came from more nimble competitors in the computer marketplace. IBM, confronted with a binary choice of change or die, ultimately survived by making radical changes in its business focus. D.A.R.E., operating in a far less rigorous marketplace, has maintained its position without making any radical change and without having to prove its value in the face of powerful evidence.

This should have been a one-sided fight. The weight of scientific evidence was overwhelming. D.A.R.E. doesn't work, and there should have been no constituency for maintaining the service. But D.A.R.E. won by intimidating and ultimately outlasting its critics. Science stopped. The number of new studies of the D.A.R.E. program has dwindled to close to zero, a predictable outcome since social scientists are reluctant to pursue research that will fall on deaf ears and funders are unwilling to commission studies that will not influence social outcomes. Meanwhile, the program lives on. Today, a dozen years beyond these studies, D.A.R.E. is still a billion-dollar enterprise, still the dominant source of antidrug programs in the schools, and still generally following the same script. The real costs go well beyond the $10 to $15 billion that donors, taxpayers, and local governments have sunk into D.A.R.E. over the last decade. The monopoly that D.A.R.E. has on the school marketplace means that new programs, new ideas, and innovative approaches to drug prevention education are effectively smothered, and this outcome is replicated across the entire charitable world.

The illogical success of D.A.R.E. is echoed, for instance, in the tale of one of the fastest-growing education programs in history, the 21st Century Community Learning Centers after-school program. Today, after-school programs are considered by many to be a natural and critical extension of the educational system, but it was not always so. The history of such services is marked by faddism, amateurish efforts to combat complicated societal problems, and confusing and often conflicting goals. The programs have their roots in the last years of the nineteenth century, when new labor laws began to liberate minors from the sweatshop and the factory floor. While social reformers cheered the reduction in child labor, many saw risks to youth in the crowded tenements, the unsavory characters on corners, and the dangerous streets, thick with horses, carriages, and the first automobiles. From this concern the first Boys Clubs were born, often small, local, and widely variable efforts to provide structured play opportunities for urban youth. In the first decade of the twentieth century, Boys and then Girls Clubs spread and multiplied and added a broad and erratic list of classes and activities: instruction in wireless telegraph, barbering, cobbling, and parliamentary laws for the boys; embroidery, etiquette, and elocution for the girls; and bookbinding, hammock making, and poster art for both. The curricula, such as they were, stemmed from a shifting welter of social goals ranging from the prevention of crime and delinquency to vocational skill building and Americanization for immigrant children, but they were more practically driven by the interests of volunteers and the local availability of class leaders. The informal network of after-school programs—which included church-supported programs and occasionally local government undertakings as well—was weakened by a reliance on poorly trained volunteers and by annual turnover of workers often topping 50 percent. Most clubs suffered from high dropout rates and complaints of inadequate resources and structure, bullying, and rough behavior.[28]

Despite the amateur quality of these charitable after-school programs, pressure to expand and formalize them began to build among policy makers in the 1960s, amid growing alarm about gang violence, the drug trade, and the general breakdown of social controls in the poorest neighborhoods. Initially, after-school programs were ignored in President Johnson's Great Society legislation in favor of early childhood programs. But in the 1970s and the 1980s, as more women entered the workforce, the demand for after-school care spread to middle-income families. Programs expanded, fueled by a patchwork of support from individuals, local governments, and foundations. But as a movement, the after-school industry lacked a common rationale. Programs were promoted variously for their ability to improve test scores, reduce delinquency, and inhibit teen pregnancy but were continually plagued by a lack of rigor and adequate staffing. To the extent that programs did not rely on volunteers, they were staffed by low-paid workers, who typically held only high school degrees and who lacked the skill set or long-term commitment to ensure that programs could follow through on their promises. Staff turnover still hovered around 40 percent, and many after-school programs operated without adequate staff for long stretches. Strained by conflicting social demands and a lack of resources, the after-school movement soon faced a battery of reports that questioned its ability to provide the most basic developmental services.[29]

Given this decades-long checkered history, what happened next may come as a surprise. In the late 1990s, the Department of Education (ED) created the 21st Century Community Learning Centers (inelegantly shortened to 21st CCLC), at first a modest-sized program designed to help facilitate opening school buildings to broader community activities. Then, despite the lack of evidence of success for after-school programs, the newly elected Bush administration latched onto 21st CCLC as a key part of its No Child Left Behind strategies, proposing that it be transformed from a small-scale facilities grant project to a comprehensive learning program. The program exploded, growing from $40 million in 1998 to $1 billion just four years later, and 21st CCLC has continued to grow to this day, though at less exaggerated rates.

The hasty and radical expansion of 21st CCLC is somewhat less surprising if seen in a political context. It was philosophically attractive to the Bush administration; academically oriented after-school programs dovetailed nicely with its bias toward longer school hours and greater educational structure. Proponents of the program could cite a Department of Justice report on the promise of after-school programs called *Safe and Smart,* despite its being a largely fact-less puff piece.[30] Finally, the concept of structured after-school programs simply sounds reasonable in the abstract. That the decision to fund 21st CCLC was divorced from any real understanding of how to design effective programs, how to research and validate new approaches to extended learning environments, and how to create effective administrative and teaching operations was in fact typical of American educational policy. Successive administrations routinely lurch from one well-meaning and attractive-sounding approach to another, a failure not of aspiration but of planning.

At the U.S. Department of Education, the mandarins were no doubt intimately familiar with politically driven, dizzying changes in educational philosophy. Recognizing that the 21st CCLC program had grown without any real evaluation of its effectiveness and that existing research on after-school programs was equivocal at best, the department commissioned one of its largest and most comprehensive studies ever, a three-year program to track more than two thousand students across twenty-six centers in twelve separate school districts.[31] Roughly twelve hundred middle and elementary school students were randomly assigned to attend 21st CCLC programs and a thousand others to a control group. The students were tracked across numerous outcomes ranging from academic achievement to social and emotional development to negative behaviors such as truancy and school suspensions. It was a massive undertaking, appropriately scaled to the billion-dollar investments being made.

When the preliminary results of the study began to leak out, they seemed likely to be a bombshell. The study showed virtually no positive effects. Most outcomes measured yielded no discernible differences between the study group and the control group, and negative effects were found in many categories. On the academic side, students who attended the 21st Century Community Learning Centers were no better off: they did not have better grades or test scores and did not even show higher incidences of completing homework. And in most behavioral categories, program participants were *more* likely to exhibit negative behaviors than their similarly situated classmates in the control group. Those who attended 21st CCLC were more likely to be suspended from school or otherwise singled out by teachers for disciplinary action. The program also had none of the expected positive impact on the families of at-risk children: the effective provision of day care did not increase the likelihood that mothers would successfully reenter the workforce. The only positive outcome at all, over twenty outcomes measured, was that the 21st CCLC participants felt moderately safer after school. In sum, the study amounted to a depressing indictment of the largest after-school effort in the country: a billion dollars a year had been spent to fund centers that had no positive effect on at-risk children. In truth, the results were not wholly shocking: they had been foreshadowed in the course of the study. After it became known that the initial results were detrimental to the program, the study was extended from two years to three years, largely in the hopes that over a longer term participants might show more, or even some, positive effects. That hope was dashed with the release of the final report.

There was another reason the results were not surprising: they dovetailed closely with a long history of social science findings that show negative effects when at-risk children are brought together in poorly structured groups. The longest-term and most famous study of such social services provided to at-risk youth began as the Cambridge-Somerville Youth Study in 1938, founded by Richard Clarke Cabot, a physician and professor of clinical medicine and social ethics. Cabot was a true Boston blue blood, a scion of the Cabot clan immortalized in the poetic phrase "And this is good old Boston, / The home of the bean and the cod, / Where the Lowells talk only to the Cabots / And the Cabots talk only to God." Cabot was fascinated with the newly developing field of total patient treatment, the concept that dealing with the patient's family, social conditions, and psychological state was an important part of health care. In his role as head of outpatient services at Massachusetts General, he became the first doctor to integrate social services into the medical treatment plan. The concept of case management by social workers was sufficiently novel at the time that Cabot had to dip into his own pockets to fund it.

In 1938, Cabot, by then at Harvard Medical School, undertook what would become one of the longest-lasting and most complete social services studies in American history. Cabot had come to believe that a network of social services could help reduce delinquency among at-risk youth, and as a scientist with a bedrock belief in quantitative evaluation he set out to prove (or disprove) it. He selected a disadvantaged area in eastern Massachusetts as his study site and deployed two groups of matched but randomly selected at-risk boys around the age of ten. The treatment group, numbering roughly three hundred children, was provided with an extensive network of personalized services from social workers, medical professionals, and psychologists. The services included monthly home visits, tutoring, psychological care and counseling, community youth activities, summer camps, and, somewhat puzzlingly, woodworking. The control group got nothing beyond what was ordinarily available to at-risk youth at the time, which was not much. Extensive data, including court files, school records, and medical histories, were collected on all the participants. The project survived Dr. Cabot's untimely death in

1939 and ran through 1945. The early evidence was encouraging, as the members of the treatment group did better than the staff of the project expected, if not necessarily better than the control group.

In most cases, that would have been that, and Cabot's experiments would have been labeled a success, except that many years later the design of the program captured the interest of a young researcher named Joan McCord. In 1957, McCord, a Harvard-trained criminologist, picked up the strands of the project, hoping to track down the participants to judge what long-term effects, if any, were produced. Dr. McCord began the detective work of finding as many past participants as possible, and despite the dislocation brought on by school graduations, family breakups, and several wars, she ultimately turned up an impressive number. She continued to track them well into the late 1970s, when most of the participants were past the age of retirement and their life stories had been more or less fully written.

At first blush, Dr. McCord's task was not promising. She set out to trace hundreds of men across two generations of time to find out whether a single program put in place during childhood would have a measurable effect on the rest of their lives, an effect that would stand out among the vast number of factors that form us, from parents, teachers, and neighbors, to marriages, children, and divorces, to jobs and military service. But against the odds, Dr. McCord came to an astonishing and truly unexpected conclusion. The involvement in the Cambridge-Somerville program did in fact play a critical, even determinative role in the participants' lives, but certainly not the hoped-for one. The youth in the treatment group fared far worse in life than those in the control group in terms of delinquency and criminality, in terms of job retention, and even in terms of health effects. Ultimately, Dr. McCord and her fellow researchers concluded that the controlling variable was exposure to summer camp. Rather than being an idyllic release from the challenges of youth, it was a cauldron of bad adolescent behavior, a laboratory where the youth modeled and reinforced the worst delinquency. The syndrome was called "deviant peer contagion," acknowledging that these types of environments could be petri dishes for the spread of behavioral diseases.[32]

The increased negative behaviors found among participants in 21st CCLC programs stemmed from the same type of dysfunction, if not in quite the same intensity. The programs, while all localized and differentiated in one form or another, shared one common attribute: the resources available after school did not match the resources available during the school day, leaving the participants with far more unstructured time and allowing them to have greater social influence on one another. The resulting "contagions" effectively hobbled the 21st Century Community Learning Centers programs.

In the wake of the disappointing ED evaluation, the Bush administration moved swiftly to reduce funding. Citing its own study, the Department of Education proposed an annual appropriation of only $600 million, a reduction of $400 million from preexisting levels though still many times higher than the original spending levels. In a letter to the editor in *The Washington Post,* Secretary of Education Rod Paige made the rather self-evident statement that "it is irresponsible to continue funding increases unless they improve academic achievement or foster positive behavior."[33] This should have been the end of the story, or at least a new chapter, but in the ways of Washington it was only the beginning. The after-school program lobby, a surprisingly effective Washington-based nonprofit called the Afterschool Alliance, fought tooth and nail to maintain full funding, despite the evidence of program failure. It rallied local after-school programs, schools, celebrities such as Arnold Schwarzenegger, who had personally started an after-school program called After-School All-Stars, and even the participants themselves in defense of the 21st Century program. The campaign was played out in a packed Senate hearing room. Russ Whitehurst, an assistant secretary of education, presented the straightforward findings of the national evaluation. In response, Senator Arlen Specter, then a Republican from Pennsylvania and a longtime advocate for after-school programs, warmly welcomed the opposing witnesses, two dozen freshly scrubbed students all waiting to testify to their personal positive experiences with after-school programs. In Washington terms, it was a one-sided fight. Whitehurst with his three-year study, one of the largest, most comprehensive research projects ever undertaken in this country, had no chance. Full funding for the program was promptly restored.

Today 21st CCLC, largely unchanged, receives more than $1.2 billion in annual funding even as the evidence challenging the effectiveness of after-school programs continues to mount. In 2011, a multiyear, randomized evaluation of Higher Achievement—a program designed in part to reinvent after-school service in light of the earlier evaluations—produced many of the same results as the national evaluation of the 21st CCLC program. Higher Achievement is one of the after-school industry's "Cadillac" projects, a resource- and time-intensive program for middle school students in Washington, D.C., that includes both after-school and summer supplemental education elements. Higher Achievement provides 650 hours a year of academic instruction, enrichment activities, and mentoring per student. Field trips, a summer academy, instruction, homework help, and even dinner during extended sessions are all part of its services. Yet despite all this, the two-year study showed only some modest positive results in terms of participants' reading and problem solving. Most of the data showed no change in test scores and a substantial increase in indicators of misconduct[34]—results that one observer described as "eerily similar" to the 21st Century testing. The research results keep mounting, but government funders show no signs of tightening the purse strings.

The 21st CCLC was not the first charitable program that Congress (or state legislatures, for that matter) has continued to fund in the face of compelling evidence of failure, and it surely will not be the last.[35] The educational sector is flush with programs and services that sound appealing but cannot withstand critical evaluations. Educational progress has stagnated in this country over the last thirty years as policy has lurched from one fad to another. Once created, education programs—whether governmental or charitable—rarely go out of business, creating a patchwork of projects and services untethered from sensible study and evaluation. As Diane Ravitch, a former assistant secretary of education for educational research and improvement, once said, "It is rare to find a program that is discontinued because it is not helping kids . . . I once concluded that the way to have eternal life is to become a federal education program."[36]

The education sector is hardly unique within the charitable community. It is astonishingly easy to start a charity; the IRS approves over 99.5 percent of all charitable applications, more than fifty thousand new charities each year.[37] New charities are begun for all sorts of reasons, many rooted in the best of intentions but only a small percentage grounded in careful analysis, strong and scalable business plans, and hard evidence. Once established, they are hard to uproot, since their standards of success are self-defined, constantly shifting, and rarely tied to data. Sometimes the pressure from big institutional funders, including the government, is irresistible, and charities are forced to conduct evaluations, but often they develop tests that are virtually certain to show positive outcomes: "happy sheets," in the terminology of one nonprofit engaged in science training. Many charities claim evidence of results, but that "evidence" often fails basic tests of independence and objectivity.

Take, for example, a charity called Chess-in-the-Schools, which provides chess instruction as part of the academic school day to elementary and middle school children in the New York City public schools. In recent years, the organization has served about fifty schools (out of over seventeen hundred New York City schools) and taught about 13,000 students (out of 1.1 million). The central conceit of Chess-in-the-Schools—and its rationale for taking students out of regular academic classes for its program—is that chess "helps promote intellectual growth and has been shown to improve academic performance."[38] This claim has helped make the organization a powerhouse on New York City's charitable circuit. Its board of trustees includes prominent members of financial and society circles, and its board of advisers is a roll call of establishment power: the current or immediate past presidents of Yale, Johns Hopkins, Cornell, the New York Public Library, and the Carnegie Corporation, as well as the U.S. senator Chuck Schumer and the journalist Robert MacNeil. For an organization of rather modest reach, it has a surprisingly large annual budget, about $3 million, reflective of the connections of its board members and its fund-raising effectiveness in the halls of city and state government. The *New York Post* bestowed upon Chess-in-the-Schools the title of "kings and queens of City Council cash" in recognition of its ability to generate over $2 million in city earmarks over the last five years.[39]

But, like many charities, Chess-in-the-Schools' bold claims of success mask a paper-thin evidentiary record. Its Web site identifies only one study, performed in the Bronx over two years in the early 1990s, to justify its claim that chess improves academic performance. That study concluded that chess programs help to increase reading scores because 15 of 22 chess program participants increased their reading scores in their second year in the program while only 491 of 1,118 nonparticipants increased their scores. Percentage-wise, the edge goes to the chess players. The study, however, proves nothing about the value of chess; in fact, its principal value is as a particularly good example of the problem of selection bias. As the GiveWell analysts note, "They're comparing *kids who volunteered to play chess* against those who didn't. Think of the chess club members at your school, and ask yourself if they would have been just like all the other kids had chess club not been offered. There's no reason to think these two groups of kids are otherwise similar or would be expected to respond similarly to school."[40] Without adequate study controls, it is impossible to know if it was chess or a thousand other independent factors that influenced the reading scores of the group. None of which is to say that the Chess-in-the-Schools program is harmful or ill intentioned. It is to say that its effectiveness is far from proven—and far from obvious given the difficulty of improving student performance in a meaningful way.

There are, fortunately, some emerging trends toward accountability in the charitable arena. They are largely limited to sectors where key institutional donors hold such sway that they can compel more effective behavior. An example is the Gates Foundation, where rigorous results testing for its grantees is now the norm. But it was not always this way. Gates's effectiveness agenda was born out of its own chastening experience. In 2000, the foundation announced a bold investment in "small schools," inspired by a trend toward putting high school and middle school students into schools of four hundred and sometimes far fewer. Small schools, it was theorized, would create a stronger sense of community among students, provide opportunities for greater individual attention, and encourage greater connectedness among students, parents, and teachers. In places where school districts were financially tethered to existing larger buildings, "schools within schools" were carved out.

The Gates investment in small schools was originally sized at $56 million, but it rapidly grew from this considerable base to more than $1 billion over five years. It's hard to overstate the influence the Gates Foundation has on American education. Because of its vast array of grants, a significant cross section of the educational community in this country is beholden to it in one form or another, and it holds a "golden leash" of consultancy fees and research grants on many of the most important figures in American education. All this gives it unrivaled sway over American education, outstripping even the Department of Education, which dispenses far more money but is limited in its funding discretion by rules and public processes. When the small-schools announcement was first made in 2000, it surprised the education community, which largely viewed the movement as a curiosity rather than a central reform strategy. The Gates Foundation's research on small schools amounted to no more than a single small-scale and inconclusive study. Ultimately, the school reform establishment came to understand that the Gates leadership had been bewitched by an evocative, essentially unproven concept. But such is the power of the Gates Foundation that the education movement fell obligingly in line, and for the next six years small-school development became a major fascination within the education community; hundreds of school systems, tied by Gates grants, developed small schools, pushing other initiatives out of the way. Potential critics muzzled themselves, cowed by the lethal combination of Gates's spending power and the foundation's famous sensitivity to criticism.

Five years and over a billion dollars later, the foundation made an extraordinary confession: the work quality of students in the model small schools was "alarmingly low." While small schools could foster a learning culture more intimate and coherent than larger schools, they suffered, among other things, from weak curriculum development, teacher burnout, and lack of infrastructure. Overall, student outcomes were not promising and certainly not commensurate with the investments poured into the schools by Gates and various school systems. In a remarkable statement, the head of education initiatives at Gates confessed that the plan was flawed from the beginning: "It's quite clear that over the last six years I created a number of grant programs that were well-intentioned but had some weak assumptions."[41] Cloaked in the polite parlance of the foundation world, this was a plain admission that core programs were fundamentally flawed. And the failure had significance beyond the specific schools affected. The Gates obsession with the small-school movement created a gravitational pull, one that diverted resources, shifted organizational agendas, and impeded a wide range of other initiatives. The period from 2000 to 2005 was a troubled one for American education reform.

The humbling lesson of the small-school debacle was not lost on

Gates. From the ashes, the foundation developed new requirements that all Gates projects and grantees be subject to rigorous and verifiable measurements. Given the reach that it has in the field, its requirements have begun to permeate the educational community. The Gates Foundation now maintains a department whose sole function is to measure and analyze results and ensure that its vast farm system of grantees is similarly focused on quantitative measures of effectiveness.

Gates is not unique; we will meet other funders in later chapters who are similarly committed to a culture of rigor and measurement, but they are still relatively rare, and their impact is more localized. Foundations only account for about 12 percent of private giving;[42] the real market power rests with individual donors and government funders, and until they too buy into the culture of results, the charitable sector will remain heavily burdened by anecdote and the culture of ineffectiveness.

TWO

The Charitable Universe

MERICAN CHARITIES DOMINATE critical sectors of public
life. They control segments of the education and health-care
fields—two large and growing economic sectors—and hold substantial positions in the environmental sectors, social services, arts, and
media and digital services. In recent years, nonprofits have even made
inroads into financial services and politics, areas not easily associated
with charitable behavior. While one might assume that charities' revenues rise in good times and fall in bad times, the sector as a whole is
actually a diversified economy with revenues from donations, government grants, and transactional services. Over the last two decades,
from 1989 to 2009, the charitable world has grown approximately
155 percent, far outstripping other business sectors and the economy
as a whole.[1]

While private associations performing public functions existed
long before the founding of the United States, their development into
such a large and important sector of the economy is mainly an American and a recent phenomenon. The American charitable sector is by
far the world's largest in absolute terms and, with the exception of the
Netherlands, which operates its equivalent of Social Security through

a charitable network, also the largest in percentage terms.[2] As far back as 1835, Alexis de Tocqueville, in a much-quoted passage, noted the tendency of Americans to come together to take on voluntary tasks more commonly associated in the Old World with government and with royalty:

> Americans of all ages, all conditions and all dispositions constantly form associations. They have not only commercial and manufacturing companies in which all take part, but associations of a thousand other kinds, religious, moral, serious, futile, general or restricted, enormous or diminutive . . . Wherever at the head of some undertaking you see the government in France, or a man of rank in England, in the United States, you will be sure to find an association.[3]

As witnessed by Tocqueville and marked by great episodes from the first communal gifts of the Puritans to the grand institutional spending of the Rockefellers, Carnegies, and Fords, the lineage of American charity looks long and unbroken. Like so much associated with American charities, it is at once an inspiring picture and badly misleading.

In fact, from the first days of the colonial era through the first hundred years of the Republic, a strong charitable sector was a generally unwelcome concept.[4] The Puritans are widely credited with inspiring a charitable blooming in America, due in part to the historical resonance of John Winthrop's sermon "A Modell of Christian Charity," which urged members of the Christian community to "beare ye one another's burthen's" but in fact they erected barriers to the creation of an effective voluntary sector. Because of the harsh treatment they suffered in England, the Puritan settlers were hostile to English legal forms, viewing them as sources of corruption and oppression. The practice of law was abolished. Thus English common law—particularly the 1601 Elizabethan Statute of Charitable Uses, which rationalized and gave rights to English charities for the first time—was unknown in the northern colonies. The Puritans celebrated *individual* acts of charity and compassion while keeping a wary eye on any institutions of corporate or associational power. Harvard University, the oldest continuously operating charity in the United States, was a rarity, and it was held in check by the fact that its board of overseers was exclusively composed of ministers from the tax-supported Congregationalist Church and by public officials sitting ex officio. It was not until 1865, when senior members of the Massachusetts State Senate lost their representation on the board, that Harvard could finally—229 years after its founding—be considered a private charity in the modern sense.

Post–Revolutionary War America continued to be deeply skeptical of charitable associations, though that skepticism had some distinct regional flavoring, with the strongest skeptics now found in the South. Democratic theory as it existed in the late eighteenth century generally viewed private interest groups to be hostile to effective representative government; the creators of the new republic were intimately familiar with the power of shadow governments such as the Freemasons and with the factionalism that almost uprooted the war effort. Inspired by Thomas Jefferson's anticorporate views—he held all private organizations to have "some trace of human weakness, some grain of corruption"—Jeffersonian Democrats made it virtually impossible for anything like a charitable organization to prosper. Virginia from its earliest days prohibited its universities from holding endowment funds, restricted private gifts, and eliminated their tax exemption. In 1792, Virginia specifically annulled the 1601 Statute of Charitable Uses and seized the endowment funds of the Anglican Church. One local jurist endorsed the move by decrying "the wretched policy of permitting the whole property of society to be swallowed up in the insatiable gulph of public charities."[5] While the anticorporate view had its fullest flower in the South, the growth of private charities was also restricted in the Federalist strongholds of New York and Pennsylvania. In part, the limitations were due to rivalries between various religious and business interests, who effectively blocked corporate charters for each other, but state law also restricted testamentary gifts to charities and set upper limits on the amount of property held by such organizations. While open hostility to the charitable world finally began to abate, as we shall see, in the second half of the nineteenth century, vestiges hung on for generations. Mississippi, for one, continued to bar charitable bequests up through the 1920s.

Even when benevolent organizations were successfully established, their work often bore little resemblance to modern notions of charity. The urban poor in post–Revolutionary War America faced many challenges: bad wages, uncertain employment, epidemics and pandemics, and poor living conditions. The response of both government and charities to widespread need was often indistinguishable from, and sometimes worse than, indifference. The most prominent charity in postwar New York was the Society for the Prevention of Pauperism (SPP), formed by a clique of prominent merchants, lawyers, and clergy. The SPP adhered to the view that poverty stemmed from "ignorance, idleness, intemperance, extravagance, imprudent marriages, and deficient childrearing practices" and that handouts and public aid would only contribute to the problem.[6] In the campaign to reduce pauperism, SPP members successfully lobbied city and state governments to *reduce* support for the poor. In 1818, not content with its victories there, the SPP launched a campaign to persuade other charities to eliminate direct relief for the needy as well. This effort was remarkably and painfully successful. The Brooklyn Humane Society closed a soup kitchen for the poor, and the Society for the Relief of Poor Widows with Small Children abolished all of its support programs on the grounds that relief encouraged unchristian pregnancies. Instead of offering food, shelter, or health care, the SPP pushed to inculcate the poor with values that would make them productive members of society: sobriety, cleanliness, industriousness, and good manners. But as it turned out, the urban gentry were not all that interested in venturing into the poorer neighborhoods and teaching punctuality and frugality to the downtrodden and the hungry. Within three years, the

SPP's programs were largely abandoned, but the Darwinian philosophy it advocated lingered on for two more generations.

The federal and state courts were only minor players in this drama for most of the first seventy years of the Republic. The Supreme Court weighed in many times on the role of charitable organizations in the early decades of the nineteenth century, but mostly on peripheral issues. That began to change in 1844 with the case of *Vidal* v. *Girard's Executors*.[7] The *Vidal* case concerned the estate of Stephen Girard, a wealthy French-born merchant and banker who died in 1831. Girard, a childless widower, left the bulk of his estate for the creation of a boarding school to educate "poor, white" boys, principally the orphaned children of coal miners. The will was attacked by various French nieces and nephews who asserted that American law would not accommodate a charitable trust such as this and that, even if it did, the terms of the gift violated public policy. In a landmark decision, the U.S. Supreme Court recognized a charitable trust in common law, for the first time giving individuals an expectation that they could leave a charitable legacy and creating a funding mechanism that could sustain a vital charitable sector.

The case proved to be enormously important, portending, as Supreme Court decisions have often done, changes not just in law but in social attitudes.[8] The first signs of widespread interest in charitable solutions to social problems began to emerge in the latter half of the nineteenth century when growing inequities in wealth and brutal exploitation of the working class stirred social upheaval. While the public was initially inclined to blame foreigners and labor unions for the violence associated with events such as the great railroad strike of 1877 and the Haymarket bombings of 1886, a new generation of thinkers such as Henry George and Edward Bellamy saw the violence as the consequence of rapid industrialization. Wealth had become polarizing, and government, riddled with corruption and captured by moneyed interests, was not a likely instrument of social justice. Under the influence of these thinkers, Americans began to view private charitable institutions as a vehicle for solving the keenest public problems.

Ironically, the notion took its deepest root among the business and professional classes, the people best served by the existing order. The great exploiters of the American working class—Andrew Carnegie, John D. Rockefeller, Henry Ford—would become the pioneers of a new American philanthropic world. Their attitude was driven by what might be called enlightened self-interest. The more forward-looking among the industrialists recognized that their steel mills, transportation syndicates, and oil empires needed the willing engagement of clerks, foremen, and common laborers; Pinkertons and other guns for hire engaged by the industrial trusts could not forever hold down the rising tide of social discontent. Many in the upper classes were also uncomfortable with the contradictions between their avowed Christian ethics and the clear evidence of widespread suffering.

The men who were to pioneer the first great American philanthropies were at the epicenter of the greatest concentration of wealth in history.[9] At the time of his death in 1831, Stephen Girard had been reputed to be the richest American, worth about $7 million. While considerable for its day, the Girard fortune was soon far outstripped by the handful of men who created the booming new industries of America—railroads, steel, and oil—and the financiers who funded them. By 1877, Cornelius Vanderbilt, known as Commodore for his control of the shipping lanes, crossed the $100 million threshold, but even his fortune was soon put to shame by the man who would become the single wealthiest person in modern history. Unlike some of his contemporaries, John D. Rockefeller never invented or really even built anything, but he perfected the art of buying low and selling high. Some twenty years after the Pennsylvania Rock Oil Company first drilled oil near Titusville in western Pennsylvania, the market for oil collapsed under the world's first glut. Rockefeller swooped in, paying a tiny fraction of what oil fields had cost just a few years before. By 1878, Rockefeller controlled 90 percent of the oil market and was able to single-handedly restore price stability. For this, he was more than handsomely rewarded; by the turn of the century, he was collecting a billion dollars a year in today's dollars, at a time before the bother of an income tax. While Rockefeller was the archetype of the Gilded Age baron, there were many others. The 4,047 millionaires reported in the 1892 census controlled an astonishing percentage of American wealth (the top 1 percent of New York families claimed well over 60 percent of the city's total income)—a concentration unrivaled in American history until the creation of the great technology and financial fortunes we know today.[10]

With so much disposable wealth, the titans of industry took to spending like modern-day pharaohs. Houses were the most visible badges of wealth, and they built towering townhomes on Park Avenue and carved vast estates out of the wilderness. George Vanderbilt constructed Biltmore in Asheville, North Carolina, to be the largest private residence in America. The maintenance of the house and its surrounding 140,000 acres was an enterprise so large that it needed a company town of two thousand inhabitants to support it. Another set of Vanderbilts, Alva and William, built a sprawling home, the Marble House, with all the modern amenities, but no doorknobs on the outside of doors to emphasize the fact that footmen were on constant standby. Like modern-day billionaires possessed of private jets and yachts, the millionaires of the Gilded Age found expensive, sometimes idiosyncratic means of getting from point A to point B. Richly appointed private railway cars were virtually the norm, and George Baker of the National City Bank built a rail siding beneath his house on Park Avenue so trains could stop in his basement. Colonel Francis Leland owned a 199-foot yacht, the *Safa-el-Bahr,* "famous for the magnificent appointments," according to *The New York Times,* and memorable for its fez-capped crew. The aforementioned William Vanderbilt's fourteen-hundred-ton yacht, *Alva,* was so massive that it was once mistaken for a ship of war by the defenders of Constantinople, who fired warning shots across its bow.[11]

The Gilded Age tycoons were ultimately best characterized by their outsized efforts to outdo all that had come before. That extended to all parts of life, even to how much they ate. Diamond Jim Brady, the legendarily gluttonous railroad executive, became famous for his nightly food orgies, so outrageous that George Rector, a prominent New York restaurateur, called him on his death "the best 25 customers I ever had."[12] They tackled their charitable activities with the same zeal to outdo their contemporaries and to leave a legacy beyond the reach of the devil. Just as they built railroads and steel plants and great ships, they built a new charitable infrastructure. Most of the robber barons had scant formal education, but in spite of that, or perhaps because of that, they commissioned an extraordinary series of world-class and largely self-referential universities: Vanderbilt, Stanford, Carnegie Mellon, Rockefeller University, and Duke. They built libraries that dotted the nation; Andrew Carnegie alone built more than twenty-five hundred, and John Jacob Astor endowed the New York Public Library. They contributed vast sums to medical science and built the world's largest telescope, the hundred-inch Hooker telescope on Mount Wilson in California. Art museums, opera halls, and magnificent theaters were all conceived and funded from their bottomless coffers. Collectively, they donated hundreds of millions of dollars in a cosmic burst of giving, and left an equal amount for foundations, many of which continue to make their marks today in fields ranging from the arts to zoology.

Yet despite all these changes and at the end of the greatest giving binge in history, the American charitable sector was still embryonic, a mere shadow of its future self. At the beginning of the Great Depression, there were still only about eighty thousand American charities (or about .5 percent of the number today), most with modest revenue and limited scope. Charities were almost entirely dependent on a very small number of givers, and despite their prodigious wealth even the Rockefellers and their contemporaries could only do so much. In the Yale University capital campaign of 1926 to 1928, just sixty-three individuals contributed over half of the $21 million raised. The sources of giving were as yet too narrow to generate a truly transformative social sector.

It took a dramatic shift in the role of government to create the conditions for today's expansive charitable world. Growth has been driven by two fundamental forces: a change in federal tax policies that encouraged widespread giving and, most important, the invention of the welfare state and a new federal practice of outsourcing much of its activity to the social sector. Given the current of government hostility to charitable forms that ran through early American history, it is a little bit ironic that the charitable sector multiplied in size only because of the passionate embrace of the central government.

The precipitating events for both changes were the Great Depression and World War II, which together altered the entire cellular structure of the U.S. government.[13] The cataclysmic events of the 1930s and 1940s left the United States the anchor of a global security system and the provider of a greatly expanded domestic social safety net. Washington, D.C., after the war was the epicenter of a new world order that included an expanded U.S. military presence; global economic commitments through the Marshall Plan, the International Monetary Fund, and the World Bank; and large-scale domestic obligations via the GI Bill.

All of this required a significant and enthusiastic expansion of federal revenue. Immediately following World War II, Congress labored for seven years to bring order and sense to the existing patchwork set of tax laws, and the result, the Internal Revenue Code of 1954, introduced a broader tax base and a new set of incentives and loopholes. For the first time, federal law provided substantial financial incentives for charitable giving, in the form of an annual deduction from taxable income and, perhaps more important, as part of estate planning. The changes spawned a new generation of tax professionals, from lawyers to accountants to estate planners, and transformed charitable giving in part into a tax-driven enterprise.

The result was an explosion in giving. Thousands of new charitable foundations were created. The foundation form was particularly attractive to the richest families because it permitted them to pass control over their enterprises to later generations without incurring tax costs. When John D. Rockefeller gave $100 million to create the Rockefeller Foundation in 1913, he derived no financial benefit from the transaction. But when Henry Ford established the Ford Foundation in 1936 as part of his estate planning, he did so in a way that preserved family control over one of the nation's largest industrial enterprises and avoided estate taxes in the process. Ford simply divided stock in his closely held company into two classes. The voting stock was retained by the family, while the nonvoting securities were donated to the newly created Ford Foundation, which in turn sold them tax-free at substantially stepped-up valuations. The family was thus able to pass control of the Ford Motor Company to the next generation without paying a penny in estate taxes.[14] In 1929, at the end of one of the most economically rewarding decades in American history, there were only 203 foundations with assets exceeding $1 million. By 1959, there were more than ten times as many.[15]

The other epochal change that fueled the growth of the charitable world was the new role of government as a funder of the nonprofit sector. The shift began incrementally in the early 1940s when the federal government began to invest heavily in applied and basic science at universities as part of the war effort. Rather than returning to prewar practices at the end of hostilities, Washington chose to cement and step up these investments in higher education by creating the National Science Foundation, the National Institutes of Health, and the GI Bill. These programs collectively transformed the balance sheets of both public and private universities nationwide by providing a massive infusion of research funds and an unprecedented supply of college students. Washington did not stop at the campus edge, expanding its funding for the hospital sector through the Hospital Survey and Construction Act of 1946 and for the insurance field by encouraging the growth of nonprofit health plans such as Blue Cross and Blue Shield.[16]

Then, in the 1960s, President Lyndon Johnson launched his war on poverty, leading to further changes in the nonprofit sector, though not in the way some had anticipated. Federal programs did not displace existing charitable activities; rather, Johnson's Great Society program spawned a whole new generation of charities. Medicare, established in 1965, provided billions of dollars to private hospitals for the care of the nation's elderly. The Social Security Act Amendments of 1967 opened the door for state and local governments to contract with nonprofit providers under the federal government's new welfare and child health programs.[17] The Economic Opportunity Act of 1964 mobilized the "resources of the Nation to combat poverty" and channeled those resources to innumerable charities to create local Head Start programs, senior citizen centers, summer youth programs, family planning services, and community health centers.

Within just two decades, the federal government had become the largest single funder of the charitable sector, far outstripping individuals, corporations, and foundations. By 1981, government funding for human service agencies, for instance, was twice as large as the revenues from all private sources combined.[18] The outsourcing of government services to a broadly dispersed group of private organizations, both for profit and not for profit, reflected a careful political strategy by successive administrations to assure widespread support. But it also reflected a specific conception of "third-party government," based upon the uniquely American idea which holds great currency today, that government agencies are poor implementers of public policy and that certain tasks of government are better delegated to organizations with operational expertise and local knowledge. Since the days of the Great Society, the nonprofit sector, especially in the areas of education, health care, and social services, has acted as an implementation arm of government.

The 1960s and 1970s were a period of historic growth for the nonprofit sector. It was widely assumed, however, that the shifting political winds that ushered in the Reagan revolution would provide a major correction to the charitable community. The association of many charities with Great Society causes and their dependence on federal funding portended ill in a conservative era promising smaller government.[19] But disaster did not strike.[20] The Reagan team championed principles of limited government, but it also valued community groups and private efforts, believing that "privatizing public initiative through the use of voluntary agencies was more flexible, responsive, economical, and 'democratic' than statist alternatives."[21] Moreover, the social sector, despite its debt to the Roosevelt and Johnson administrations, had become far more politically diverse than many had realized; for more than a decade, wealthy conservatives had fueled an expansion of conservative foundations, think tanks, and advocacy groups in the South and the West; church-related charities also constituted a substantial slice of the social sector—and the Reagan administration had little interest in cutting their funding. The concern of the Reagan White House was reflected in high-profile undertakings such as its Task Force on Private Sector Initiatives, which focused both on assuring adequate government support for charities and on fostering diversification of revenues in the social sector.

In truth, the incoming administration found itself with a rhetorical dilemma. Although it was strongly supportive of private, volunteer activity, its proposed reductions in Great Society programs threatened key revenue streams for hundreds of thousands of social service charities—a fact that only gradually dawned on the administration. The implications for the nonprofit sector, as well as political realities in Congress, had a moderating effect on some of the more draconian ideas of the new administration. In the end, government funding to charities shrank by about 6 percent in Reagan's first year. While cuts in funding hit some nonprofit organizations hard (legal services and advocacy, housing and community services, and employment and training in particular), the charitable sector as a whole was able to make up the shortfalls in other ways. Overall, funding for the nonprofit sector rose, against all expectations, during the Reagan years. A number of factors contributed to this modest rise in revenues. A wave of judicial decisions had the effect of pushing government responsibilities into the charitable sector. In the early 1980s, for example, the federal courts ordered that tens of thousands of mentally disabled persons be deinstitutionalized and placed in smaller, less restrictive group homes. Unwilling to provide the services directly, most states funded thousands of newly created nonprofit organizations to do so. In addition, private charitable contributions rose during the period, though only enough to offset about 25 percent of the decline in government funding. Finally, the largest increase in nonprofit revenue during this period came not from government or philanthropic sources but from raising fees—or implementing new fees—for services. Charities more than replaced the funds lost to government cuts by charging clients more than before or by instituting fees where none had existed. The winners during the Reagan administration were thus charities in fields such as health, education, and the arts that could charge fees and serve a broad or relatively well-to-do clientele. Those that suffered were in sectors in which poor customers could not make up for reductions in government funding. But overall, after eight years of the Reagan revolution, while the ground had shifted, the social sector had grown by another 30 percent. The George H. W. Bush years, too, saw direct federal services reduced in favor of "a thousand points of light," a constellation of voluntary community groups charged with caring for the disabled and the dependent.[22] The charitable world continued to grow.

Since World War II, despite the shuffling of political parties and changes in political philosophy, the growth of the nonprofit sector has been unbroken and geometric. In 1940, there were only about 12,000 nonprofits in the country. That number had quadrupled to 50,000 by 1950, but that was only the beginning. By 1967, there were 367,000; by 1977, 790,000; by the end of the Reagan administration in 1989, almost 1 million; and today, 1.4 million.[23] In all, that reflects a 115-fold growth—a rate that far outstrips the growth of private businesses, government, and national economic activity in general, making the charitable sector the fastest-growing business segment in this country over the last seventy years.

Today, the huge growth and reach of charities in the United States is rarely if ever thought of as a serious public policy issue. Charities are fully integrated into American life, and both parties have strong ties to the charitable sector. To the extent that there are regular critics, they tend to be people like Senator Chuck Grassley of Iowa, dubbed "the man museums love to hate,"[24] who from time to time challenges some of the more egregious compensation and fund-raising practices of the sector (explored in chapter 6). But no one seriously questions the scope and role of the charitable world. The consensus in support of this expansive role of charities is of surprisingly recent vintage. Throughout the 1950s, 1960s, and 1970s, the rapid rise of foundations and charities was greeted with suspicion and concern in some quarters. The most virulent attacks centered on foundations, which had an unenviable combination of opponents. Progressives viewed them as inequitable tax shelters; conservatives and McCarthyites challenged them as un-American and pro-communist; and a broad spectrum in Congress viewed their policy activities with suspicion and distaste. Senator Al Gore, Democrat of Tennessee and father of the future senator and vice president of the same name, was an early opponent, in 1969 proposing a legislative sunset on foundations that would require them to go out of business after forty years. While his proposal did not directly implicate most operating charities, his rationale was a warning to the entire sector:

> We are subsidizing bogus, phony charities . . . [O]nce an organization has achieved tax-exempt status, there is no Federal Agency adequately equipped for regulation, supervision, record keeping or knowledge of what happens. Under our present law, the organization enjoys that status forever.[25]

While Gore's proposal melted away, he was not alone in his critique of the sector. The most persistent critic of the charitable world was John William Wright Patman, the powerful Democratic congressman whose long tenure spanned the Hoover administration on one end and the Ford administration on the other. Patman was born in the most modest circumstances, in the tiny hollow of Patman's Switch, near the small town of Hughes Springs in Cass County, Texas. Even today, Cass County is a sparsely populated, largely poor stretch of land, hard up against the Arkansas border. The area is predictably conservative and avowedly regional in its outlook, perhaps most keenly reflected in the fact that it clung to its adopted name of Davis County in honor of Jefferson Davis for a number of years after the Civil War. First elected from the area in 1928, Patman quickly proved to be the star of his class—brilliant, self-assured, and stubbornly independent in his views. Patman was a populist in the fullest sense of the word, deeply suspicious of any nondemocratic sources of civil authority. He was passionate in his pursuit of stronger antitrust laws and in his time was the most relentless critic of the Federal Reserve Board. But he reserved some of his strongest views for the charitable world. For the most part, he focused his fire on the great foundations, which he viewed as vehicles for the wealthy to preserve their reach and influence outside the tax laws. But he viewed the charitable world and the foundation world as interlinked, and throughout the 1950s and 1960s he pursued legislation to restrict the entire nonprofit sector. In 1965, for instance, he proposed a twenty-five-year sunset on foundations and a moratorium on the creation of any new tax-exempt organization.[26]

Patman's foil in the charitable arena was born about as far away from Cass County as can be imagined. John D. Rockefeller III carried the most storied name in American business. As the eldest son of John D. Rockefeller Jr., he was predestined to go into the family business, which by this time was no longer oil but philanthropy. Upon graduating from Princeton in 1929, he joined his father, universally known as Junior, in the "family office," shorthand for the extensive staff that handled the Rockefeller investments and oversaw the family's charitable and public commitments. Junior's philanthropic activities showed extraordinary range, extending from conservation and the creation of national parks to the great historical restoration at Colonial Williamsburg to medical research at Rockefeller University.

Unlike his more outgoing brothers Nelson and Winthrop, John was never cut out for politics and was better suited to follow in the footsteps of his father: "John was frail, excessively serious, almost pathologically shy and self-conscious, overburdened with a sense of responsibility."[27] For more than two decades, John toiled in relative obscurity—to the extent that a Rockefeller can ever really be obscure—under the heavy thumb of his father. John took on many of the family philanthropic obligations, becoming a trustee of more than a dozen charitable organizations, but he largely served in these roles at the pleasure of his father. It wasn't until the early 1950s, after a dispute with his father over the future of Colonial Williamsburg, that John began to chart his own course.

Once going, however, John developed an extraordinary range of interests and activities. In late 1950, he accompanied John Foster Dulles to Japan and commenced a long love affair with the Far East. He led the revival of the Japan Society in 1952, a risky action in the still raw atmosphere in the decade following World War II, and founded the Asia Society just a few years later. His passions included population (an interest sparked by a conversation begun, oddly enough, in the men's room on the fifty-sixth floor of Rockefeller Center[28]) and the performing arts—leading to the creation of the Population Council and the building of Lincoln Center. Underlying all of his work was a deep concern over the direction of American philanthropy and volunteerism. He was surprised and distressed in the wake of Patman's first assaults on foundations to find that most Americans did not understand or much care for the charitable world. For the next decade of his life John made it his goal not only to protect the privileges of the charitable sector but also to create new structures to promote charitable effectiveness and common purpose. Rockefeller understood that in doing so, he risked being perceived as merely defending the hereditary rights of the manor house, so he began to rebrand himself (well before "rebranding" was a word) as an intellectual leader of the charitable community, taking the unusual step for the day of hiring a public relations firm to help burnish this image.[29]

John's work in this area began in the early 1960s in the form of published writings and extensive testimony before Congress. Unlike many in the charitable arena, he recognized that the relationship between government and philanthropy had changed since World War II, and he advocated for new, less political institutions to bring rational policy and order to the burgeoning charitable sector. In part, his motivation was protectionist—to neutralize the threat from the Patmans of the political world—but he also wanted to help rationalize a charitable world that was growing and changing every day. His early words on the subject were barely noted, and John began to realize that his solitary efforts—famous name and deep pockets notwithstanding—would have little effect on public discourse and political outcomes. He thus began to seek a new vehicle through which to put his mark on the charitable sector and found it by creating first the Peterson Commission[30] to influence the legislative process and then the Filer Commission to rethink charitable structures more broadly.

The Commission on Private Philanthropy and Public Needs was named for its chairman, John Filer, the president of Aetna Life and Casualty. It had an unusual pedigree. The Filer Commission was a private-sector initiative, as its name suggested, but it was publicly announced by Secretary of the Treasury George Shultz and Wilbur Mills, the powerful chairman of the House Ways and Means Committee. Nonetheless, it had John Rockefeller III stamped all over it. Unlike earlier commissions that were largely focused on the technical details of the tax code as it applied to charities and were constructed to influence particular pieces of legislation, the Filer Commission was organized to take on larger issues created by the mostly unplanned growth of the social sector. Among the key questions was whether "society's resources devoted to satisfying community needs [were] being appropriately allocated among the many purposes, organizations and institutions which depend on private support."[31] For Rockefeller, the commission's challenge was to develop new institutions that could answer such questions and create common rules for the charitable sector. These were knotty problems fraught with political challenges for a commission that included liberals and conservatives, Democrats and Republicans, representatives of business, government, academia, the foundation world, media, law, and the civil rights movement and had no fewer than 106 associated groups of consultants, special consultants, and advisers. And even this unwieldy crowd was deemed insufficiently inclusive, and a "pickup" group representing the donee community was granted quasi-official status within the commission framework.

The commission labored for two years and in 1975 produced a report of great scope, a six-volume tract that surveyed the charitable sector in all its dimensions and analyzed the role of nonprofits as providers of educational, health, and social services and as a force in political life. Most important, the report, practically for the first time, gave voice to the notion of the charitable world—or the voluntary sector, as the commission called it—as a unified and distinct sector within American life.[32] This was perhaps the commission's most lasting impact, since its specific recommendations satisfied no one and offended many, even those on its board. The final report drew more than twenty pages of dissents and criticisms from commissioners, and the Donee Group prepared a separate critique titled *Private Philanthropy: Vital and Innovative or Passive and Irrelevant?* The ten core recommendations, the results of a consensus drawn from widely divergent perspectives, were predictably tepid. But one important recommendation, reflecting John's goals, survived the internal negotiations: a call on Congress to create a permanent national commission on the nonprofit sector modeled after England's Charity Commission to act as a quasi-governmental rule maker, regulator, and adviser for the charitable community. While politics and discordant views prevented the Filer Commission from delineating a specific role for the proposed commission, it was a serious attempt to bring structure and supervision to the charitable world. The Donee Group produced an even stronger recommendation, a call for a permanent, standing committee in both the House and the Senate to supervise the growth and effectiveness of the voluntary sector.

At first, the political prospects for the Filer Commission recommendations were promising. John had friends in the highest places. His younger brother Nelson was the vice president of the United States and presumably sympathetic to the efforts of his eldest brother. It was well known that William Simon, who had replaced Shultz as secretary of the Treasury, supported the national commission recommendation. And Mills, enlisted in the commission process from the beginning, could be counted on to give the recommendations a favorable hearing in his powerful congressional committee.

But within months of the publication of the final report, both Nelson Rockefeller and Mills were gone from office: Rockefeller the victim of the Democratic wave that drove Republicans from the White House, and Mills the author of a notorious sex scandal that ended with his mistress, an Argentinian stripper with the stage name Fanne Foxe, paddling furiously and drunkenly across the Tidal Basin in a futile attempt to escape the U.S. Park Police. The incoming Carter administration was suspicious of, bordering on hostile to, the proposals of Rockefeller and the Filer Commission. President Carter and his Georgia mafia had campaigned on a platform of reducing the privileges of Washington elites, including the welter of advisory groups, panels, and blue-ribbon commissions typically populated by political insiders and friends of the administration. In this atmosphere, a new commission with broad regulatory authority—especially one championed by someone named Rockefeller—was doomed to find little purchase. After a few encounters between Rockefeller and the incoming Carter team, the White House and the Treasury Department declared their opposition to a new charity commission. The public announcement was a bitter pill for John, who had spent the last decade trying to craft a new vision for American philanthropy. When Rockefeller died months later in a car accident, the light of charitable reform was extinguished with him.

In the thirty-four years since Rockefeller's death, there has been no similar effort to shape and manage the charitable world. The non-profit sector has continued to explode, adding tens of thousands of new organizations each year, and it would probably be unrecognizable to John if he had lived to see it. And, as we will shortly see, the unchecked growth of the charitable world has diluted the very definition of what charities mean and do.

THREE

The Spaghetti Factory

The Story of the Uncharitable Charity

I N THE 2009 movie *Whip It,* Ellen Page plays Bliss Cavendar, an attractive, engaging seventeen-year-old from Bodeen, Texas. Bliss is a social misfit, constrained by narrow-minded small-town culture and yearning for new outlets for her energies. After spotting a flyer on a trip to Austin, she finds fulfillment in the speed, drama, violence, and underground appeal of Roller Derby. Skating under the pseudonym of Babe Ruthless, she becomes a star, a vision of youth and purity amid the tattoos and the beer-soaked sexuality of the sport. Unfortunately for her, but fortunately for the narrative arc of the movie, her passion for Roller Derby collides with her mother's view of female propriety. Mom pushes Bliss unwillingly into the beauty pageant circuit, creating the core conflict of the movie. When Mom finds out about her daughter's surreptitious and decidedly unladylike passion for Roller Derby, she is horrified and rejects Bliss's pleas to be allowed to participate in the championship match.

What Bliss needed was a better strategy. Instead of hiding her Roller Derby activities, she should have promoted her skating as a socially sanctioned charitable activity, akin to working for the Red Cross or, better yet, the Junior League. Meet the Renegade

Roller Girls, a Roller Derby league in Bend, Oregon. The Renegade Roller Girls have much in common with their fictional Texas
sisters. Like the Texas league, they promise violent, scantily clad
action in the "hottest show in town, with our no holds barred play,"
and they display the same affection for bumps, bruises, and blood
that are the badges of honor in the movie. But there are differences
too: unlike the fictional league of *Whip It,* they do not operate in
the shadows by taking over an abandoned warehouse for race night.
Instead, they operate openly, as a 501(c)(3) organization approved as
a public service charity by the Internal Revenue Service.

This classification of the Renegade Roller Girls might come as a surprise to Bliss's mother, but there are many equally improbable public
charities. Numerous organizations qualified by the IRS as tax-exempt
charitable organizations fail to pass the laugh test. For example, in
2008 the IRS approved tax exemption for the All Colorado Beer Fes-
tival, an annual two-day beer tasting and drinking event in Boulder
and Colorado Springs. Self-described as a "fun distribution" event, it
also has been approved by the IRS as a charity, notwithstanding the
socially questionable, if economically gratifying, decision to hold the
celebration of Colorado alcoholic beverages in two college towns.

The IRS also approved the 501(c)(3) application of the Grand
Canyon Sisters of Perpetual Indulgence. The sisterhood is a cheery
proponent of the drag queen lifestyle. Its Web site promises frank
discussions of sex, cucumbers, condoms, drag, and dignity. Just so
that the public does not confuse members of the sisterhood with
more traditional and conservative sororities, the sisters can be recognized by their flamboyant and colorful outfits, heavy makeup and
face paint, and heels so high that they would make the stiletto queen
Mariah Carey stagger. The tongue-firmly-planted-in-cheek nature
of the organization is reflected in the sisters' names as well: Father
Craven Moorehead, Sister Atopa Sleepur-Sofa (the Broyhill Harlot),
Sister Inga von Schlappenheinie (Barer of the Bodacious Ta-Tas), and,
a personal favorite, Sister FarmaSue Tickle (of the Flaming Habit).

The inclusion of these organizations on a list of official charities might only be an amusing story of bureaucratic ineptitude were it not symptomatic of a larger concern. The Internal Revenue Service, charged with reviewing applications for tax-exempt status and weeding out applicants that do not meet charitable requirements, does not act as an effective adjudicator of what constitutes a charity and what does not. In recent years, according to a Stanford University study, the IRS has approved more than 99.5 percent of all charitable applications. This statistic reveals the first troubling truth about our process for deciding what is a charity and what is not: we don't have one. We permit almost anyone with a basic facility with government forms to start a charity. The failure of the IRS and other regulatory organizations to act as a gatekeeper for the charitable sector has real consequences. There are of course substantial economic costs to the public in the form of income tax and property tax exemptions for charities and for charitable deductions taken by donors. It also means that more and more charities compete for a finite set of dollars from public and private donors, diminishing the effectiveness of individual charities. And it produces confusion and mistrust when so many charities seem frankly uncharitable.

The modern understanding of what constitutes a charity can be traced back to a surprisingly specific point in time, a British legal decision issued in 1891. Prior to that date, the definition of charity was generally restricted to relief for the poor. Then the Moravian Church appealed a denial of tax exemption from the Board of Inland Revenue, the English equivalent of the IRS. The presiding judge, Lord Macnaghten, in a decision still cited in both American and Commonwealth courts to this day, rejected the government's position, holding that the definition of charity was far broader than relief of the poor: " 'Charity' in its legal sense comprises four principal divisions: trusts for the relief of poverty; trusts for the advancement of education; trusts for the advancement of religion; and trusts for other purposes beneficial to the community, not falling under any of the preceding heads."[1] This catchall notion of charity was quickly adopted by the American Congress in the Tariff Act of 1894, the first law that took notice of the special tax status of charitable institutions, in that case by exempting them from corporate income taxes. Subsequent tax acts have gradually added to and clarified the definition of charity. To the 1894 list of charitable, religious, and educational organizations, Congress added organizations dedicated to scientific discovery (in 1913), prevention of cruelty to children and animals (in 1918), literary purposes (in 1921), testing for public safety (in 1934), and amateur athletics (in 1976), but throughout all this expansion the Macnaghten formulation of "purposes beneficial to the community" has remained at the heart of the American understanding of public charity.

The interpretation of what exactly is beneficial to the community has always allowed for broad and highly idiosyncratic views, leaving both judges and regulators in an "I know it when I see it" posture. That posture has been tempered over time by the development by courts and legislatures of a couple of key interpretative principles. First is the acknowledgment that the charitable tax exemption and special charitable status exist to relieve the government of having to provide and pay for certain services. This "public functions" test puts significant bounds around what constitutes a charity, including the implication that charities should not replicate the actions of the private marketplace.[2] Second, the charity cannot operate for private benefit; its value must be felt broadly within the community. While this rule does not require that charitable services be open to all—this would wreak havoc on private school and university admission processes, for example—it does require that charities provide services on some evenhanded and equitable basis, one not wholly shaped by the ability to pay.

It is difficult to fit the Renegade Rollers under these or any definition of charity, but the individual cases that fall through the cracks are not the most serious problem. Rather, there are entire industries that stretch and contort our current definition of charity while claiming tens of billions of dollars each year in tax benefits. In this chapter, we will look at two segments of the charitable sector that once operated as charities but now are indistinguishable from for-profit businesses. We will also examine organizations that are widely accepted as charities but fail the second of the two key elements that define charitable service, serving the community at large. These stories of "uncharitable charities" reveal a troubling truth about the charitable sector: having once conferred charitable status, we have few opportunities to reassess that decision even as the organizations themselves change. While it is technically possible for a charity to lose its tax-exempt status, in practical terms the IRS lacks any meaningful system for reassessment. Realistically, once a charity, always a charity. Yet charities, like all other institutions, may shift with changing times, altering business practices and sometimes even core missions. Such is the case for charitable hospitals.

When Chicago's John H. Stroger Jr. Hospital opened in 2002, it was touted for its state-of-the-art facility and for having the latest in diagnostic and therapeutic equipment. But just a decade later, it has already fallen on tough times due to outsized demands on its resources. Dirty and overcrowded, it is an uninviting place at the best of times, sometimes unfavorably compared by patients to third-world medical centers. As the main public, county-operated hospital in Chicago, Stroger is free to all, and people come from across the city despite long waits, frustrating admission rules, and sometimes coarse treatment at the hands of overwhelmed medical staff.[3] The hallways are often lined with uninsured and underinsured patients. Some of those patients have come to Stroger because they know that it is the hospital of last resort for those without financial means. Others, however, have come via a more indirect route. These patients have gone first to other hospitals and have been transferred to Stroger. They bear discharge slips, prescriptions, and even Google and Yahoo! maps. "Go to Cook County Hospital immediately," says a discharge slip for a man with a broken jaw. "Go to Cook County ER to be evaluated for admission," reads another, this one for a man with a tumor. Across the city and even in adjacent counties, hospitals routinely off-load uninsured and risky patients to Stroger and other Cook County medical facilities, transferring the cost of free treatment or the risk of bad debt to government-run hospitals.[4]

In this age of bottom-line health-care management, this type of behavior might be expected, except that the patient-dumping practices described here are committed not by for-profit hospitals organized for the purpose of maximizing economic returns but by charitable hospitals chartered to provide services to the community as a whole. These organizations, often founded as hospitals for the poor and the indigent, have increasingly taken on business and compensation practices that are virtually indistinguishable from for-profit institutions and, in some cases, involve predatory financial practices that their commercial brethren shy away from.

Quinton White became an unlikely celebrity because of these very practices. Born in 1927, White married his wife, Jeanette, in 1946. He lived an unremarkable working-class life: four sons, a steady job as a dry-cleaning worker, a small house in a quiet neighborhood in Bridgeport, Connecticut. In 1982, Jeanette was diagnosed with throat cancer and made two inpatient visits to Yale–New Haven Hospital, the renowned nonprofit hospital owned and operated by Yale University. The treatments, while perhaps prolonging her life, were ultimately unsuccessful, and Mrs. White died of her cancer in 1993. She left behind a host of hospital bills and no Medicaid or private insurance to cover the expenses.

At the time of the 1982 treatment, the Whites plainly lacked the financial wherewithal to pay off the medical care. They initially offered to pay the hospital at a rate of $25 per month. Deeming that offer inadequate, the hospital's lawyers went to court, placing a lien on the Whites' house and obtaining a summary judgment for $19,000 in medical charges plus $3,000 in interest and attorneys' fees. The judge approved a payment schedule of $5 a week, essentially the same as the Whites' offer. Though Mr. White dutifully made the court-ordered payments to Yale–New Haven, the payments did not even cover the accruing interest on the bills, a fact that did not escape the attention of the hospital's lawyers. In 1996, three years after Mrs. White's death, the hospital returned to court, seeking higher payment. The judge eventually agreed, tripling payments to $15 a week. The hospital also sought to seize Mr. White's thin savings and ultimately collected $9,600, leaving White with only about $5,000 in savings that could not be legally seized because they were Social Security payments. Mr. White continued to make regular payments on his debt, which was mounting faster than he could pay it. In 2002, White was himself hospitalized for serious kidney and heart conditions and missed a series of payments (all in all, he missed only seventeen payments in twenty years, most of them when he was hospitalized). The hospital's lawyers promptly returned to court, seeking to seize Mr. White's remaining savings. With judgment in hand, the hospital instructed the state marshals to proceed to White's bank and seize up to $32,000 in any savings and checking accounts. Yale–New Haven only ceased its efforts when the marshals reported back that Mr. White's assets had by now dwindled to $491 and were only the legally protected Social Security payments.[5]

By 2002, White had made payments to the hospital totaling almost $16,000, a number almost equal to the original bill, but still owed almost $40,000 due to compounded interest and fees. In 2003, he told *The Wall Street Journal* that he believed he would never be able to get out from under that debt: "They will never get the whole amount. I am not gonna live that long." The debt had outlived his wife and seemed likely to outlive him as well. When revealed by the *New Haven Advocate* and *The Wall Street Journal*, the portrait of a dying man buried under twenty years of medical bills was a shock to the New Haven community; it was made worse by the fact that

Yale–New Haven controlled a multimillion-dollar fund to help out-patients just like Jeanette White but had never told the Whites of its existence. Instead, Yale–New Haven outsourced collection of debts to private attorneys, some of whom made millions of dollars in fees from the practice and had every financial incentive to pursue the Whites to the end of their lives, and beyond.

The story of the Whites has been repeated time and again across the country. Numerous newspaper stories, lawsuits, and civil enforcement actions by attorneys general attest to predatory collection practices in charitable hospitals. At least the Whites' story had what passes for a happy ending. Embarrassed by press accounts and pressured by the attorney general of Connecticut, Yale–New Haven cleared Quinton White's debt in 2004, twenty-two years after Jeanette's hospital visits and more than a decade after she passed away.

Charitable hospitals have become some of the most aggressive debt collectors in the country.[6] Their weapons of choice include lawsuits, garnishment of wages, seizing of savings accounts, and placing liens upon property. Some charitable hospitals have outdone their peers by availing themselves of the rarely used legal process called "body attachments." This legal tactic of arresting a debtor who fails to comply with a court order or appear for a debt-related hearing is considered so extreme that many major commercial creditors have policies expressly prohibiting their collection agencies from petitioning the court for arrest warrants. Ford Credit and Sears Roebuck, to name just two, have specifically eschewed the practice, which smacks of the excesses of Dickensian England. But some charitable hospitals do pursue such aggressive measures, and a few have become notorious for their efforts. In Illinois, the Department of Revenue was so shocked by the conduct of two hospitals—Carle Foundation Hospital (the primary teaching hospital of the University of Illinois) and Provena Covenant Medical Center (a Catholic hospital in Urbana)—that it took the virtually unprecedented step of attempting to revoke the charitable property tax exemption for both. The agency was unsuccessful with Carle, but it was ultimately successful, after nine years of litigation, in persuading the Illinois Supreme Court that the Provena hospital was not entitled to property tax relief.[7]

The outrageousness of these collection practices is compounded by the fact that the hospitals are often seeking much higher payments from uninsured patients than from similar patients who are privately insured or covered by Medicaid. Both public and private insurers negotiate deep discounts from price lists prepared by hospitals and doctors. Uninsured patients, who have no negotiating leverage, are charged the medical equivalent of rack rate, a price unrelated to the prevailing value of services in the marketplace. Take, for instance, Paul Shipman, a middle-aged furniture salesman who underwent a cardiac procedure at Inova Fairfax, a well-regarded charitable hospital in Northern Virginia. Shipman and his wife, like fifty-five million other Americans in 2004, were uninsured at the time of the operation, and he was presented with a bill for more than $29,000 for twenty-one hours of care. This bill was roughly twice as much as Medicaid would have paid Inova in full satisfaction for this service. Ironically, Shipman was able to negotiate a discounted rate for similar services from Reston Hospital Center, a for-profit institution, but was unable to secure any type of fee parity from Inova. He was soon set upon by the hospital's collection agencies.[8] Shipman's story is not unique. Cases like his have been widely reported in the press,[9] and they are only a small part of a larger, unsettling effort to maximize revenues by many charitable hospitals, some of whom have now gone so far as to station bill collectors in hospital emergency rooms.[10]

It is unlikely that charitable hospitals have specifically targeted the uninsured with these predatory billing practices. The "rack rates" are a relic of the 1980s, when hospitals were required by law to maintain one set of prices for all patients. But several significant changes occurred in the health-care industry. Medicare and Medicaid began to set uniform payments across the industry, and HMOs and insurers became large enough to negotiate discounted rates from hospitals. Hospitals now had an incentive to maintain high published prices, often significantly higher than their costs, in order to support their negotiations with the insurance industry. The unintentional result has been a tiered pricing system that charges the uninsured 140 percent more than insured patients.[11]

The apparent callousness of many charitable hospitals has not gone unnoticed by some regulators. A number of states, including Illinois, Minnesota, and California, have crafted indigent care procedures, placing limits on billing and collection procedures and creating funding pools to support care for the destitute and uninsured. New York, for instance, operates a $1.2 billion Indigent Care Pool (ICP) for the more than 2.8 million uninsured and underinsured residents of the state. In 2007, it enacted the Hospital Financial Assistance Law (HFAL), requiring stricter procedures and greater transparency for hospitals wanting access to the ICP funds. HFAL is informally known as Manny's Law, named for Manny Lanza, a young employee of the Wendy's fast-food chain. In 2004, Lanza was admitted to St. Luke's Hospital, a prestigious charitable hospital affiliated with Columbia University, with a severe brain condition called arteriovenous malformation (AVM). Lanza had been referred there by another Manhattan hospital since St. Luke's specialized in the treatment of AVM. Despite its expertise and the urgency of Lanza's condition, staff at St. Luke's repeatedly postponed his treatment, telling his family that they would not treat him until he obtained Medicaid coverage. Lanza died in January 2005 at the age of twenty-four while appealing a denial of coverage because his income from a low-level fast-food job exceeded the Medicaid income threshold. After his death, debt collectors for St. Luke's called Lanza's family, seeking resolution of more than $42,000 in hospital bills.

HFAL was intended to cure these problems by providing clear accountability for hospitals and requiring them to assist patients in need, both medically and by helping them apply for state assistance. But a 2012 study found that more than two-thirds of New York hospitals were not complying with Manny's Law and that hospitals continue to turn to collection agencies and sue when collection fails.[12]

Ironically, the unpaid bills—still reflecting much higher rates than what insurers or the government will pay for identical services—are then reported by the hospitals as charity care.[13]

The issue in New York is now made even more urgent by the implementation of federal health-care reform, the Affordable Care Act (ACA). The ACA is expected to reduce, but not eliminate, the rolls of the uninsured; New York is projected to still have up to 1.8 million uninsured citizens after full implementation of the law. But the ACA will also virtually eliminate federal support for indigent care, meaning that there will be far less money in state coffers to pay hospitals for care of the uninsured. The poor and the indigent will thus have to increasingly rely on the good graces of charitable hospitals, a not entirely promising prospect given current practices.

In most ways, charitable hospitals are not worse than for-profit hospitals. Rather, they are exactly the same. Uncompensated nuns, scuffed floors, and Jell-O on the meal tray are things of the past. Today, charitable hospitals are some of the richest medical institutions in the world. Just down the street from scruffy Stroger Hospital is Northwestern Memorial Hospital, which in 1999 opened a new $1 billion campus, complete with a marble lobby, a thousand works of art, and a roof topped with ten thousand square feet of gardens. Patients in Northwestern's state-of-the-art birthing center can watch TV or surf the Web on forty-two-inch flat-screen televisions, order twenty-four-hour room service meals, and connect with nurses and doctors via a wireless paging system. The services are consistent with the neighborhood, the fashionable Gold Coast of Chicago, and so are the profits and compensation practices. In 2006, the hospital rewarded its outgoing CEO, Gary Mecklenburg, for quintupling patient revenue during his tenure with a $16.4 million exit package. The only thing frugal about nonprofit Northwestern is its charity spending practices; its annual spending on uncompensated care is a reported $20 million, or 2 percent of patient spending[14]—a percentage below average for all hospitals and a total that is only a fraction of the tax breaks it receives from property tax abatement and from exemptions from sales and income taxes.

In a competitive environment in which many hospitals, including charitable institutions, compete for an elite clientele willing to spend above and beyond insurance reimbursements, Northwestern barely stands out from its peers. Many charitable hospitals have invested heavily in "amenities suites" to serve the wealthiest patrons. The New York–Presbyterian Hospital/Weill Cornell Medical Center calls its Greenberg Pavilion a "very special luxury accommodations" experience and promotes whisper-quiet rooms and hotel-like services that include a kitchen, marbled bathrooms with Euro-style walk-in showers, Frette bed linens, and original, framed works of art. These luxuries come with a price: $1,500 a night on top of whatever private insurance or Medicare pays. New York–Presbyterian is one of the most prominent hospitals in the country, and it attracts high-end donors as well as high-end customers. Sandy Weill, the former chairman of Citigroup whose name graces the front door to the hospital, has contributed tens of millions of dollars. The luxury wing itself is named for Hank Greenberg, another major contributor and the former CEO of AIG—the insurance company at the heart of the mortgage-backed securities crisis—and it is more than a little ironic that his millions in tax-deductible contributions have gone to underwrite a hospital unit that serves only the wealthiest clientele. But New York–Presbyterian is not alone; it has competition from other charitable hospitals for the richest customers: Cedars-Sinai Medical Center in Los Angeles promises the "ultimate in pampering," and Mount Sinai Medical Center in New York touts its personalized service to its high-end clientele. Its director of hospitality bragged to *The New York Times* in 2012 that "we pride ourselves on getting anything the patient wants. If they have a craving for lobster tails and we don't have them on the menu, we'll go out and get them."[15]

This high-end arms race extends to CEO pay as well. Perks such as country-club memberships, spousal travel, car allowances, and interest-free loans are piled on top of extraordinary salaries like the compensation package of more than $7 million a year for the head of the Cleveland Clinic and the packages of over $5 million for the heads of NorthShore University HealthSystem, Catholic Healthcare West, McLaren Health Care, and AHS Hospital Corporation.

Nonprofit hospitals are actually more likely to be profitable than their for-profit counterparts. In 2008, *The Wall Street Journal* reported[16] that 77 percent of nonprofit hospitals were profitable as compared with only 61 percent of for-profit hospitals. The combined net income of the fifty largest nonprofit hospitals jumped nearly eightfold to $4.27 billion in the first half of the last decade. Ascension Health, a Catholic nonprofit system that runs a string of hospitals in the Midwest, reported net income of $1.2 billion in 2007 and cash on hand of $7.4 billion—more cash than the Walt Disney Company. Children's hospitals are particularly profitable. The thirty-nine largest children's hospitals—all of them charities—reported more than $1.5 billion in profits in 2009 and had combined net assets of more than $23 billion. Boston Children's Hospital, recently cited in a critical government report for having some of the highest charges in the state, has investment assets of $2.6 billion, an astonishing number for a single hospital not part of a larger group.[17]

Profitable companies do not necessarily like to sit on their cash. For-profit businesses can distribute profits to owners and shareholders or use them for acquisitions. Profitable charities have fewer outlets, but they also like to put their profits to work. This has spurred a huge building boom in hospitals, even where they are not needed. In the last decade, more than $16 billion has been spent on new and expanded children's hospitals alone. Orlando is now getting its *third* children's hospital, a ninety-five-bed, $400 million facility courtesy of the Nemours Foundation. State officials twice rejected the proposed hospital, noting that cities the size of Orlando typically have only one such center. Regulators reversed themselves in 2008, after Nemours, a wealthy and well-connected Jacksonville foundation, launched an extensive marketing campaign and signed up the support of leading state politicians. The Children's Hospital of Philadelphia has spent more than $1 billion on new facilities and plans to spend $1 billion more over the next few years. A new hospital in Pittsburgh will cost $625 million, more than, as a report in *Kaiser Health News* noted, the combined cost of Heinz Field and PNC Park, the homes of the Steelers and the Pirates. All this building comes with a significant public cost in direct subsidies, tax-exempt financing, and tax benefits for the hospitals and their donors alike. Little of this public investment is repaid in charitable service: on average, the top-tier children's hospitals reported less than 2 percent in free medical care, and some, like the Texas Children's Hospital in Houston, dipped under .5 percent.[18]

Charitable hospitals will tell you that the cases cited here are mere outliers and that they provide a vast range of charitable services including treating indigent patients, serving underserved communities, and providing care in less profitable medical fields. As Dr. Neil Rosenberg, medical director of the intensive care unit at Westlake Hospital in Chicago, told *The New York Times* in 2004, "We give away care routinely. I don't think there's another business alive that comes close to what we do."[19] To the extent that charitable hospitals acknowledge their occasional overzealous pursuit of nonpaying patients, they place it in the context of hundreds of thousands of properly served customers and in a business environment that puts a premium on processing claims quickly and on careful cash flow management techniques. The nonprofit hospitals contend that in the end they fully discharge their charitable and religious responsibilities to help indigent and uninsured patients to justify a massive indirect federal and state tax subsidy that runs into the billions of dollars. Sadly, their story is just not true.

The nonprofit sector plays a huge role in the American health-care system. Of the approximately 630,000 Medicare-certified hospital beds in this country, 68 percent are in charitable hospitals, typically run either by religiously affiliated organizations or by community groups. The remaining beds are roughly equally divided between for-profit hospitals and hospitals that are government owned and operated, usually county or municipal facilities. In 2006, the nonpartisan

Congressional Budget Office (CBO) undertook at the behest of the Senate Committee on Finance a groundbreaking study of the non-profit hospital sector.[20] Rather than study the value of nonprofit hospitals in isolation, the CBO studied the services of all three sectors of the hospital industry to find out whether charitable hospitals actually provide more charitable services than for-profit or government hospitals. The CBO defined charity as: (1) the provision of uncompensated services,[21] (2) the provision of Medicare and Medicaid services at lower than market rates, (3) the provision of specialized and uneconomical medical services to the community, and (4) the provision of services to economically deprived and underserved communities. The findings of the CBO study—that the nonprofit sector behaves in the aggregate virtually identically to the for-profit sector (and in a far less public-spirited manner than government-owned hospitals)—would have been shocking but for the fact that they largely confirmed the findings of a series of earlier, though less comprehensive, evaluations.

For their study of uncompensated care, the CBO researchers studied hospitals in five states: Florida, California, Georgia, Texas, and Indiana. They found that the "average uncompensated care share"—that is, the cost of uncompensated care as a percentage of the hospitals' total operating expenses—was quite high at government hospitals (about 13 percent) and that the uncompensated care share at both nonprofit (4.7 percent) and for-profit hospitals (4.2 percent) was significantly lower than government hospitals and virtually identical to each other. The slightly higher rate of uncompensated care at non-profit hospitals was attributable to just a handful of highly charitable hospitals that drove up the average.

When it came to providing Medicare and Medicaid services, an important metric because Medicare and Medicaid typically reimburse at rates below actual costs and hospitals underwrite the difference, the CBO found that these services actually account for a higher percentage of activities at for-profit hospitals (17.2 share) than at nonprofit hospitals (15.6 share) and both are substantially lower than at government hospitals (27.0 share). The provision of specialized services—in this case, intensive care for burn victims, emergency room care, high-level trauma care, and labor and delivery services—was also studied on the theory that these services were important to the community and generally unprofitable to the hospital. To their credit, nonprofit hospitals were found to provide significantly greater specialized services than their for-profit counterparts, especially with respect to emergency room care and labor and delivery services. Finally, the CBO studied the locations of various hospital groups and found that the nonprofit hospitals were, counterintuitively, more likely to be located in prosperous and economically advantaged communities than for-profit hospitals.

Taken collectively, these numbers show that the differences in charitable behavior between for-profit and nonprofit hospitals are negligible at best and nonexistent at worst. The two sectors have functionally merged. In a number of cases, for-profit hospital chains have actually acquired nonprofit hospitals, raising concerns in their communities about the loss of specialized and charitable services. But the changes in ownership structure in all these cases have not led to any material decline in services.[22] This was not, as some might postulate, because of a fear of popular backlash but because, for these charitable hospitals, the transition to for-profit management proved to be business as usual.

The CBO study and other reporting on the practices of charitable hospitals did in fact spur reform efforts, including a proposal in Congress to require a minimum uncompensated care rate of 5 percent in return for tax-exempt status. All the major proposals, however, have been beaten back, with reform advocates having to settle for greater public reporting obligations for charitable hospitals on the theory that greater transparency would ratchet up pressure for change. It hasn't worked. A 2012 nationwide study found continuing low levels of uncompensated care, only 1.51 percent on average, a number less than half the profit margins for the same group of hospitals.[23]

The issues here have substantial economic consequences. Hospitals are the single largest component of the charitable sector, and the value of tax incentives is enormous, if judged by the $66 million property tax bill recently sent to the Prentice Women's Hospital, a sparkling new hospital in Chicago's upscale Streeterville neighborhood. Prentice, one of three hospitals targeted by the Illinois Department of Revenue, was deemed uncharitable because Northwestern Memorial, its sister facility, provided free care amounting to only 1.85 percent of revenues—a standard, if widely applied, that would call into question the charitable status of hundreds of hospitals nationwide. While estimates vary, the value of local, state, and federal tax incentives to nonprofit hospitals almost certainly exceeds $20 billion a year, and perhaps by a good bit. Since charitable hospitals return only a fraction of that in charitable care, it raises the possibility that the public would be far better served by removing or reducing the subsidy and using the savings to buy better health care from the best and most efficient providers. And it raises the question: When a charity stops being charitable, does anyone notice?

At the core of our charitable system is the notion that charities perform critical social functions and thereby save the government and the taxpayer the effort and expense of providing the service. But the charitable sector is filled with organizations doing things that no government would care to do and that would scandalize taxpayers if they understood they were underwriting the effort. That brings us to the Allstate Sugar Bowl in New Orleans, an annual college football matchup now completing its seventy-eighth year. It is a much-anticipated game, not only by the football faithful, but by the city's beleaguered merchants and hoteliers. The football game itself lasts only three hours, but the party runs for days—from the pregame concerts to the corporate festivals scattered across the French Quarter to the bacchanalia of Bourbon Street. For four days, the streets run thick with drunken college students tripping in and out of strip clubs, music joints, and quick-serve bars. Given this backdrop, we might be able to forgive the collected fans—drunk or sober—for not realizing that they had gathered in New Orleans for a grand charity event.

The first college football bowl game was played in 1902 as the culmination of the Tournament of Roses in Pasadena, California, giving truth to ABC's Keith Jackson's evocative description of the Rose Bowl as "the granddaddy of them all." The game was launched to shore up the finances of the flagging Tournament of Roses, and to an extent the ploy was successful, with more than eight thousand fans attending. Unfortunately, while a financial success, the contest was a competitive mismatch: the University of Michigan squad of Coach Fielding "Hurry Up" Yost annihilated Stanford 49–0. Fearing that the crowds would not return to watch another mismatch, the Tournament of Roses organizers replaced the football game the next year with a polo match, which proved far too rarefied and calm for the rowdy turn-of-the-century California crowd. In 1904, inspired by a recent Broadway adaptation of General Lew Wallace's national best seller *Ben-Hur: A Tale of the Christ*, the Rose Committee unexpectedly shifted to amateur chariot races, which held the allure of speed, gambling, and quite possibly grievous bodily damage.[24] The races were an immediate success, marked by large crowds and unforgettable moments of drama. In the second year, Ed Off, one of the racers and a member of the Tournament of Roses organizing committee, lost control of his horses and was nearly flung from his chariot. When his team was finally brought under control, Off carefully dismounted, presented himself to the tournament queen, gave a courtly bow, and then promptly fell flat on his face as his rubbery legs gave out. The next year, Off was thrown from his chariot and sustained injuries that were happily not life threatening but encouraged his permanent retirement from the games. Though the races continued to draw crowds approaching twenty thousand, eventually the novelty of chariot racing began to wane. The Rose Committee valiantly tried to pump up interest in the races in 1913 by supplementing them with ostrich races and a race between a camel and an elephant. These attempts proved to be in vain. In 1916, with the Michigan blowout only a distant echo, the Rose Bowl football game returned with Washington State prevailing over Brown 14–0.

With the successful return of the Rose Bowl, the growth of college football as an American institution began. Because the Rose Bowl grew out of a public charity, the Tournament of Roses, it and all future bowl games were organized along the same lines, claiming all the tax exemptions and privileges permitted by law. Over the years, the bowl system has grown, with its first growth spurt coming, oddly enough, in the 1930s, smack in the middle of the Great Depression. The Orange Bowl and the Sugar Bowl both began in 1935, the Sun Bowl and the Cotton Bowl in 1936 and 1937, respectively. After World War II came another burst, this time of mostly transient but often amusingly titled games: the Cigar Bowl in Tampa, the Raisin Bowl in Fresno, and the Salad Bowl in Phoenix. Among the most colorful was the Bacardi Bowl, informally named after the distilling company, which was played seven times in Havana between 1907 and 1946. It typically pitted an American college squad against a Cuban club team and often offered an interesting political sideshow, including the 1937 match that the Cuban dictator Fulgencio Batista threatened to cancel because his picture was not included in the game program. Only the last-minute work of an agile printer saved the day. From the 1950s to the 1970s, new bowls would pop up from time to time, including the much-revered Poulan Weed-Eater Independence Bowl. Some would last a year, some a decade, but there were always fewer than ten in any one year. That changed in the 1980s with the emergence of lavish television contracts and the related rise in corporate sponsorship. In 1988, the Sugar Bowl became the USF&G Sugar Bowl, and the flow of money began in earnest. In 2010–11, there were thirty-five bowl games, virtually all of them titled with a sponsoring corporation that can be loosely grouped into providers of food (Kraft Fight Hunger Bowl, Outback Bowl, Chick-fil-A Bowl, Little Caesars Pizza Bowl, Tostitos Fiesta Bowl, and Beef 'O' Brady St. Petersburg Bowl), technology (uDrove Humanitarian Bowl, GoDaddy.com Bowl, and

AT&T Cotton Bowl), and financial services (EagleBank Bowl, Discover Orange Bowl, and Citi National Championship Bowl Game).

It is no doubt puzzling to most Americans that this string of open-air parties, football games, and corporate promotion events have the same charitable designation as Habitat for Humanity, Teach for America, or the local food bank. And the bowl games are not only tax privileged but also the frequent recipients of governmental support. The Sugar Bowl, for instance, took in over $5.4 million in federal government subsidies from 2007 to 2009; the Orange Bowl received $1.2 million in 2009; and the Fiesta Bowl has received frequent and generous support from the State of Arizona.[25] The bowl games have defended their charitable status by claiming that revenues flow through them in significant amounts to other charities that provide vital social support to the needy; it is an interesting if not entirely persuasive argument that an entity that gives away some of its profits is in fact a charity (which would lump bowl games with JPMorgan Chase, Bernie Madoff, and the government of Saudi Arabia), but it is beside the point since the bowl games contribute well under 2 percent of their annual revenue to other charities.[26] Where, then, do the revenues from bowl games go? The bulk of the proceeds goes not to the needy but to the sponsoring committees and their staff for plainly non-charitable expenses.

The bowl games spend an extraordinary amount on executive and staff salaries, benefits, and perks.[27] The Sugar Bowl's executive director, Paul Hoolahan, made $645,386 in 2009, over 5 percent of the organization's total revenue. When Hoolahan's two top deputies were added in, their salaries amounted to over $1.2 million, or a full 10 percent of total revenues. Second on the compensation list among bowl executives was John Junker, then CEO of the Fiesta Bowl, who took in $592,418 in 2009. The perks that come with these jobs are also substantial and certainly exceed those to be had at comparably sized for-profit businesses. Top executives and their spouses are rewarded with first-class travel and luxury accommodations: the

Orange Bowl alone spent more than $750,000 on travel in 2009, a stunning amount for an organization that comprises only a handful of employees and volunteer board members. The Fiesta Bowl provides complimentary health and social club memberships for its executives and grosses up their salaries to pay for the tax consequences of these perks. The Sugar Bowl annually spends more than $150,000 on executive meeting expenses, and its Football Committee, which foots the bill for bowl insiders to travel to college football games all over the country, spends over half a million dollars a year.

While no doubt these jobs have their challenges, it is still fair to question what these positions are worth. The bowl committees produce only one event a year, and that event is essentially the same event year after year. The Fiesta Bowl effectively conceded this point in its public filings when it noted that Junker only works twenty-one hours a week in return for his nearly $600,000 in compensation. The admission that bowl games can be run with a half-time executive director largely confirmed what many had long suspected: other than the requirement to wear garishly bright sport jackets, the job of bowl director has to be one of the least onerous in America.

The bowl committees are not shy about spreading their good fortune to others within the college football community. The Orange Bowl, for instance, holds an annual Summer Splash, which in 2010 brought together forty-six athletic directors and conference commissioners and their spouses with the Orange Bowl Committee leadership for a cruise on Royal Caribbean's *Majesty of the Seas*. The *Majesty of the Seas* boasts of its conference facilities, but it needn't have bothered, since the Summer Splash cruise week was fully booked with leisure activities. Attendees were offered a full day at the ship's private island CocoCay in the Bahamas and a day at the Atlantis Paradise Island, complete with an Orange Bowl private bar and pool lounge area. If pools and slides weren't their thing, options for attendees included snorkeling, parasailing, gambling at the Casino Royale, a Thriller powerboat adventure—virtually anything other than work related to the Orange Bowl. The Orange Bowl annually spends about $1.6 million on entertainment and catering and so much money on golf that it receives a separate line item in the Orange Bowl's federal filings.

Golf is a particularly large expense for the bowl committees. The Sugar Bowl actually maintains a Standing Committee on Golf. Not to be outdone by its longer-tenured rivals, the Fiesta Bowl spends more than $300,000 a year on an annual Fiesta Frolic, a weekend of golf and entertainment for college football officials at a Phoenix-area resort. The Fiesta Bowl in addition gave $120,000 in interest-free, non-secured loans to its two top executives so that they could join the exclusive Whisper Rock Golf Club in Scottsdale. Beyond that, the bowl games lavish gifts on their employees, on their committee members, and on other people of significance within the sporting world. The Orange Bowl spent $535,000 in gifts in 2006, and the Sugar Bowl passed out more than $200,000 in gifts and bonuses in 2008, a year in which the organization lost money. The Sugar Bowl topped that with a secretive fund called only "special appropriations," which exceeded $700,000 over a recent two-year period.

These expenditures are magnified by the fact that the bowl games are not particularly large organizations, even by charitable standards; the Fiesta Bowl's annual revenue is only about $17.5 million. With such a large percentage of revenues being lavishly washed over salaries, events, and expense accounts, it is clear that the principal beneficiaries of these charities are not the public in any meaningful way but a small club of bowl employees, committee members, and the athletic directors and conference commissioners who have been the loudest and proudest defenders of the current bowl system.

Some of the schools playing in the bowl games are additional economic beneficiaries of this system. The bowls at the bottom of the food chain provide relatively modest support, sometimes not even enough to cover the considerable travel costs of a large football squad and accompanying entourage. The New Orleans Bowl (a lower-tier bowl held at the Superdome) pays out only about $350,000 per team, the Hawaii Bowl a little under $400,000, and the San Diego County

Credit Union Poinsettia Bowl about $750,000 per side. The payouts get considerably richer as the teams move up the bowl ladder: a mid-level bowl like the Capital One Bowl in Orlando guarantees a payout of about $4.25 million a team; the Chick-fil-A Bowl nets about $5.8 million. But at the top, the money really flows. Arkansas and Ohio State each pocketed about $18 million in 2011 for their trips down the Mississippi to the Sugar Bowl. It is little wonder that both schools fought hard to get into the game, and it is little wonder that the major conferences fight hard to preserve their protected position within the bowl system.

In a certain sense, the $18 million payout was the least of the financial inducements for Ohio State and Arkansas. College presidents and university fund-raisers know that victory on the playing field, more than academic honors, more than naming opportunities, more than the economy, drives fresh contributions.[28] As Bear Bryant, the long-time Alabama football coach, once observed, "It's kind of hard to rally round a math class," but it is easy for a happy alumnus to show his pleasure with a big football win.

Some of those donations come in small checks, but a number come in large and occasionally in astronomical chunks. The largest athletic department gift ever was a grant of $165 million in 2006 by the oil tycoon T. Boone Pickens to his alma mater, Oklahoma State University (OSU). By itself, it was one of the top ten gifts ever to an institution of higher learning; in combination with similarly directed gifts from Pickens to the OSU Athletic Department, it may have been the biggest piece of the largest charitable gift ever to an American university.

T. Boone never did things in a small way. He built Mesa Petroleum into one of the largest independent oil development firms in the world by taking on and often swallowing much bigger competitors. He gained a reputation in the 1980s as one of the more aggressive and ruthless corporate raiders of his generation and reaped billions in profits both from successful acquisitions and from the payoffs from failed takeovers. His outsized reputation followed him into public life.

Pickens gained greater notoriety for funding the Swift Boat attack ads that were instrumental in unnerving John Kerry and ultimately derailing his presidential bid in 2004. Not content to be the private banker for the effort, he stepped directly into the controversy when he openly challenged, with a $1 million prize, anyone to disprove any of the factual assertions contained in the Swift Boat attack ads. When Kerry himself and then separately a group of swift boat veterans stepped forward with evidence, he publicly rejected the claims and declined to make good on the prize. In subsequent years, he has become the personal pitchman for the Pickens Plan, a campaign to alter both public policy and public perception in favor of domestic sources of energy production, many in which Pickens has invested. From business to politics, much of what Pickens does comes with his personal involvement and control. T. Boone likes to call the shots.

Pickens's gift to OSU was no different. His millions were designated principally for the building of a new west end of the Boone Pickens Stadium and secondarily for various fields and practice facilities, for an athletes' residential village, and to support "Las Vegas–style" buffets for OSU athletes—all to create a new Shangri-La for OSU sports cheerily known to the denizens of Stillwater as Boone World. The gift did come with some strings, one of which was T. Boone himself. Since the gift, Pickens has attended every OSU football game and is reported to exercise veto power over every important decision within the university's sports programs.[29] He is the godfather of OSU sports.

The donation also came with specific financial instructions. Less than an hour after the gift arrived in the bank accounts of Cowboy Golf (later renamed Cowboy Athletics), one of the charitable arms of the OSU Athletic Department, the funds were routed straight back to Pickens's hedge fund, BP Capital Management. The gift was accompanied into BP Capital by another $37 million in unrelated donor funds that the university apparently agreed to invest as a condition of the grant—in bold disregard of principles of investment diversification.[30]

With the money for stadium expansion locked up in Pickens's hedge fund, OSU ended up borrowing the funds for the stadium construction. That action by itself is not unusual. Even when they have sufficient available funds for a project, charities often leverage their tax-exempt status to borrow funds at low rates and invest their available funds in matching higher-yield taxable securities. The difference in returns produces an "arbitrage," a low-risk cash flow that favors the charities. But this only works when the charity puts its money in a matching, typically safe bond investment. When the money, as in this case, goes into an oil and gas fund betting on changes in commodities prices, the charity will either win big or lose big. At first, OSU won big, as BP's bets paid off, and the value of OSU's investments spiked to over $300 million. But the recessionary plunge in oil prices in 2008 nearly brought BP Capital Management to its knees; the fund lost more than $1 billion in investment value, taking with it a substantial percentage of the OSU donation. The losses took OSU underwater—it owed more on the loan than it had in investment assets—and imperiled much of the project, with the exception of the west end zone project already well under way. When word spilled into the blogosphere that the entire donation had been lost to margin calls, Pickens quickly announced that he would return the surviving $125 million and pledged sufficient additional funds to ensure that the project would be completed.[31]

The gift from Pickens in support of the Athletic Department was so large that it could not help but raise eyebrows—both with local commentators and with the editors of *The New York Times*[32]—about whether this was really the highest and best investment in Oklahoma State University. To provoke people to question support of a college football team in Oklahoma takes quite a lot. Oklahoma is the state, after all, where the president of the University of Oklahoma once promised "a university the football team could be proud of." When financing for OSU education programs was imperiled in the great recession, those eyebrows arched a shade higher. But in truth there was less controversy than mere carping, because people accepted the fact that it was Pickens's money and he had the right to dispense with it as he pleased.

It's a fair argument. The same system let Andrew Carnegie build libraries and museums and lets Bill Gates lead the fight against global poverty and disease; it also let Ace Greenberg, the onetime CEO of Bear Stearns, contribute $1 million to provide Viagra for financially needy men on the grounds that it would "give a lot of pleasure to a lot of people."[33] But the debate must also account for the fact that these acts are not entirely private affairs; they all have a significant public component. Pickens's donation to Cowboy Golf entitled him to a substantial set of deductions, made larger by the fact that Pickens could avail himself in that year of special tax incentives prompted by Hurricane Katrina. In the end, the public does pick up the tab for a significant portion of such gifts, and it is entitled to question whether they are a wise use of public resources. We should not forget that when the oversized members of the OSU offensive line belly up to that Las Vegas–style buffet, they are literally and figuratively eating the educational system out of house and home.

College bowl games and college sports are by no means the only charities now tied up with big-money sports. The United States Golf Association (USGA), for instance, which runs the U.S. Open golf tournament, washes through tens of millions of dollars each year in prize money, ticket sales, corporate sponsorships, and television dollars. It wasn't always that way. The USGA was just months old in October 1895 when eleven players competed in a new golf contest on a nine-hole course at the Newport Country Club in Newport, Rhode Island. In a single day, the players made four laps of the course, and the winner, an unheralded twenty-one-year-old Englishman named Horace Rawlins, took home the princely sum of $150, plus an oversized trophy. The USGA was at the time an embryonic charity, a coalition of eastern country clubs seeking to codify the rules of golf. The tiny event received virtually no notice.

The 2011 edition of the U.S. Open was something entirely different. When that tournament took place at Congressional Country Club in Bethesda, Maryland, the golfers were international superstars like Lee Westwood, Phil Mickelson, and the eventual winner, Rory McIlroy, competing for a prize purse of $7.5 million. The top prize, somewhere in the range of $1.35 million, while four hundred times larger than Rawlins's purse even in inflation-adjusted dollars, was in fact far less meaningful to the top players in golf, all worth anywhere from tens of millions of dollars to an estimated pre-divorce net worth of nearly a billion dollars for Tiger Woods. Much of that wealth comes from endorsements, a concept that would have been utterly foreign to the players at the inaugural U.S. Open. Most top professional golfers are walking billboards for their sponsoring companies, who will have paid handsomely to have the players wear their shoes, hats, watches, and shirts and to play with their golf clubs and golf balls. Congressional Country Club itself speaks to the wealth and exclusivity of this rarefied form of the game. It is a playground for the Washington elite, including seven presidents dating back to William Howard Taft. Its sprawling red-roofed clubhouse overlooks rolling hills, deep blue water hazards, and its famous close-shaved bluegrass greens. Membership is open to anyone with the right social connections, the patience to wait about eight years, and the deep pockets to pony up $150,000 in initiation fees. While Congressional is typically insulated from commercial considerations, for the U.S. Open it permitted its clubhouse to be surrounded by the tents of prime sponsors and advertisers, who shelled out hundreds of thousands or even millions for the privilege.

The USGA itself bears little resemblance to the fledgling charity organization that held that first Newport championship. Now headquartered at Golf House in Far Hills, New Jersey, it is a $150 million a year sports giant whose revenues principally come from television rights and ticket sales from the U.S. Open and a handful of other televised tournaments such as the U.S. Senior Open and the U.S. Women's Open. The only thing that is a constant from 1895 is that the USGA remains a charity, even though its principal activities are virtually indistinguishable in substance from the for-profit Daytona 500 and Kentucky Derby. As with the hospital system, it is now nearly impossible to tell the difference between for-profit sports organizations and charitable ones, in purpose or in practice, and equally difficult to justify any public subsidy from the taxpayer.

There is precedent for attempting to strip such charities of their charitable status. In the late 1940s, when grateful alumni donated the Mueller Macaroni Company to New York University Law School to be a long-term source of institutional support, competitors in the pasta business cried foul. They argued that it was an unfair competitive advantage for Mueller to be tax-exempt, but the courts upheld the arrangement, finding that all parts of a charitable organization, since they operated to the benefit of the parent charity, were by their nature charitable. Under pressure from the spaghetti lobby, Congress responded and in 1950 enacted the Unrelated Business Income Tax (UBIT). Under the UBIT rules, nonprofits have to pay income tax at ordinary corporate rates for regularly recurring revenues generated from activities unrelated to their charitable purposes. The rationale for the act was both fairness in the marketplace and the fiscal needs of the Treasury; as one congressman put it at the time, "Eventually all the noodles in the country will be produced by corporations held or created by universities . . . and there will be no revenues in the Federal Treasury from this industry."[34]

The UBIT rules, however, have not kept pace with the times. In the half century since Congress acted in the wake of the Mueller Macaroni acquisition, the nonprofit sector has gone through enormous changes, and the industry is now pocked with organizations that are no different from their commercial competitors. From hospitals to universities, the public is effectively supporting these "spaghetti factories" to the tune of many billions of dollars a year. Much of this is not secret: it is known in charitable quarters, at the IRS, and in the halls of Congress and is reported from time to time in the popular press. But there are strong institutional factors that weigh against remedying it. Universities and hospitals have powerful lobbies; all members of Congress have universities or hospitals in their districts, meaning that there is a cost to fighting for change and little clear political return. Despite those barriers, Congress has on at least one occasion acknowledged the need to prune back eligibility in light of changing times. In 1998, Congress eliminated the federal tax-exempt status for some of the Blue Cross and Blue Shield Associations and for TIAA-CREF, a giant financial services company that serves the hospital and education fields, acknowledging that their activities were now market-driven and transactional and that they stood on a similar footing as many for-profit businesses. While all those organizations are still often tax-exempt under state rules, they are no longer treated as charities under federal law. These were not trivial changes, but such piecemeal decision making is inadequate to resolve the inconsistencies and loopholes that mar the charitable field.

Our final category of uncharitable charity is one that defies the concept of public benefit. Rooted in ordinary notions of fairness and public good, the public benefit principle requires that a service must support, directly or indirectly, the broader population and not principally dispense a private good. In concept, it seems both obvious and straightforward; in practice, it creates significant line-drawing issues. While other countries have challenged the tax exemption of exclusive organizations, in the United States we have largely avoided challenging the major charitable institutions that are increasingly inaccessible to the average American.

The Metropolitan Opera is such an institution. Opening night for its 2009 season was a glittering affair. Jewels and gowns, ties and tails, were standard dress, and tickets ran into the hundreds of dollars, topping out at $1,750 for access to a cocktail party and dinner. Celebrities mingled with the stars of classical music, and sprinkled among them were the people who are the economic heart of the Metropolitan Opera: oil barons, hedge fund managers, senior Wall Street executives, even the man who devised the now infamous mortgage-backed securities. The entire event testified to the enduring glamour of New York society and was a reminder that "the opera house remains a playground for the wealthy in our society."[35] Even in the middle of the deepest recession in seventy years, the event sold out.

Charities hold fancy fund-raisers all the time; society pages routinely chronicle swanky charity balls, auctions, and concerts. Virtually every nonprofit holds some form of high-end donor event at some point; it is a generally accepted, sometimes effective form of fund-raising. But rarely are the attendees the direct and principal beneficiaries of the service. Those in attendance at the Metropolitan's opening night were largely underwriting their own entertainment. Opera falls into that odd class of charities where the principal beneficiaries of the service are defined primarily by their wealth—not the lack thereof, as is usually the case. Tens of thousands of charities serve the poor, but the opera principally serves those who can afford high-priced tickets to attend performances. With most tickets running into the hundreds of dollars, the opera is not just the playground of the wealthy; it is their gated community.

These types of means-tested organizations—which include a range of private schools, clubs, operas, and other arts institutions—raise serious questions about the use of tax incentives to subsidize entertainment for the privileged few. The dollars at stake, while tiny in comparison to the nonprofit hospital industry, are still considerable.

The Metropolitan Opera's budget exceeds $250 million a year, and even smaller opera companies can raise tens of millions of dollars in donations each year.

To be sure, some opera companies do engage in outreach beyond their core constituencies; the Metropolitan Opera, for one, gives away some tickets and has some lower-priced sections. It also runs an extensive free broadcast operation, and on opening night in September 2009 it simulcast the performance to three thousand spectators in the plaza outside Lincoln Center. Setting aside the vaguely *Titanic* sensibility of having the masses watch in the cold while the swells sip champagne and relax in comfortable seats, the Metropolitan's efforts extend the reach of its services but cannot obscure the fact that its core services are essentially a closed benefit.

The Metropolitan Opera and other arts organizations that serve a high-income audience are just one example of private groups taking advantage of the tax codes. Fraternal organizations and other voluntary social organizations, while not typically defined as charities under federal law, are often immune from income and property tax. This is not an inconsiderable benefit for those groups, ranging from the Masons to golf clubs that control high-value real estate. In addition, many fraternal organizations, including the eating clubs at Princeton and the secret societies like Skull and Bones at Yale, have set up charitable foundations to underwrite a portion of their activities. In a system where virtually all applications for charitable status are approved, the result is charity for all, even for those among us who are least in need of it.

FOUR

Money for People

Fraud in the Charitable Sector, Fraud on the Charitable Sector

WITHIN HOURS OF the devastating Haiti earthquake, thousands of charities—perhaps tens of thousands—sprang into action, marshaling resources, activating emergency plans, and sending out pleas for support to tens of millions of people around the world by every conceivable means of conveyance. One such solicitation, an e-mail from the M.E. Foundation, referred potential contributors to a lavishly produced Web site complete with pictures of neat rows of white tents at its refugee camp just outside Port-au-Prince. The Web site made a stirring case for supporting the foundation in its valiant undertakings in Haiti and helpfully provided several easy-to-use methods for donating to the relief effort. The M.E. Foundation's pitch was not easily distinguishable from many others seeking to do urgent work in Haiti, making it all the more a shame that the foundation was entirely a fiction, the pictures of the refugee camp cut and pasted from a site depicting a real refugee camp in Pakistan, the stories entirely fabricated, and the proceeds flowing directly to the pockets of the con men behind the site.

The people behind the M.E. Foundation were hardly alone in trying to take advantage of the Haiti crisis. The urgency of the situation, the huge range of choices facing donors, and the lack of oversight of charitable fund-raising created a fertile field for fraud. Grifters, scammers, and charlatans have always gravitated to the nonprofit world, but technology now allows scam artists to take their schemes to new heights. After Katrina, the FBI estimated that twenty-four hundred fake charity Web sites, many with plausible names like katrinafamilies .com and parishdonations.org, were set up to relieve well-meaning but careless donors of their cash.[1] After Haiti, the scam artists displayed even greater speed and technological prowess. E-mail, Facebook, and Twitter are part of the arsenal of the modern con man; within hours of the earthquake, hundreds of fake appeals were sent out over social media channels, often urging the youthful audiences that tend to use those services to make small (and harder to trace) donations using their mobile phones.

Crooks gravitate to crises. The huge, largely unregulated, and rapid flow of cash (the top U.S. charities raised $528 million in just the first fifteen days following the 2010 Haiti earthquake) makes for an irresistible target. But the problem extends well beyond the emergency response field; the charitable world is pocked with fraud and self-enrichment, and it is often hard to tell, even for regulators, when organizations are treading close to or over the line. The qualifications for setting up a charity are little more than the price of a stamp and a very modest filing fee, a certain facility with government forms, and the patience to wait thirty days or so. Once that process is complete, only the most egregious facts, combined with rotten luck and bad timing, will bring regulators to your door.[2] Ineffective supervision, unclear legal standards, and enormous consumer confusion all create a situation where it is astonishingly easy to set up, operate, and maintain charities that principally benefit their fund-raisers and managers.

The U.S. Navy Veterans Association (USNVA), for instance, is by most appearances a high-performing public charity. Founded in 2002 to provide support and medical care to naval veterans in need, the organization boasts forty-one state chapters and sixty-six thousand members. Over an incredibly short period, the USNVA recorded astonishing financial success. In the ten years since the IRS approved its charitable status, it has raised more than $100 million in donations, almost all of it through aggressive telemarketing campaigns. This highly efficient organization has been run by an all-volunteer staff of eighty-five dedicated souls, who report up through the CEO— a silver-haired former naval captain named Jack L. Nimitz—to a five-member executive board in Washington, D.C.

In the pantheon of charities serving veterans, the USNVA is one of the fastest growing and would be one of the most admirable, except that virtually everything about the organization is fraudulent and deceptive. The entire organizational apparatus of the USNVA is a mirage: there are no local chapters, no sixty-six thousand members, no eighty-five-person staff, no straight-talking, lantern-jawed CEO with a name redolent of naval history. Its business addresses have turned out to be post office boxes in most cases and vacant lots in others. Its only real employee, and apparent mastermind, is a disheveled man named Bobby Thompson working from a run-down Ybor City, Florida, duplex, with a view of the concertina wire surrounding the parking lot of the Cuesta-Rey cigar factory.[3]

There is some substance to the USNVA. The $100 million, at least, is real, raised from small donors by a Michigan-based telemarketing firm with the conveniently generic name of Associated Community Services (ACS). Most of that money stayed with ACS, which charged the USNVA sixty cents of every dollar raised, a figure that soars up to eighty cents per dollar once overhead and administrative fees are piled on. Less than 1 percent, perhaps much less than 1 percent, ever went to actual veterans in need. The rest presumably stayed with Thompson, though some was funneled out through an associated political action committee called Navy Veterans for Good Government to a wide variety of local and federal elected officials. The respectability that these contributions brought to the USNVA is captured in a series of photographs framing Thompson with prominent politicians: Senator John McCain, Speaker of the House John Boehner, Karl Rove, and even President George W. Bush.

The other real element of the USNVA is that it was lawfully organized and approved by the IRS. It took the IRS only thirty-three days to approve the original application for charitable status, and that, in normal circumstances, would have been its last substantive interaction with the charity, probably forever. But either by happenstance or on a tip, the IRS conducted an audit of the USNVA in 2008. Field audits are a very rare occurrence for the IRS, and by all rights this one should have created one of the few triumphs for its beleaguered and understaffed charities division, but the audit—rather astonishingly given the thinness of the deceit here—produced "a clean bill of health."[4] It is surprising that the audit staff of the IRS, with its wide-ranging investigative authority, failed to uncover that the USNVA was a stack of lies, that its only living, breathing employee had stolen his identity from someone in Washington state and was impersonating a navy commander, that everyone else associated with the organization was simply a fiction, and that if an IRS auditor had tried to knock on the door of any of the many listed offices of the company, he would have found himself in a vacant lot or at a Mail Boxes Etc. Even if we acknowledge the stretched resources and limited investigative expertise of the IRS, it is still virtually impossible to fathom how it missed such a plain fraud. Just months after the IRS finished its review of the USNVA, two reporters from the *St. Petersburg Times,* Jeff Testerman and John Martin, stumbled upon the USNVA story. They were initially interested only in some modest contributions that the affiliated political action committee had made to a candidate for county commissioner, but Thompson's nervous and dissembling responses to their inquiries sent them down a new trail. After several months of dogged reporting, the *Times* published its first article in a series that spanned more than a year, and the USNVA fraud began to unravel. Within a few months, an Ohio grand jury issued indictments, though by then Thompson was to the wind.[5] But even after all these events and revelations, the USNVA is still recognized by the IRS as a legally constituted charity and is still listed in the IRS databases as a viable and going public concern.

The failure of the IRS in the USNVA case is not unusual; it reflects serious resource constraints. Even as the number of tax-exempt organizations has exploded over the last four decades, the resources devoted to supervising the charitable sector have stagnated or in some cases even shrunk. In 1969, the IRS commissioner at the time, Randolph Thrower, forecasting the explosion of the social sector, committed to doubling the resources dedicated to the Exempt Organizations Division (now folded into the Tax Exempt and Government Entities Division). Under Thrower, the division did grow, though not as much as he promised. But since then, it has suffered cutbacks and consolidation, leaving it inadequately prepared to do its job, even as its responsibilities have expanded. In a typical year, the IRS examines approximately one-tenth of 1 percent of all charitable returns, and these are typically little more than a review of the documents submitted by the charity.[6] This leaves the states, which share overlapping jurisdiction for charity oversight with the IRS, with all the more responsibility for fraud enforcement. But while the IRS is permitted to cooperate closely and share information with state revenue offices on tax collection matters, federal privacy law prevents coordination between the IRS and state charity regulators. That alone would not be fatal if state charitable oversight offices were adequately resourced, but in fact they generally don't even exist. Only thirteen states perform some sort of charity oversight function,[7] and it has been estimated that there are fewer than a hundred state officials, spread out across fifty states and 1.4 million charities, charged with full-time responsibility for supervising charities.[8]

Even in the rare event when a state regulatory authority responds to an instance of abuse, its hands are often tied, as was the case when California pursued charges against the Association for Firefighters and Paramedics (AFP). The AFP claims to support burn victims and burn centers across the country, directing "much needed funds to help the survivors of catastrophic fires." Not many funds, however. In its most recent filings, the AFP acknowledged that of the $2.6 million it raised, $2.3 million went to fund-raising expenses, $230,000 went to administrative expenses (with roughly half of that going in salary to its CEO), and a miserly $82,000, or about 3 percent, went to actual program expenditures. That number only modestly exceeded the funds that the AFP spent on out-of-town board meetings in San Diego and Las Vegas and for a Caribbean cruise for board members and their families. In 2010, Jerry Brown, then the attorney general of California, sued the AFP, alleging false and misleading fund-raising practices, including the mailing of fulfillment cards for pledges that were never made. On the surface, it would seem to be an easy case, a self-enrichment scheme masquerading as a charity. But the standards for charitable practices are so unclear and the lines between illegal fraud and lawful inefficiency are so blurry that Brown's case was hobbled from the beginning, and he eventually settled it for a modest fine ($100,000, or about two weeks of billings for the AFP's fund-raisers). The fact that its entire business is effectively structured to benefit its employees and fund-raisers and not burn victims and burn centers did not apparently violate any laws, at least not in a way that was sanctionable by the State of California. Today, the AFP remains in business, with largely unreformed practices and a Web site that is a marvel of obfuscation, revealing not a single fact of relevance to the donor: no financial information, no specific disclosures about how donated dollars are spent, and certainly no information on the largesse showered on the AFP's commercial fund-raisers, staff, and board.

No better testament to the weakness of state nonprofit regulation can be found than in Oregon, where a list is published annually of the state's twenty worst charities, focusing on organizations that spend virtually no money on actual charitable service. The charities on the list all have public-spirited and generally indistinguishable names: the Law Enforcement Legal Defense Fund, the Disabled Police Officers of America, the Disabled Police Officers Counseling Center, the Firefighters Charitable Foundation, the National Vietnam Veterans Foundation, the National Veterans Services Fund, Project C.U.R.E., the Foundation for Children with Cancer, and so forth. Most of these organizations retain the vast majority of contributions for their own expenses: the Shiloh International Ministries spends less than 4 percent on charitable causes, while the Law Enforcement Education Program distributes less than 7 percent, and the Korean War Veterans National Museum and Library spends less than 8 percent. But the most remarkable thing about this annual list is not the contents but the source: the Oregon attorney general, the state's chief law enforcement officer, who apparently can resort only to press releases and a bully pulpit rather than criminal or civil enforcement to bring these egregious matters to light. The attorney general was forced into this posture because of the lack of regulatory and enforcement authority in his state and because of uncertainty over what constitutes fraud versus mere inefficiencies. His efforts to obtain greater authority and clarity through new state laws have stalled in the Oregon legislature.[9]

The greatest irony of the USNVA story is not the failure of law enforcement but the fact that Thompson probably could have realized his enrichment scheme without ever breaking the law. There is a strikingly large group of apparently legal but dubious charities clustered around veterans, firefighters, and police support issues, perhaps not a surprise since there are more than fifty-nine thousand American charities with the word "veteran" in the title alone. This creates fertile terrain for telemarketers who can take advantage of both the compelling nature of the cause and the confusion sown by so many similarly named organizations.[10] For instance, the Firefighters Charitable Foundation (FFCF) is a lawfully organized charity based in New York known for its aggressive phone-banking efforts. It is perhaps not surprising that its telemarketers are so hardworking since they are the principal beneficiaries of the charity. Only about 8 percent of donations go to support fire victims, educational programs, and local fire departments, while 87 percent goes to fund-raising expenses, mostly to the commercial call centers that raise the bulk of its donations. The FFCF looks positively efficient compared with the Disabled Veterans Association (DVA), an Ohio-based charity that purportedly works to improve the lives of veterans and their families. Its Web site is draped with flags and all-American images—and mentions catchy programs such as VETS (Veterans Entrepreneurial Training Seminars) and HAVE (Helping and Assisting Veterans in Emergency). In reality, the DVA seems more keenly interested in improving the lives of its fund-raisers, who take away 95 percent of the $9 million in annual revenues. The DVA regularly shows up on lists of ineffective charities, but that is of limited use in alerting the people who make pledges to telemarketers. And even if the elderly and the harried who are often the targets of telemarketers were able to responsibly evaluate the solicitation, it would still take an expert to distinguish the DVA from other virtually identically named organizations such as the DAV (Disabled American Veterans) and the Disabled American Veterans Charitable Service Trust.

The opportunity for confusion is also demonstrated by the case of the Coalition for Breast Cancer Cures (CBCC) and its for-profit fund-raising arm, the Resource Center. The executives of the Nassau County, New York, organization confessed to the New York attorney general in 2011 to running a sham charity, mailing false invoices to donors, and repeatedly charging donors' credit cards without authorization. Proceeds from these extracurricular activities went not to charitable purposes but instead to decidedly private ends such as expensive steak-house dinners, lavish vacations, and the sorority dues of the daughter of the two ringleaders. The Coalition for Breast Cancer Cures case should not be confused with the entirely unrelated matter of the Coalition Against Breast Cancer (CABC) and its for-profit fund-raiser, the Campaign Center, which also operated out of Long Island. Just weeks before the CBCC confession, the attorney general of New York sued the CABC, charging that it also violated various nonprofit and antifraud laws. The suit charged that the CABC raised more than $9 million over five years, distributed less than $45,000 of that amount to legitimate causes, and kept the rest for the cost of fund-raising, salaries, and personal services.[11] The existence of these two virtually indistinguishable organizations just twenty miles apart captures well the disorder that exists in the marketplace. And they are by no means alone. The National Breast Cancer Coalition Fund, the National Breast Cancer Coalition, the Breast Cancer Research Foundation, and the American Breast Cancer Foundation, to name just a few, are also on the scene. With so many virtually identically named charities and so little meaningful marketplace information, the opportunities for duplicitous solicitors to take advantage of donor confusion are immense.

The charitable world includes many organizations that tread the blurry line between legitimate and illegitimate. For many years, the aggressive solicitors for the United Homeless Organization (UHO) were one of the signature sights of the streetscape of New York City. On any given day, more than a hundred solicitors, working in two shifts, fanned out across the city, toting their folding tables and big blue empty watercooler containers out to sidewalks and seeking contributions "of any size" to help the homeless. Wearing UHO-branded aprons and brandishing laminated legal documents, the UHO teams asked passersby for money to support food pantries, homeless shelters, detox centers, or whatever else sounded plausible in this context. The "jug band," like Salvation Army bell ringers at the holidays, created an easy, though sometimes socially awkward, opportunity for direct, point-of-purchase donations. These face-to-face solicitations were enormously effective, raising, according to the New York attorney general, millions of dollars over twenty-five years.

If you looked past the badly laminated IDs, the UHO had all the indicia of fraud: no business office, shoddy record keeping, and a bank account that was raided for personal expenses at GameStop, the Home Shopping Network, and Weight Watchers. In fact, the UHO was a deeply unsavory organization with an ingeniously simple business model. The organization rented out its jugs and tables for $15 a shift, and the solicitors pocketed whatever they raised in excess of that amount. The rent went directly to the UHO and thereafter into the pockets of its two founders, Stephen Riley and Myra Walker, whom the New York *Daily News* once pleasingly described as a "lowdown, slithering, conniving pair."[12] Where the money never went was to any of the social service efforts that the UHO purported to support.

While it can't be too shocking to find out that a group of street people with folding tables and water jugs are not entirely on the up-and-up, the UHO nonetheless was a lawfully established public charity that operated openly and notoriously for almost two and a half decades before it drew the attention of a state regulator (and never, to this day, of federal regulators).[13] The *New York Post* and *The New York Times* first reported on its deceptive business practices in 2001, and yet it was not until 2010 that Andrew Cuomo, the attorney general at the time, succeeded in shutting it down. In the intervening years, the UHO pulled millions of dollars in small-change donations out of the charitable economy. The UHO was far from a secret. For almost a quarter century, it was perhaps the most ubiquitous charity in New York City, and its very public business model should have, and did, set off warning bells. The fact that it took regulators decades to answer those bells is a prime indicator of their ineffectiveness.

The fake charity and the con man are American archetypes running from the grifters of *Maverick* to George Costanza on *Seinfeld.* Remember the Human Fund? In an episode called "The Strike," George, tiring of the year-end gift exchange ritual with co-workers, distributes cards to colleagues indicating that a gift has been given in their names to the Human Fund, an organization with the wonderfully generic slogan "Money for People." It's the jolliest of holiday seasons for George until his plan unravels. George's boss, the lugubrious but occasionally prophetic Mr. Kruger, decides to give the company's annual charitable gift of $20,000 to the Human Fund because "they all seem the same to me, so, what's the difference?" When the company's accounting department discovers there is no such charity, Kruger confronts George with the fact that there is no Human Fund, to which George replies: "Well, there could be." Costanza, in fact, was just a little ahead of his time. Eight years after the *Seinfeld* episode first aired in 1997, two Cleveland-based entrepreneurs established a real Human Fund, an arts education organization serving underprivileged youth. The Human Fund—the Ohio version—has no employees, a pleasant-looking Web site that most high school students could replicate in a few hours, and no significant paper trail: no newspaper articles, no online ratings of substantial dimension, no offices, and no financial information posted on its Web site. Without substantial insider knowledge about how to research charities, it is really not so easy to tell which charity was developed by a team of comedy writers.[14]

Charities that deceive donors are only part of the story, and the lesser part at that. There is a whole other category of guile: stealing from legitimate charities themselves. Andrew Liersch was a pillar of the Santa Clara community: a leader of one of the biggest and most respected nonprofits in the county, a member of numerous community and church organizations, a family man. He also oversaw one of the longest-running financial frauds in American nonprofit history.[15] For seventeen years, he and a small group of confidants systematically looted more than $20 million from the Santa Clara Goodwill, which he ran as CEO. The scam was simple: when donors dropped off goods at any one of a dozen or more Goodwill storefronts, the members of Liersch's syndicate would skim off the best material. As goods came in the front door, they would shovel the best out the back door, pack it into barrels, and put the diverted goods on a truck that made daily runs. These daily activities, if not the criminal purpose behind them, occurred in plain sight of employees, volunteers, and donors and were widely known within the Goodwill community. Liersch became so bold in his scheme that he even charged the costs of the trucks to Goodwill. Compared with the brazen nature of the thefts, Liersch's manner of secreting away the money was virtually the opposite—furtive and sophisticated, spreading his gains across accounts in Switzerland, Austria, and the Isle of Man. In effect,

Liersch was far more concerned with the prying eyes of the federal tax man than he was with detection from within the Goodwill family.

How could such an inelegant fraud continue for such a long period of time? There was no shortage of clues for honest employees, auditors, and the board of directors: from goods marching out the back door to Liersch's uncanny ability to match revenues to projections (as the prosecutor subsequently noted, "They would project a $10 million budget for the year and come within $38 of that"). The answer lies with the structural failures from which so many charities suffer. Goodwill failed to make necessary and critical overhead investments. It lacked the accounting systems and internal auditing functions necessary for a business of its size and complexity; its board lacked expertise and failed to understand its governance role in ensuring adequate checks and balances within the organization. Like many mission-driven organizations, Goodwill staffers were susceptible to the notion that their colleagues shared their passion for the enterprise, so they were less rigorous about oversight and more open to passable explanations for suspicious behaviors. In the end, after seventeen years, no one ever caught Liersch and his fellow thieves; they were only undone when one of his co-conspirators blew the whistle on the scheme.[16]

Heads of charities—whether they are founders, religious figures, or longtime leaders—are often trusted figures with wide-ranging authority. They can be subject to astonishingly little internal oversight. Father Kevin Gray was a popular priest in a largely poor, immigrant parish in Waterbury, Connecticut. He lived humbly, didn't own a car, and dressed modestly, all consistent with a man who made less than $28,000 a year. But it was not consistent with a man who managed to steal about $1.3 million from parish accounts over the course of his seven years at Sacred Heart. At first blush, it is hard to figure out how Father Gray spent this money—no fancy homes, no cars, no clothes, no family—but it turns out that during frequent absences from the parish, Father Gray's life was very different. He stayed at fancy hotels like the Waldorf-Astoria, the New York Palace, and

Copley Square in Boston, dined out regularly at Tavern on the Green and Arturo's in New York and at Abe & Louie's Restaurant in Boston, and acquired clothing from expensive labels such as Saks Fifth Avenue, Brooks Brothers, and Armani. But the majority of the money was spent at strip clubs and on escort services, as well as through Gray's generosity to others: he rewarded his male escorts with American Express cards, and three young men in turn ran up hundreds of thousands of dollars in charges, financing their own lifestyles and in two cases their continuing education.[17] As with Goodwill of Santa Clara, the fraud was not especially clever, though it was no less successful for its lack of sophistication. For the most part, Father Gray simply wrote checks on the church's account to himself, to his friends, or to American Express. When he tapped out the account, he brazenly sold access to the church's steeple to a cell phone company for $200,000 and pocketed the proceeds.

It turns out to be rather easy to steal money when no one is looking. Sacred Heart had no finance committee, no internal auditor, no trustee or parish council. The financial records, such as they were, were contained on a QuickBooks account on Father Gray's computer, and he controlled the only password. When representatives of the church financial hierarchy came to review financial statements, Father Gray always absented himself with the excuse of needing to go to New York City for treatment of his colon cancer—a claim now known to be fabricated in furtherance of his scheme—and the records went unexamined for want of the password. It apparently never occurred to anyone to reschedule the diocesian auditor's visits or to find anything suspicious in the uncanny coincidence of financial reviews with medical appointments, and Father Gray's fraud continued for seven years until a prolonged and unexplained disappearance from his parish led to a deeper investigation by the Archdiocese of Hartford. The consequence of the theft was dramatic for the poor, largely immigrant parish. Before the thefts, Sacred Heart had a substantial financial cushion, but Father Gray spent all of the parish's reserves and even dipped into operating funds, leaving Sacred Heart with a string of unpaid insurance invoices. In 2011, Father Gray pleaded no contest to the charges and was sentenced to three years in jail. In an odd codicil to the events, the Archdiocese of Hartford announced at the time of sentencing that since Father Gray had shown contrition and accepted responsibility for his actions, he would be eligible to continue to serve as a priest, though not in a position of financial responsibility.

Father Gray is a particularly salacious example but by no means an isolated one. A 2007 survey of the Catholic Church by researchers at Villanova University found that 85 percent of dioceses had discovered embezzlements in the last five years, with 11 percent reporting losses of more than $500,000.[18] Some instances were due to the lack of controls around cash contributions, but those were the minority. Most frauds exceeded $50,000, with some of extraordinary size and duration, such as one case in Delray Beach, Florida, in which two priests spent $8.6 million on trips to Las Vegas, dental work, and other personal expenses over the course of four decades.[19] The Catholic Church is hardly alone in its problems: the Presbyterian Church has had similar embarrassing internal theft problems; allegations of misappropriation of funds led to the ouster of the chancellor of the Orthodox Church in America in 2006; and senior leaders of Shuvah Yisrael, a messianic Jewish congregation, are as of this writing under investigation for stealing millions of dollars,[20] but the problems are particularly acute for the Catholic Church. Under canonical law, all parishes are required to have finance committees, but those are often dormant or populated with people unwilling or lacking in the skills to challenge the authority of the parish priests on financial matters. The ingredients for substantial fraud are irresistible: a largely cash economy, individuals with unfettered local authority, no checks and balances, and a religious hierarchy unwilling or unable to put reasonable financial controls in place. Many nonprofits, including local dioceses, are often too small and unsophisticated to separate financial record keeping from asset, including cash, management and are reluctant to make necessary investments in accounting staff and financial management systems. And it is almost certainly true that the Villanova numbers understate the issue, since they do not include estimates of undiscovered frauds and likely reflect some underreporting by organizations loath to admit embarrassing problems that might diminish public trust in them.

Charity fraud is not always as straightforward as theft of assets. Charities can also be convenient vehicles for the exchange of political favors. Vito Lopez has perfected this form of corruption by charity. He is an old-style political boss: chairman of the Kings County (better known as Brooklyn) Democratic Party, a long-serving member of the New York State Assembly, and the onetime chairman of its powerful Housing Committee.[21] But Lopez's power grows not so much out of his political affiliations as from his control of a large local nonprofit. The Ridgewood Bushwick Senior Citizens Council is a $100 million a year social services charity that is entirely funded through state and city grants to provide affordable housing, meals to the elderly, and after-school programs. Lopez founded Ridgewood Bushwick in 1973, and though as a member of the assembly he is unable to be officially involved in the organization, he remains in complete control, through his close alliances with the organization's leaders. The entire range of Ridgewood Bushwick assets are at Lopez's political disposal; it is commonly understood that its employees, contractors, and beneficiaries are all expected to support the various electoral causes of Lopez and the Bushwick United Democratic Club.[22] It is largely through Ridgewood Bushwick that Lopez has been able to generate thousands of Election Day volunteers and reliable votes over the years.[23] The culture of Ridgewood Bushwick is built around furthering the political causes of Lopez and his club. It is Lopez's political machine.

Reporters and state investigators have repeatedly uncovered close links between campaign contributions made to Lopez and contracts received from Ridgewood Bushwick. Real estate developers, architects, accountants, security firms, and land surveyors have all lined up to make large contributions to Lopez and the Kings County Democratic Party, and many subsequently obtained large and lucrative service contracts from Ridgewood Bushwick. Often, as public records reveal, the checks have been written immediately before or immediately after the award of the contract.[24] Given the context, it is perhaps not surprising that the charity is not entirely punctilious about internal record keeping and financial accuracy. In 2010, the arrest (and later conviction) of a young employee for submitting falsified time sheets led state and federal authorities to launch a broader inquiry into Ridgewood Bushwick. Those probes, still ongoing, have uncovered hundreds of thousands of dollars in questionable bills submitted to the city by Ridgewood Bushwick and affiliated charities.[25]

Once again one wonders how a prominent organization could so long evade detection (and enforcement) by the state or federal government or from internal checks and balances. As we have seen, the federal government is largely absent from these matters because the IRS lacks the resources to act as an effective check on the vast charitable world. The capacities of states are highly variable. New York State, one of the few states with a charity division within the Attorney General's Office, is a relatively aggressive regulator, yet it has proven to be ineffective and highly reactive due to the huge number of charities paired with very limited resources. And internal checks and balances were certainly lacking at Ridgewood Bushwick since the executive director doubled as Lopez's campaign manager and the next-highest-ranking employee of Ridgewood Bushwick was Lopez's girlfriend. Both were handsomely rewarded for their loyalty. Christiana Fisher, the executive director, earned more than $650,000 in 2009 from Ridgewood Bushwick, in addition to her compensation from the Lopez campaign and the Kings County Democratic Committee. Angela Battaglia, Lopez's longtime girlfriend, drew a salary of more than $330,000 as director of housing for Ridgewood Bushwick, in addition to her salary from a position on the city's Planning Commission. She was also a major developer of publicly funded apartments in northern Brooklyn, as well as a major contributor and political adjunct to Lopez. Given their multiple jobs and commitments, even if Fisher and Battaglia were inclined to instill good management and ethics practices, they would hardly have the time for it.[26] Fisher was finally fired in January 2012 (a development cheerfully covered by the *New York Post* with an article headlined "Vito's Golden Girl Gets Booted by City") for "re-creating" missing and likely fictitious documents to justify her pay package, though her dismissal came only after New York City threatened to yank more than $69 million in contracts. As of this writing, Battaglia remains gainfully employed at Ridgewood Bushwick.[27]

Ridgewood Bushwick is by no means the most prominent example of misuse of a charity by a politician. That honor probably goes, at least in recent years, to Vincent Fumo, a long-serving and powerful state senator from Philadelphia. In 1991, Fumo founded Citizens Alliance for Better Neighborhoods to offer services, mostly in his district, that the city government was unable or unwilling to provide. With a small army of laborers and vehicles, the charity cleaned streets, cleared snow, trimmed trees, and tidied up alleys and abandoned lots. From the very beginning, Fumo was the funding fairy godfather for Citizens Alliance, ensuring a steady flow of government grants from his perch as the ranking Democratic member of the powerful Senate Appropriations Committee. When direct state funding proved insufficient, Fumo began to trade favors for large-scale corporate contributions to Citizens Alliance. In the biggest case, PECO, a Pennsylvania-based electrical and natural gas concern, donated $17 million to Citizens Alliance in return for Fumo taking a position favorable to the company in the senate's power deregulation proceedings.

Not all these funds, however, went to public services. A good chunk went to enrich Fumo, who had adopted a strict policy of only spending OPM, other people's money. Consistent with this thrifty philosophy, Fumo directed Citizens Alliance on a spectacular spending spree for more than a decade, procuring via the charity all manner of highly expensive, and deeply unnecessary, items. The list is extensive, comprising goods and services valued into the millions, including at least three cars; $75,000 in tools (Fumo was a tool collector); $600,000 in renovations and improvements for Fumo's offices; a bulldozer, tractor, backhoe, ATV, and pickup truck for Fumo's farm; and a long list of items for Fumo's summer home that included a high-end meat grinder (worth $450) and more than $3,900 in mosquito magnets. Fumo also freely drafted Citizens Alliance employees to work as unpaid laborers to paint his dock at his Jersey shore home, collect and dispose of vast quantities of Christmas decorations at his Spring Garden home, and transport items to his Harrisburg farm, among other numerous personal chores. Citizens Alliance also funded various dirty political tricks for Fumo—including a stalking horse lawsuit against a senate rival, political push polling, and the cost of a private investigator to help a 2002 gubernatorial candidate—and it doled out $60,000 to support a grassroots group that sought to stop the building of dunes along the Jersey shore, which Fumo feared would block the unimpeded ocean view from his Margate home. Among this astonishingly productive and idiosyncratic list, one item stood out. The purchase that eventually drew the most public attention and wonderment was paint—not just any paint, but a Dutch paint called Hollandlac that, at $100 per gallon, was described as the most expensive commercially available paint in the world.[28]

It is tempting to dismiss these as isolated cases, but they are not. Politicians, including the disgraced (and convicted) Detroit mayor Kwame Kilpatrick and many members of the Illinois legislature, have found charities to be convenient vehicles to launder public dollars. In Washington, D.C., the city council member Harry Thomas used his wide-ranging political influence to direct more than $300,000 in city money to Team Thomas, a local youth sports charity that he controlled. Instead of being used for youth baseball programs, as it was intended, the money ended up funding a $60,000 Audi automobile for Thomas, trips to Florida and Las Vegas, and various political activities. Thomas was forced in 2011 to return the money to the city and, in 2012, resigned from the city council just before pleading guilty to federal fraud charges.

The roll call of charitable thefts is long: $1.5 million stolen by the president of Philadelphia's Independence Seaport Museum; $112,000 lifted by the treasurer of the Downers Grove Panther Junior Football

League in Illinois; $3.6 million taken by the chief financial officer of the San Francisco–based Music Concourse Community Partnership.[29] To be sure, fraud and theft occur across government, in private business, and wherever money is a temptation, but the institutional limitations of the charitable world—the lack of investment in internal accounting, cash management, and financial tracking systems and the lack of will and expertise to implement effective internal checks and balances—make the problem more insidious and widespread. A 2008 study put the likely annual loss within the charitable sector at $40 billion. The problem is far greater than petty theft, the breakage from people dipping into petty cash accounts, or in-kind donations never quite making it into the ledger. The *average* charitable theft is estimated to be $100,000, meaning that money is walking out in large chunks.[30] Given that the average bank robber in the United States gets away with only about $4,000 and runs a far higher risk of apprehension, one might expect that in a sensible theft marketplace, more people would be attracted to the soft targets of charities.

It is highly likely that the $40 billion projection, like the Villanova study of Catholic dioceses, underestimates the real loss from charitable thefts. The 2008 study did not take into account the underreporting of thefts by charities, out of fears that such disclosures would undermine donor confidence, and it did not account for the continuing failure of charities to detect internal thefts. Whatever the right number, it is clear that loss of funds due to fraud is an enormous, sector-wide failure.

Unfortunately, the problems are not addressed simply by locking drawers and bird-dogging collection plates. As we have seen, charities tend to be ineffective overall because they are discouraged from investing in infrastructure. The normal speed governors of effective organizations—strong boards, empowered auditors, internal checks and balances, and active regulators—are broadly absent in the charitable system. And until that is addressed, charities will remain an easy mark for con men, criminals, and thieves.

FIVE

The Donors

B Y THE EARLY winter of 2003, I had worked at NPR for four years as its chief operating officer and was responsible for, among other things, managing the revenues of the company. The bursting of the Internet bubble had caused some shaky months for us, but overall NPR was in very good shape: our audience was growing despite the difficult media environment, and revenues were rising again. But while most of the measures of financial performance were solid, one problem was particularly bedeviling to NPR. When I started at NPR in the late 1990s, operating reserves and endowment—the organization's financial cushion—were virtually nonexistent; if revenues had been disrupted for even a matter of weeks, NPR would have been insolvent. That may sound a touch melodramatic, but in fact NPR had brushed up against financial failure in the past. In 1983, its lawyers were rushing to file bankruptcy papers before a midnight infusion from the Corporation for Public Broadcasting rescued NPR. A generation later, the memory of 1983 still lingered throughout public radio.

One of NPR's principal goals was to build financial assets and create long-term economic stability. We had made important strides by increasing corporate sponsorship and raising fees paid by stations for NPR programming, but we were still a long way from our goal of reaching the standard benchmark for charities: having an endowment and operating reserves at least equal to the annual budget, for us in the range of $125 million. On its face, this should have been a relatively modest goal. NPR has a strong and intimate relationship with its audience of almost thirty million; for its most dedicated listeners, it is often the first voice heard in the morning and the last heard at night. NPR is a marker of identity: millions of people describe themselves as NPR listeners in personal ads, on bumper stickers, and now on Facebook. The NPR audience is also uncommonly affluent, a fact frequently pointed out in political debates, in parodies, and in NPR's own internal research reports. Suffice it to say that the NPR audience has enormous potential for major gifts. But for the first thirty-plus years of NPR's existence, those gifts did not happen. There was a reason for this. The internal politics of public radio had for decades inhibited NPR from undertaking any significant effort to find and cultivate major donors. While, to most listeners, public radio is one seamless service generically known as NPR, each station is in fact an independent operator, responsible for its own finances and its own future, and stations are at once both heavily dependent on and deeply wary of NPR. Potential donors to NPR are almost by definition existing or potential donors to their local public radio stations as well, and station executives have long been concerned that their donors could be lost to NPR. Nothing, of course, stops donors from supporting both a national and a local service—and virtually all NPR donors also support a local station—but many of the public radio stations that controlled NPR through its board and that counted on listeners for their revenues were eager to draw all sorts of red lines to keep NPR away from these donors. Thus, in 2003, more than thirty years after NPR's birth, it barely had a working endowment, and its major gifts program was rudimentary at best.

All that changed swiftly and dramatically in October 2003. Joan Kroc, the widow of the McDonald's founder Ray Kroc, died that month, scattering about $2 billion in charitable bequests to various organizations, including a gift to NPR that eventually totaled almost $250 million. The gift was not only stunning in size (we called it the largest gift ever to an American cultural institution) but also disproportionate to anything that NPR had ever received. In its thirty-two years of existence, NPR had received only three gifts from individuals that equaled or exceeded $1 million, and one of those had been from Mrs. Kroc herself just a few months before her death. When Kevin Klose, the president of NPR and my then boss, came down to my office to tell me the details of the call he had just received from the trustees of the Kroc estate, I was so nonplussed that I ended up chasing him back up the hallway toward his office to make sure that I had heard the number correctly. A few weeks later, we broke the news to the NPR board on a hastily scheduled conference call. We had countless such telephone meetings during my time at NPR, and they were almost always routine events, frequently characterized by board members (and NPR staff as well) drifting away from the call as they attended to more pressing or interesting activities. This one started out no different, and I could distinctly hear the clatter of a keyboard as one board member checked his e-mail or worked on a memo. When Klose finished a long windup with the titanic news of the Kroc gift, there was a stunned silence broken only by a loud "say what?" from that distracted board member as he tried to grapple with the news he had just half heard. When we announced the gift publicly days later, we connected the bequest with Mrs. Kroc's longtime passion for NPR and her personal and deep connection with the public-radio-listening experience. The NPR press release read, "Joan Kroc believed deeply in the power of public radio to serve the communities of America. She made this extraordinary gift from the steadfast conviction that NPR and its member stations provide a vital connection to millions of listeners." Joan Kroc was in our narrative a dedicated and passionate NPR listener,[1] a story that resonated with many, though it was a story made less impressive to me by the fact that I knew it was not particularly true.

NPR was never supposed to get the Kroc gift. Years before we ever met Joan Kroc, she donated $3 million for the studio expansion of KPBS, the local PBS and NPR affiliate in her hometown of San Diego. The gift was very large for an organization of KPBS's size, and it was made quite clear to the staff at KPBS that the gift from Mrs. Kroc was intended to be the capstone of her relationship with the station. But Stephanie Bergsma, the head of fund-raising at KPBS and the person who had cultivated the Kroc relationship, cleverly reasoned that if she could connect Kroc with one of the national public broadcasting organizations, the relationship might redound somehow to the further financial benefit of KPBS. Since Mrs. Kroc's interest in KPBS had been expressed through her support for public television, Bergsma reached out to the then president of PBS and invited her to come meet on the West Coast with Mrs. Kroc. Rather surprisingly, the offer was declined. A number of requests and entreaties from Bergsma followed, all rebuffed for a variety of scheduling issues. Frustrated, Bergsma reasoned that one national broadcasting organization was as good as another, and she called NPR's Klose, inviting him to meet with Kroc near her home in Rancho Santa Fe.

You never had to ask Kevin Klose twice to meet a major donor, especially one sitting atop billions of dollars in fast-food profits. Klose had all the traits of a great fund-raiser: he was energetic, personable, eloquent, and passionate about NPR. Tall, patrician, and topped by a shock of white hair, Klose even looked the part of a leader of a great charitable organization; as a longtime journalist and former foreign correspondent for *The Washington Post,* he had the bona fides to speak about the important role that journalism plays in American society. Within weeks of Bergsma's call, we, along with Barbara Hall, NPR's head of fund-raising at the time, were on a plane to California for breakfast with Mrs. Kroc. By then in her mid-seventies, she was no longer the "blond beauty" who had captivated Ray Kroc when he saw her play piano in a St. Paul, Minnesota, bar in 1957, but she was still a carefully pressed, well-preserved figure. The breakfast went very well, though not because Kroc had a deep and long-standing interest in NPR. In fact, throughout the breakfast, it was clear that Kroc did not listen to NPR, and she frequently confused NPR (as many people do) with other public media organizations ranging from PBS to the BBC to other public radio producers. But Kroc was also plainly captivated by Klose. Less than two months later, it became clear how successful the breakfast was. A check for $1 million arrived in December 2002, an early Christmas present for NPR. Several more visits from Klose followed, and in the spring of 2003 Kroc sent an emissary, an energetic former McDonald's communications executive named Dick Starmann, to Washington to kick NPR's tires. In October 2003, almost exactly one year after our first meeting with her, Joan Kroc died of brain cancer, and shortly thereafter the trustees of her estate were announcing some of the largest bequests in history: more than $200 million for NPR, another $5 million for KPBS, $50 million each for Notre Dame and the University of San Diego, $10 million for the San Diego Zoo, $20 million for the San Diego Hospice, and eventually $1.5 billion to the Salvation Army to build two dozen community centers across the country.

It usually takes years for a charitable organization to build a successful relationship with a major donor, and even then the relationship is often built on a direct and personal connection between the donor and the institution: an alma mater, a hospital that treated the donor, a lifelong love of the symphony. Mrs. Kroc's gift was notable not only for its size but for the surprisingly brief intersection between her life and NPR. But in fact for Mrs. Kroc, it was not all that unusual, as she had developed over time a very personal giving style. Like many donors, she responded to stories and personal impressions. Earlier in her philanthropic career, Kroc had established a foundation, as many wealthy donors do, to direct and focus her charitable activity. There are tax advantages to personal foundations, but there is also a loss of control; donation decisions are made by professional staff and a theoretically independent board of trustees. After several years of this structure, Mrs. Kroc abolished her foundation, as she wanted to be personally and directly involved in giving decisions. And directly involved she was, responding, often instantly, to the news of the day, giving money, often anonymously, to flood victims, to individual victims of diseases, to school districts to balance budgets, to an HIV/AIDS laundry that had been flatteringly portrayed on the local news. Kroc would hear a story of need, often through the media or through her network of friends and associates, and a check could follow within hours. This method of giving is in fact the norm for many donors: reactive to news and events, and responsive to individual stories and needs. It reflects the intimate and individualistic nature of giving in this country, and this generosity and willingness to open up pocketbooks has created the largest philanthropic sector in the world by far. But, as we have seen in earlier chapters, it also shapes charities into storytellers and provides little incentive toward organizational effectiveness and results-driven management. Americans' investments in charities are impulsive, driven by anecdote, and, as we shall shortly see, occasionally even destructive. I daresay that if Joan Kroc had employed similar strategies to invest her wealth, she would have had much less of it to spread around at her death.

Donor psychology—the goals and style of American giving—plays a determinative role in shaping the charitable sector. Donors like Mrs. Kroc are more often than not well-intentioned and generous individuals whom charities pursue with the ardor of romantic suitors. Yet even well-meaning donors unintentionally form a key barrier to the kind of change the charitable sector desperately needs. I use Joan Kroc as an example of this with some regret. Her generosity and commitment to the less fortunate among us should be honored. There are many who have done far less. To the extent that I frame her story in the pages that follow as a cautionary tale, it is only because it forms an unusually vivid example of the charitable ethos of our time, and the challenge of good intentions and bad results that is endemic to our system.

The question of why people donate has fascinated academics since the 1950s. In 2011, two prominent students of giving behavior, René Bekkers and Pamala Wiepking of the Free University in Amsterdam, undertook a survey of recent studies of philanthropy and ended up collecting over five hundred peer-reviewed articles from such widely disparate disciplines as marketing, economics, social psychology, political science, anthropology, biological psychology, neurology and brain science, and sociology.[2] From a scientific perspective, the act of giving to strangers is considered to be somewhere between counter-intuitive and irrational, and researchers have struggled mightily to understand this evolutionarily puzzling behavior. They have tested the effects of mood, time of year, income, familial relationships, types of solicitations, and numerous other variables on giving. One study looked at the effect of temperature on donations to the Salvation Army between Thanksgiving and Christmas and found a sizable positive effect of more temperate weather.[3] Scholars have conducted hundreds of experiments using tools such as "dictator games" and blind testing, and they have filled pages with sophisticated mathematical equations.[4] Yet virtually every paper on the subject concludes that the author has been unable to develop a satisfying theory of donor behavior and that further and substantial analysis and testing will be required. Of course, that might be a clever job-preservation strategy for the academic community, but it more likely reflects a complicated set of motivations not easily summed up in a single formula.

Still, if you had to boil down a generation of work on donor psychology, it would come to this divide: people give either out of altruism or to get personal benefits. Those benefits are sometimes tangible (tax benefits, public acclaim through naming rights) but also include intangible feel-good benefits in the form of the "warm glow," a phrase first coined by James Andreoni, a professor of economics at the University of California, San Diego. Proponents of the altruistic theory look for behaviors that suggest that donors care only about outcomes and direct their funds accordingly. Thus, if a donor believes that an activity needs $1 and someone else, either a governmental funder or another donor, provides that $1, the altruistic or strategic donor would direct his or her $1 to the next-most-worthy recipient. This is labeled the "crowding out" effect and is considered evidence of altruistic behavior. Conversely, those who support the "warm glow" effect point to the signs of personal benefits from voluntary activity: the joy of giving, the prestige of being acknowledged as a donor, and the strengthening of self-image. Studies of brain activity centers tend to support this view, revealing that gifts to charity "elicit neural activity in areas linked to reward processing."[5] Academics frequently point to the example of public radio drives in support of this theory, noting that listeners continue to give even after goals are met, which suggests that private benefits are at work. The effectiveness of listener gifts such as mugs, bumper stickers, and the much-mocked but also highly coveted tote bag, as well as on-air announcements of donor names, is also indicative of private benefits or at least of mixed motivations. Over the years, the research has tended more and more to support the theory that people donate to obtain personal benefits, either because they want the warm glow of giving or because of the availability of more tangible benefits.[6]

The difference between altruistic giving and warm-glow giving may seem small, perhaps even trivial. The United States has the most vibrant social sector in the world, and it has continued to grow over time, even through the economic troughs of the last few decades; whatever the motivation for giving, it seems to be working in terms of delivering money to the charitable sector. So long as people give and give generously, it would hardly seem to make much of a difference whether the act of "detached and disinterested generosity," as the Supreme Court has defined a gift,[7] masks complicated and sometimes self-rewarding emotions. This is an appealing perspective, but it turns out that it matters a great deal why people give. Simply put, warm-glow donors behave differently than altruistic ones. They put greater value on emotional connections and derive value from direct links to charitable causes. They are more likely to be "point of purchase" buyers, responding to face-to-face requests and less influenced by analytical tools. They tend to value settled relationships with established institutions. And because they are motivated by emotional reward, they are driven to specific projects and appeals and are less inclined to concern themselves with questions of organizational effectiveness. It is not that donors are indifferent to the quality of their charitable investments—they would lose considerable value if they thought their money was being wasted—but it pushes effectiveness far down their list of priorities. They are the kinds of donors who make charities passive toward rigorous measures of performance.

When Nicholas Kristof gave his "advice to save the world," he did not tout new technologies, nor new medicines, nor new ideas of how to house and feed people. Nor did he advocate for better charitable organizations to carry out the best ideas in the most effective manner. Rather, he looked to Madison Avenue and marketing departments for lessons on how to better connect with potential donors. Kristof marveled at the fact that social psychologists have found that people are more responsive to individual stories of success than to overwhelming stories of need—the more specific and personal the better.[8] Donors are more likely to respond to an appeal to provide water to a village of a hundred people than to provide the exact same service to a hundred identical people in a city of one million people—and are more likely to respond to the needs of a single identifiable person within that village than to the needs of the village as a whole. Fund-raisers and product marketers have known this for years: stories, anecdotes, pictures, and individual case studies sell far better than more generalized facts, figures, and results. For decades, international relief agencies have raised money by having a donor sponsor an individual child in need, complete with picture, bio, and regular thank-you letters. In many ways, it was the perfect charitable marketing device: highly engaged, personal, and deepening over time. The fact that the charities understood that it made no particular sense to allocate resources in such a highly tailored manner was less important than finding the right formula to encourage donations. Good stories sell.

This fact is reflected in research that has highlighted the importance of the "identifiable victim" in giving decisions. In one famous experiment, participants were given the opportunity to help the needy through contributions to Save the Children, a global relief and social services organization. Potential donors were exposed to three giving scenarios: the first focused on the needs caused by the fact that "food shortages in Malawi are affecting more than three million children," a second scenario focused on one desperately poor seven-year-old Malian girl named Rokia, and a third scenario described both the Malawian problem and Rokia's plight. The second group—who heard the Rokia-only story—in every instance gave substantially more than the other groups. When a second identifiable child was added to Rokia's story, contributions declined. The results reflect what philosopher Peter Singer of Princeton has called the "rule of rescue," that we will give more, both financially and emotionally, to assist a relatable rather than a statistical victim. The call on resources will be most compelling when the cause is comprehensible, human, and specific. The fact that people respond to stories with a human face is hardly surprising, but it can lead to the misallocation of scarce resources, with significant implications. The Rokia study is not alone in revealing this challenge. In a recent study, one group was told that a single child needed lifesaving treatment that would cost $300,000. A second group was told that eight children could be saved with similar treatment that cumulatively cost $300,000. The first group always gave more.[9]

The social science experiments are replicated in real life in haunting ways. In 1983, John Donvan of ABC News was reporting from Beirut in the midst of some of the worst sectarian violence of the Lebanese civil war. He rushed to the scene of a particularly horrific car bombing in time to capture the tragic image of a small girl, no more than four, being borne aloft on a stretcher by rescue crews. After Donvan's graphic report aired on the nightly news, hundreds of people flooded ABC News with offers of support for the girl. As Donvan recounted to me many years later, the ABC newsroom referred callers to relevant relief agencies—both because ABC had no mechanisms for delivering aid to individual victims and because the young girl in Donvan's report tragically was already dead—but the overwhelming mass of callers were connected only to that child and uninterested in providing support to a broad group of victims. Instead, they were focused entirely on getting resources to that one little girl who was in no known way different from the dozens of other victims of that terrible bombing and the hundreds of thousands of other victims of the Lebanese civil war. It is a scenario well known to reporters—and well known to charities as well. Charities know that they are rewarded not for finding cost-effective solutions to problems—nor solutions to problems at all—but for finding ways to personalize, humanize, and convey needs. This does not make charities indifferent to impact, but it also does not ensure that resources will be driven to the institutions best equipped to make broader impact. Like all institutions, charities are shaped by financial incentives, and here market forces encourage focus on individual efforts not reasonably calculated to solve broader social problems.

Charity fund-raisers deploy varied strategies for raising money, from raffles to direct mail to walkathons to face-to-face solicitations to high-end charity balls. But among the most effective ways to attract warm-glow donors is to give them recognition and prestige. Association with a cause can be a matter of personal identity—support for Habitat for Humanity, the Nature Conservancy, or the local opera or symphony is shorthand for a set of interests and values—and donors get positive reinforcement if their support of charities can be demonstrated.[10] Since you can't just walk down the street and shout out your latest charitable contribution, charities have come up with endless ways to provide recognition for donors. At the low end are the yellow wristband and the pink ribbon. Higher up the dollar food chain are published or broadcast donor acknowledgments, right up to naming rights for grand buildings (this explains the Eugene and Agnes Meyer Women's Restroom at the Arena Stage in Washington, D.C.). This phenomenon has been cleverly labeled "conspicuous compassion," reflecting the odd alchemy of charitable impulse and self-promotion.[11] Fund-raisers know that the availability of greater rewards for greater gifts provides strong incentive for donors to give more.[12]

At the top of the hierarchy of benefits is direct involvement in the organization, either on its board of directors or through some other form of direct control over the dispensation of funds. These roles may be styled as service and volunteer opportunities, but in reality board appointments are often effectively economic deals. Charities expect board members to make financial contributions of often very specific amounts, and in return donors get prestige, recognition, and some level of control over how their gifts are used and over the institution itself. This is not to say that donors do not make good board members—they may or they may not—but capacity to give is not a reliable indicator that the donor has the subject matter or strategic expertise to help manage a charity. Most important, when board seats are awarded as part of a tacit exchange, some donors, not unreasonably, believe that they have purchased the right to have say over projects and matters better left to professional staff. When a charity creates the conditions for donors to feel this sense of entitlement, the consequences for the charity's service can be considerable.

Given the location of the Metropolitan Opera in New York, Amarillo, Texas, would seem an unlikely well of major funding. Hot, dry, and lonely, 362 miles from Dallas to the east, 288 miles from Albuquerque to the west, Amarillo has ridden the booms and busts of the Texas Panhandle, cresting with the cattle trade and resurging with the oil boom. The public image of Amarillo, if it has one at all, is a cliché of the American West: pianos plinking between swinging bar doors, cowboys and cows roped together on the long drive, roughnecks from the oil fields drinking and brawling on a Saturday night. But the truth is quite different. Today, in spite of, or perhaps because of, its physical isolation, Amarillo has developed a vibrant cultural scene, centered on the Globe-News Center, a bold soaring performance center that houses the local opera, symphony, ballet, and theater company. Arrayed around the Globe are the trappings of a thriving arts community: schools, galleries, libraries, and cafés.

Much of the original energy, and money, for the Amarillo arts scene came from the local oil barons, especially Don and Sybil Harrington. Don Harrington arrived in Amarillo in 1926, during the early years of its oil and gas boom, and within a few years had established himself as one of the leading local energy developers. The Harringtons married in 1935, and they quickly developed a reputation for generous funding of philanthropic ventures in the Panhandle, everything from football fields to local libraries to a regional cancer clinic. But the Harringtons' cultural writ extended well beyond west Texas; their bank accounts brimming with oil dollars, they scoured Europe for paintings, bringing back works by Picasso, Monet, Degas, and Renoir to fill their home. And they climbed the New York cultural scene, making lavish and prolific donations to some of the most prominent arts charities in the city. Beginning in 1978, Sybil Harrington became the Metropolitan Opera's largest donor, funding numerous productions and facilities. And Mrs. Harrington's involvement went beyond funding; she demanded and received extraordinary say in the selection of performances for the Met season, down to the choice of directors and the style of production. Her tastes ran to the most traditional of operas and presentations and drove the Met to become one of the most conservative opera companies in the world. Mrs. Harrington was not alone in claiming approval rights over Met decisions; the investment banker Alberto Vilar exercised similar if not quite as broad control over productions as well, but Mrs. Harrington proved unique in trying to maintain control from the grave. Her will provided additional funding for only "traditional/grand opera productions . . . set in a place and time and staged as the composer placed it." This controlling hand from the grave proved problematic for the Met as it tried to walk a tightrope between donors such as Vilar who designated their funds for more modern productions and the legal demands of the Harrington will. It was an impossible balancing act, and Mrs. Harrington's estate eventually sued, arguing that the staging of a particular Wagner performance in 2001 was not sufficiently traditional by the standards of the late Mrs. Harrington.

The Harrington case ended up entangling the courts for many years, no doubt perplexing jurists asked to adjudicate operatic style, and it stands as a cautionary tale for many charities. The care and feeding of donors who make highly personal gifts can distract from core charitable purposes and matters of organizational effectiveness. There is little more central to the Metropolitan Opera than its artistic vision—the selection of operas, their staging, the singers, and the directors—and that vision was compromised by following the dictates of donors. Vilar ultimately took his demands elsewhere. Convicted in 2008 of a dozen counts of federal securities fraud, he left many cultural institutions, including the Met, on the wrong end of multimillion-dollar pledges. Struggling under the weight of $33 million of unfulfilled pledges from Vilar and the stigma of criminal association, the Met quietly removed the placarding on the Vilar Grand Tier. The naming rights are available once again for a more law-abiding but potentially no less intrusive donor.

Donor dictates can even bring a charity to the brink of failure. For years, the Washington National Opera company teetered on a financial knife's edge, due to a paralyzing funding situation. As the second opera house in a one-opera town, it had always been plagued by a narrow and inadequate funding base and had to rely on a small group of influential donors to keep it from insolvency. By 2005, the funding situation at the opera had become increasingly precarious, in part because of the lofty, expensive, and largely unrealized ambitions of its famous artistic director, Plácido Domingo. It was clear to virtually everyone that the days of the National Opera as a viable independent organization were numbered and the only realistic course was to fold or seek a merger with the Kennedy Center, the dominant player in the local opera market. The Kennedy Center was fortunately willing to play the white knight, and all the conditions were set for a successful merger. One thing, however, stood in the way: the core asset of the National Opera was a $20 million endowment gift from Betty Brown Casey, a local philanthropist, who made the gift over a decade before but had permanently tied it to the continued independence of the National Opera. Should the opera ever merge or be acquired, the gift would go instead to the New York Metropolitan Opera, a galling prospect to the D.C. cultural community, always chafing against the far loftier reputation and reach of their New York City counterparts. As the merger moved from rumor toward reality, Mrs. Casey retained the notoriously combative lawyer Brendan Sullivan to assure that the terms of her gift would be protected to the letter. The Casey challenge brought merger talks to an abrupt halt, and the National Opera limped on for five more years, always on the verge of extinction. The story, however, ends sensibly, as these stories sometimes do. When it became clear even to Mrs. Casey that the National Opera could no longer exist as an independent organization, she removed the limitations from her gift in 2011, and the merger with the Kennedy Center finally took place.

Donor dictates may also extend to personnel decisions, even when donors lack the expertise to assess candidate qualifications.[13] For instance, donors have frequently claimed the right to appoint or approve candidates for endowed chairs. Clashes between Yale University and the oilman and alumnus Lee Bass over such appointments led Yale in 1994 to the highly unusual step of returning a $20 million gift, an act that only one of the largest and best-funded charities in America could even contemplate. In January 2011, the largest donor to the University of Connecticut Athletic Department, a Greenwich hedge fund manager named Robert Burton, exploded in anger and in print because, in his view, he had not been sufficiently consulted over the hiring of the new head football coach at the school. He demanded the immediate return of more than $3 million in gifts. It took four weeks and shuttle diplomacy that included the university president and the governor of Connecticut to calm the roiled waters and ensure the continued flow of Burton family money to the university. Burton's position was widely panned by both the press and the public alike. Only one commentator rose to his defense: T. Boone Pickens, who opined that athletic departments should always have time to hear the views of their major donors, a not surprising view from the man who reportedly hand selected his quail-hunting buddy to be the Oklahoma State athletic director and blessed the hiring of the head football coach.[14]

A more serious controversy erupted just months later, in May 2011, at Florida State University (FSU) when it was revealed that FSU had given the Charles G. Koch Charitable Foundation full hiring participation and veto authority over Koch-funded endowed chairs in political economy and free enterprise. Charles and his brother David had gained considerable fame, or notoriety, in the previous few years by aggressively funding conservative political candidates and libertarian causes across the country. The flames of controversy in Tallahassee were fanned by the widespread suspicion, which the Koch brothers did not bother to refute, that the investment in the Florida State Economics Department was part of a broader strategy to promote the teaching of libertarian thought and the hiring of sympathetic academics at colleges around the country.[15] As part of the overall gift, Koch provided matching grants, an offer that was taken up by the BB&T Foundation, the charitable funding arm of a large North Carolina bank holding company. The BB&T Foundation gave FSU $500,000 to create economics courses that prominently featured the writings of Ayn Rand. This was one of approximately twenty-five similar gifts that the BB&T Foundation spread across American universities, all requiring the creation or expansion of Rand-related courses. The involvement of a corporate foundation in a controversial and politically charged field is a little surprising; most corporate giving is deeply conservative, not in the political sense, but in the desire to avoid any tinge of controversy. Corporate philanthropy thus tends to veer toward supporting hometown institutions, charities already popular with employees and shareholders, and charities that have some connection to the business goals of the company. The Walmart Foundation, for instance, touts its support of hunger relief, military veterans, and education. In BB&T's case, the gifts reflected the interests and political tendencies of its then CEO John Allison, making the contributions more controversial since the money came from shareholder, not personal, assets.[16]

The use of donor gifts as ammunition in the culture wars is just one way donor control can reshape organizations in ways that have little to do with charitable effectiveness. The desire of donors to put a personal stamp on charities is not a new one, and indeed concepts of donor control date back to English common law. Our modern laws and courts, too, have established donor rights that oblige charities to be accountable to their supporters, but the open question is accountable toward what—the goals and specific outcomes of the charitable mission or the specific personal or social views of the donor? Those goals are often not the same and can drive wildly different actions and results.

The donor accountability movement has a modern godmother, Adele Smithers-Fornaci.[17] For many years, Mrs. Smithers-Fornaci has played a pivotal role in the world of alcohol-abuse treatment as president of the Christopher D. Smithers Foundation, the nation's most important foundation in the fight against alcoholism. The foundation was established in 1952 with the first in a series of large gifts from Smithers-Fornaci's husband, Brinkley Smithers, the son of a wealthy investment banker for whom the foundation was named. The foundation's focus was not an accident; it stemmed from Brinkley's own battle with alcoholism. At the time, alcoholism was rarely studied and never treated as a medical condition; rather, it was viewed in polite society as a failure of the poor, a challenge for the working class, and something between a social handicap and a charming foible for the well-to-do. The purpose of the foundation was to educate the public that alcoholism was a widespread disease, not limited, in Mrs.

Smithers-Fornaci's words, to "skid row bums."[18] As Brinkley Smithers put it, the foundation's mission was to convince the American public that "alcoholism is a respectable disease, from which people can and do recover." The statement captures much about the ethic of the Smithers Foundation, a mix of medical and social viewpoints with perhaps a dash of self-justification. Whatever the personal psychology behind it, the Smithers Foundation made an extraordinary impact on the field. It is fair to say that its investments over a half century helped revolutionize and, one could argue, invent the alcohol and addiction treatment fields, and its grants dominated everything from research to education to treatment centers to social campaigns.

However, the Smithers Foundation's largesse came with strings attached. Brinkley Smithers and later Adele Smithers-Fornaci, who succeeded her late husband as president of the foundation, had decided views on the causes and treatments of alcoholism, and any institution or researcher the foundation supported who challenged their views was in for a fight. This attitude engendered a series of battles between the foundation and the Smithers Alcoholism Treatment and Training Center at St. Luke's–Roosevelt Hospital in New York City. The conflict began in 1994 when Mrs. Smithers-Fornaci discovered that the hospital was using designated endowment funds for purposes unrelated to the treatment of alcoholism. She sued for the return of the money, ultimately winning back millions of dollars and new rights for donors and their heirs to seek redress in the courts to enforce the terms of charitable gifts, a right previously held in New York only by the attorney general. Then, in the middle of this contentious litigation, another conflict emerged out of the tight strings attached to every Smithers dollar.

In July 2000, *New York* magazine published an article on the Smithers Center at St. Luke's–Roosevelt, noting, largely in passing, that doctors at the center were testing a range of treatment models. The writer briefly described its flirtations with "moderation models" that did not at least immediately demand complete abstinence from alcohol. While the article described these as experiments, in truth the extent of the innovation was not really clear: the moderation model was a decade-old concept, part of an evidence-based pretreatment option largely for nondependent drinkers that fell well within the wide norms of accepted practice.[19] The article quoted Alexander DeLuca, the center's medical director: "We do find that people who go to twelve-step meetings do better. But it doesn't work for some and I'm not going to tell them 'Come back after you've suffered some more and are ready to do it our way.'" The suggestion that moderation management (or MM, as it is known in the field) was a potential alternative to total abstinence for some was heretical to the view of the Smithers Foundation. Smithers viewed the MM perspective as something akin to the notion that a little bit of malaria is okay. (In that view, the foundation is not alone, and to this day the scientific evidence remains equivocal.) Mrs. Smithers-Fornaci reacted angrily and immediately to the magazine article, taking the extraordinary step of placing a full-page ad in *The New York Times,* excoriating both the hospital and Dr. DeLuca for their views and accusing them of destroying families and causing the needless loss of lives through the use of moderation management. The hospital, already embroiled in one fight with its largest donor, was unwilling to begin another one. Within days, Dr. DeLuca was fired and his program erased, all without scientific evaluation or professional debate. Smithers's viewpoint on abstinence may ultimately be proved the right one, or it may not, but the use of the foundation's funding power in this way plainly did not advance research and knowledge in the field.

Ironically, good ideas imposed on a charity can be almost as harmful as bad ideas, by disrupting planning, service focus, and attention to the goals and metrics of an organization. Which brings us back to Joan Kroc. When NPR announced the massive Kroc donation, it was not yet publicly known that the NPR gift was dwarfed by a much,

much larger bequest to the Salvation Army, originally reported as $1.5 billion. The delay was not at the hands of the Kroc trustees but at the behest of the Salvation Army, which spent many months considering whether to take the gift. Charities are not in the business of rejecting donations, and it took extraordinary circumstances to prompt the Salvation Army to consider turning down the largest single gift ever made to an American charity.

When you and I stuff a holiday dollar into the red kettle in front of the supermarket, the money goes to the general funding of the Salvation Army, most of which is spent on programs to feed the hungry, shelter the needy, and provide relief to the victims of disasters. These are the core services of the Salvation Army, evolved over the 150 years since its founder William Booth walked the streets of London preaching to the downtrodden. The Army's programs have been refined, changed, and in some cases abandoned over time, prompted by evolving measures of effectiveness, the emerging needs of society, and its own fixed values. We small-dollar, or loose-change, donors have little say in how the Salvation Army develops and implements its programs, except in one sense. If it appears to do an effective job, we will donate again. If it fails to deliver on the promise of effective services to the needy, we have the opportunity and perhaps even the responsibility to brush by the bell ringer next holiday season.

Mrs. Kroc did not stuff $1.5 billion into a kettle. Instead, she offered the Salvation Army a deal, one that promised unheard-of up-front dollars but also required a substantial reorientation of the Salvation Army's focus and some risk to its resources. Before her death, Mrs. Kroc had funded a new Salvation Army community center in her hometown of San Diego. The Salvation Army had built community centers before, as anchors for food distribution activities and for its classroom and devotional activities, but never anything like this. The entrance to the San Diego center is graced by a Henry Moore sculpture, which charmingly doubles as a jungle gym for kids, albeit, at $2.5 million, a very, very expensive jungle gym. The $87 million complex boasts three swimming pools, an indoor skating rink, skateboarding ramps, and a six-hundred-seat theater. The center is based in a low-income neighborhood of San Diego and outstrips in services all but the toniest country clubs in town. Mrs. Kroc's posthumous offer to the Salvation Army was this: she would give funds to build approximately thirty more centers across the country, with enough left over for endowments to cover approximately half of the operating costs. The rest of the operating costs would come from service fees, other voluntary contributions, or the Salvation Army's general operating funds.[20]

It's hard for anyone, let alone a charity that rings bells for spare change, not to get moony over a billion and a half dollars, but in fact the Kroc gift was met with considerable trepidation within the Army's headquarters. It was not the value of the community centers per se that concerned the organization's leadership but the risk of undermining its core efforts. High-end community centers—even those subsidized to support all income classes—are a long way from the Salvation Army's mission of providing food for the needy, shelter for the elderly and for struggling families, drug rehabilitation services, and disaster relief. The Kroc gift carried substantial risk for the Salvation Army: management distraction and inattention to core services, public confusion over the operations and brand of the Salvation Army, and potential diversion of funds from core operations if the Kroc centers did not prove self-sufficient. Moreover, while the San Diego Kroc Center was beautiful, the service value of the center was unclear and untested by meaningful measures. These were all persuasive arguments against taking the gift, but ultimately the magnetic pull of $1.5 billion was simply too strong. In January 2004, about three months after the death of Mrs. Kroc, the Salvation Army finally announced the historic gift.

The Kroc estate began the distribution in January 2005; by that time, investment gains had grown the gift to $1.8 billion, sufficient to fund a planned twenty-seven centers around the country. As of this writing, the Salvation Army has built about half those centers. Typical is a recently opened center in a tired, rapidly declining neighborhood in North Philadelphia. The factories of North Philadelphia once made car parts and Tastykakes but have since been shuttered and shattered, gifts to vandals and climbing weeds. The new Kroc Center is a lovely and surprising oasis on a particularly depressing stretch of Wissahickon Avenue. The facility, all blond wood and rounded edges, is anchored by a bright four-hundred-seat worship center—though only about eighty excited camp kids were bouncing up and down to the movie *Ice Age* on the day I visited. It has a two-story workout facility, classrooms, child-care facilities, a fashionable café, and a small computer center, but the pools are the real revelation: a children's aquatic park, a small lazy river, and an expansive competition pool, overseen by Jim Ellis, the swim coach made famous in the movie *Pride*. It would be forgivable to think you had taken a wrong turn into a wealthy Main Line Philadelphia country club, except for the urban moonscape clearly visible just beyond the habitat trails of the Kroc Center.

The 130,000 square feet of the North Philly Kroc Center came with a very hefty price tag: $132 million, of which only about half was covered by the Kroc gift. The other $60 million came from local fund-raising and from borrowing. Membership fees cover the operating costs. And because of that, the Kroc Center has the feel of a commercial operation. Family memberships are not cheap: there is a $149 initiation fee and a $99 monthly charge, fees virtually identical to an L.A. Fitness center three miles down the road in Bala Cynwyd. And the Salvation Army has begun to offer specialized classes at an extra charge to boost revenues, classes with names like BLT (butt, legs, and thighs) and Shreddin' for the Weddin'—jingly titles not easily associated with the Salvation Army.

The Kroc Center in North Philadelphia is beautiful, a beacon in a neighborhood where hope is in short supply. But it is, like many charitable investments, long on imagery, short on provable results. It is an unlikely anchor for economic revitalization of the neighborhood, and the services it provides are hard to measure, their value difficult to gauge—a problem for any charitable activity but especially problematic in a community with a tall stack of measurable needs starting with housing, jobs, and support services for the poor. For the Salvation Army, the Kroc Centers are a mixed blessing. It is hard to escape the fear that running a vast network of athletic centers, which require revenue flows for operations, maintenance, and life cycle investments, may disadvantage the core mission of the organization. Mrs. Kroc had a vision of service to poor communities around the country and the wealth and generosity to pull it off, but her gift was not reasonably calculated to make the Salvation Army better at its central functions; it is more likely to leave it stretched and more thinly resourced for the long run. In that sense, the Kroc gift was a classically flawed donor gift and not an effective investment in building a strong, healthy, and self-sufficient charity.

To Mrs. Kroc's credit, she at least invested in an existing nonprofit, which in theory is more likely to be prepared to expand proven services. That is frequently not the case. In a system with virtually no barriers to entry, rich and modestly resourced enthusiasts alike frequently dispense with gifts to existing charities in favor of setting up new nonprofits—often leading to the creation of overlapping, redundant, and inefficient services. The IRS has been the handmaiden for this by rubber-stamping applications or, as in New Orleans, fast-tracking the creation of new charities regardless of their likely efficacy. The ease of opening has spawned a new trend, that of "celanthropist," the painfully awkward label given to celebrity philanthropists.[21] Celebrities, with their ability to generate publicity, attention, and dollars for a cause, have shown a propensity to create their own charities, which offer them control and maximum prominence. In 2007, Madonna, following her adoption tour of Malawi, pledged to build a $15 million school to educate four hundred girls there. Madonna promised $11 million of her own money to jump-start the effort and raised another $7 million from a combination of boldfaced names such as Tom Cruise, Gwyneth Paltrow, and Alex Rodriguez and less famous and well-heeled donors as well. Instead of investing that money through an existing organization possessed of infrastructure, local expertise, and a proven track record, she, along with officials from the Kabbalah Centre in Los Angeles, created Raising Malawi. The new charity did not aspire to create a new model of service or offer any particular innovations. It was just new, meaning new staff, new offices, new infrastructure, new oversight mechanisms, new checks and balances, which Madonna and her team proceeded to create with stunning ineffectiveness. Four years after birth, Raising Malawi officially abandoned the school project, having spent $3.8 million of donor money without ever breaking ground or even taking title to land.[22] Instead, the money went for office space, salaries, architects' fees, two cars for staff who had not yet been hired, and staff benefits that included golf course membership, free housing, and a car and driver for the prospective school director. An internal investigation was unable to track all the expenditures due to lack of internal financial ·systems and inadequate oversight—not surprising since management was more than ten thousand miles away and lacked necessary expertise. Just months before calling off the project amid internal upheavals, Madonna recruited outside experts who advised her that building an expensive school was an ineffective investment in the first place and suggested using funds to finance education programs through existing organizations. But even as she confessed to the failure of the project and even as eight staff members filed suit against the charity citing illegal dismissal and failure to pay benefits,[23] Madonna reiterated her support of the organization and expressed her desire to use it as a vehicle for raising and distributing donations. Raising Malawi is an easy example of how unprofessional efforts can waste money and frustrate effective service. Unfortunately, this example is replicated every day in efforts big and small across the charitable sector.

Most readers will recognize little of themselves in Madonna's or Joan Kroc's stories, since most donors see themselves as sensible supporters of established charities. Indeed, research on donor self-image shows a strong correlation between the willingness of donors to give to a specific organization and their belief in the organization's effectiveness. In a 2010 major-donor survey conducted by Hope Consulting, a San Francisco–based philanthropy advisory firm, "organizational effectiveness" was the most cited factor in choosing a charity, identified by 90 percent of surveyed givers.[24] Yet when the Hope Consulting team began to look at the actual behavior of these very same donors, an entirely different picture emerged. While the vast majority of donors say they care about charitable effectiveness, few make serious efforts to confirm it. Fully 65 percent of donors confess that they never do any research. Of the remaining 35 percent, the effort level is trivial. About half of this research is completed in under an hour, two-thirds in less than two hours. Only 3 percent of donors claim to have done more than six hours of research over the course of a year. And even that modest investment of time tends to have limited value. Donors say about half of their research is drawn from the charity itself, either by looking at its Web site or by talking to one of its volunteers or employees, and opinions of friends and family stand second in rank. Thus, as well-meaning as those donors may be, their research veers heavily toward the anecdotal and subjective.

When Hope Consulting pressed donors to explain their individual donations, effectiveness got pushed even further down the list. Most of the givers explained their own donations on very specific grounds: the desire to reward an alma mater, the need to support a church, the opportunity to support a friend's request. One subset limited donations to small charities, where they could see that their contributions make a difference. All these reasons have little or nothing to do with the effectiveness of the charity. Only one subset of donors, whom the Hope Consulting team labeled "High Impact" and who accounted for about 15 percent of the population, focused on giving to nonprofits that are generating the greatest social good.

Unfortunately, even for the very small group who care about charitable effectiveness and are willing to do some research, they are often not asking the right questions. Most turn to the hoariest of charitable myths: the overhead equation. The single "most important piece of information sought out before giving" is how much money a charity spends on overhead.[25] Even putting aside for the moment the real limitations of the concept, which were explored in the introduction, the analysis is still likely flawed, since much of the data on overhead spending is predicated upon self-reporting. A number of charities even report zero overhead expenses in their annual 990 filings with the federal government, a virtual impossibility. More systematic studies have shown substantial discrepancies between what charities are willing to put in their public disclosure forms and what they compile for private, more closely scrutinized filings. A 2003 study found that California hospitals reported a robust 83 percent of spending on programs in their public disclosure forms, but less public regulatory filings for the same hospitals for the same periods revealed only a 68 percent program allocation.[26] Even the minimal effort that people make to assess charitable effectiveness may be frustrated by misleading data.

In the absence of useful information, donors concerned about effectiveness look for evidence of commitment from other donors: friends, public figures, people in the know. This is called "signaling," and it is why charities announce major gifts at the beginning of every campaign, to assure potential donors of their institutional quality and the likelihood of success of the campaign. In New York City, Brooke Astor, the socialite and heiress by marriage to the last large chunk of the Astor family fortune, for many years played a powerful signaling role.[27] Her contributions were closely monitored and followed by other major donors, though for reasons more related to social status than to evidence of her acumen in analyzing charitable quality. Major charities jockeyed for her donations, knowing that larger checks usually followed from other deep-pocketed donors. There is some logic in following careful charitable investors, just as the moves of Warren Buffett are followed by the investment marketplace. But in reality, major donors often have as little knowledge and are subject to the same behavioral flaws as everybody else.

However, a new set of "signalers" is emerging in the charitable field that may better bear the Buffett comparison, donor organizations that make careful and long-term charitable investment decisions and offer management and strategic expertise to the charities in their portfolios. These new types of donors look and act very different from Kroc, Pickens, and the Astors. One such group is New Profit, based at the upscale address of 2 Canal Park in Cambridge, Massachusetts.

The New Profit lobby looks more like that of a well-heeled consulting firm than a small nonprofit; its sleek waiting area is lined with modern art, and most of the serious young staffers striding between meetings look as if they were stamped from a Harvard Business School admissions catalog. In fact, they may have been, cycled straight from the corridors of Aldrich Hall to the offices of the Monitor Group, a prestigious global management consulting firm that has a symbiotic relationship with New Profit. Though smaller and less well known than its competitors at McKinsey and Boston Consulting Group, Monitor has developed a strong reputation for careful economic analysis and innovative business practices.[28] New Profit occupies a floor in the Monitor office, and, more important, Monitor provides some of the analytical DNA that has shaped New Profit since it was launched in 1999.

New Profit is the brainchild of Vanessa Kirsch, a veteran nonprofit manager. In 1995, Kirsch traveled the world interviewing social entrepreneurs in twenty-two countries. In a small Vietnamese village, she met a local social entrepreneur who had discovered that the tiny shrimps found in the region's rice paddies were a marvelous food supplement, producing a noticeable enhancement in the health and nutrition of the village children. But when Kirsch traveled to the next village downriver, she found the same rice paddies, the same tiny shrimps, but no knowledge of the neighboring village's innovation.

Health and nutrition in the second village were decidedly lacking in comparison to its upstream neighbor. It was not that the villages lived in isolation from each other. They shared the same transportation hubs and for that matter the same Coca-Cola distributor, but while the Coca-Cola team easily found the keys to marketing and distributing across a vast network of villages, the local social innovators lacked the expertise, the capital, and perhaps even the incentive to spread their ideas beyond their immediate horizon. Her Vietnam experience was not unique. Kirsch observed the same barriers over and over in her year of travel and study; everywhere, social entrepreneurs struggled to create broad impact for their charitable enterprises.

When Kirsch returned home, she realized that the challenges facing American charities were really no different. To be sure, there was more money flowing through the charity system here, more access to expertise and resources, but the fundamental challenge of "growing beyond their village" was similar. Indeed, the scale and complexity of the social problems facing the United States—a sagging multibillion-dollar education system, a frayed safety net that permits rampant homelessness and food insecurity, growing inequities in income between the top and the bottom quartiles—made the challenges of the Vietnamese social entrepreneurs seem quaint by comparison. To address the problem, she engaged a group of local business leaders, nonprofit managers, and enterprise thinkers to grapple with the question of how to create and grow effective charities. From these roundtable discussions New Profit was born, a new form of hybrid investment vehicle that would provide multiyear grants to early-stage charitable organizations along with a range of consulting services and a suite of top-flight financial, business, and planning tools. Much of the consulting is done by Monitor Group staff who provide sophisticated expertise not usually available to start-up social entrepreneurs. Explicit in the New Profit ethic is that each client organization is a business, a service business, to be sure, but one that has to have innovative services, a sound and scalable business plan, a tiered strategy to move out of New Profit support within a few years, and the ability to demonstrate results anchored in research. The funding capital for New Profit has come from a growing list of fifty or so wealthy donors who believe that their impact on society can be heightened if their money is directed not by anecdote or relationships but by non-profit investment professionals. In effect, New Profit is a charitable mutual fund, an intermediate organization that gathers the resources of individual donors and directs them in the most targeted and careful manner—putting in time and leveraging expertise that individual donors cannot realistically match.

In its first year, New Profit invested in Jumpstart and Citizen Schools—two early-stage educational charities—and Freelancers Union—a then-new charity providing benefits and advocacy for independent workers—and over the past dozen years has gradually expanded its portfolio into education, workforce development, poverty alleviation, and public health. In over a decade of operation, it has worked with twenty-seven nonprofits, the majority of which have graduated from the New Profit portfolio into self-sustaining operation. Its graduates include some of the most forward-thinking, empirically driven charities in the country, organizations that are in many ways models for the entire charitable community.

But while New Profit has grown considerably, its portfolio remains small. Even as it preaches the benefits of growth and the need for large-scale organizations to combat large-scale social problems, it has struggled to find scale and wider social impact itself—and it is not alone in this struggle. New Profit is at the leading edge of the social entrepreneurship movement that took hold in the late 1990s, rooted in the idea that business innovation could propel the charitable sector forward. Over the last fifteen to twenty years this notion generated an enormous amount of attention and interest. Forums such as the TED conference and the Clinton Global Initiative have made rock stars of some social entrepreneurs, and one of them, Muhammad Yunus, the Bangladeshi founder of Grameen Bank and a father of micro-lending, has even won the Nobel Peace Prize. But for all its prominence, the social entrepreneurship movement has hardly put a dent in the American charitable world.

To its credit, after almost a decade of operation, New Profit began to recognize the limitations of its model. It could continue to slowly recruit major donors into its fold, always fighting the desire of most donors to get personal value out of directing their own donations. Or it could seek a disruptive solution, a bold effort to change the funding equation. In 2005, Kirsch and her team founded Action Tank and America Forward to advocate for public-private initiatives that could support social innovations on a much broader scale. Action Tank implicitly acknowledged that the resources necessary to bring scalable solutions to major problems were likely beyond the reach of the social entrepreneurship movement as it then stood. But not if the resources of the federal government could be marshaled and directed to the best social innovators. And the Obama administration seemed to agree. In 2010, with initial funding of $50 million, the White House launched the Social Innovation Fund to support the next generation of innovative charities and social entrepreneurs. Unlike a traditional government direct-grant program, the Social Innovation Fund pushed out its resources to grant-making organizations, including New Profit, which had the expertise to invest the money in the most promising nonprofits and provide them with strategic support and oversight.[29]

At $50 million, the Social Innovation Fund is a drop in the bucket. But its importance lies in the subversive notion that there is a better way for government to spend its money on social programs. Government agencies are often subject to political undertows and lacking in expertise to evaluate organizational effectiveness. Government programs are also often structured by law to be cost-driven rather than output-driven; they are charged with buying specific services at low-bidder prices instead of ensuring desired social outcomes. One of the early, bipartisan goals of the health reform efforts that culminated in the passage of the Affordable Care Act of 2010, for example, was to move from a system that pays health-care providers on a transaction basis—for each operation, drug treatment, or night in a hospital bed—to one that pays for healthy outcomes instead, giving doctors incentives to provide preventive care and adhere to cost-effective treatments rather than churning through medical tests. This conceptual shift proved too dramatic to survive the political process, and government health programs, along with the vast majority of other federal programs, remain input oriented. Nonetheless, Action Tank's vision of a role for organizations like New Profit in facilitating federal spending has become a hallmark of Obama administration thinking, reflected not only in the Social Innovation Fund but also in the $650 million Investing in Innovation program at the Department of Education. The hope is that intermediate organizations can do what government cannot: drive resources toward charities that produce results and starve the rest. If this vision was realized across all federal programs, it could fundamentally reshape the charitable sector.

At twelve years of age, New Profit is still trying to find its footing, one of many small-scale reform organizations operating at the margins of a massive, seemingly immovable charitable sector. But its record of achievement is clear and unequivocal. Its twenty-seven portfolio companies, ranging from nationally recognized leaders such as KIPP to the fast-growing entrepreneurial education program at BUILD, have compiled an enviable record of growth and evidence-based results. New Profit is an audacious model for the future: one that takes us from a capricious donor world to a rational investment world. Currently, people wanting to make sensible, results-oriented giving decisions are left to their own devices and their own intuition. Billions of dollars are thus misallocated to underperforming, nonperforming, or even fraudulent charities. But New Profit and its handful of peers envision a future in which individuals and governments entrust their funds to professionals able to support, monitor, and incentivize charities toward more effective operations. This is not just a business change; it is also a cultural shift, requiring donors, large and small, public and private, to rethink the rewards they seek from giving. In this new world, donors earn their warm glow from supporting a system that builds the most effective charities possible and leaves the laggards behind. The shift from a donor mentality to a charitable investment mind-set is no simple matter, since it requires the disruption of long-settled charitable practices and assumptions, but the payoff is potentially immense—much greater charitable effectiveness at a time of rising needs and diminishing public resources. This is the promise of New Profit.

SIX

Million-Dollar Babies

CHARLIE QUATT IS an unlikely catalyst for a heated public controversy. He is slightly built, always neatly dressed in muted business attire, and speaks in the quiet tones of an academic—and indeed he is a Harvard Ph.D. Quatt is unfailingly pleasant, to the point of an almost curious courtliness. His offices are modest, located in a nondescript building on a busy commercial strip near but not in a fashionable section of Washington, D.C. But his modest environment belies the influence that Quatt has had in his field, a field he helped create just a handful of years ago. Charlie Quatt is one of the nation's premier nonprofit compensation consultants, listened to by nearly every major nonprofit in this country. Before Quatt and a handful of other pay consultants came along, compensation practices at charities were best described as idiosyncratic, based on individual negotiations and highly subjective notions of propriety and fairness. Quatt helped standardize them by creating new compensation models based on pay data from a mix of nonprofit, for-profit, and government sources. And by developing industry databases of nonprofit executive compensation, he created a new market transparency that has fostered a vigorous spirit of "keeping up with the Joneses" among many larger charities.

As a result, executive pay at charities has become increasingly uniform, more competitive, and significantly higher. Over the last decade, non-profit executive pay has rapidly escalated at a rate of 7–8 percent a year—twice the rate of increase for comparable for-profit or governmental jobs. Even in 2009, during the worst domestic recession in seventy years, and amid widespread layoffs across the charitable sector, the average pay for charity CEOs rose 6 percent.[1]

The evidence of this inflation can be seen all over the charitable world. Salaries in excess of $500,000 are now routine at larger charities; compensation packages that top $1 million are not uncommon in certain select corners of the nonprofit world. Not surprisingly, the highest salaries are found at the charitable institutions that for all intents and purposes operate as for-profit corporations. The most rarefied air can be found in the health-care sector, where nonprofit hospital leaders are lavishly paid. Average compensation for CEOs of elite charitable hospitals is $1.4 million and can extend upward from there by a considerable amount. In New York state, the CEOs of twenty-one top charitable hospitals brought home a collective $64.3 million: the head of New York–Presbyterian made $9.8 million in 2007, and the head of Bronx-Lebanon collected $4.8 million. Michael Dowling, the president of North Shore–Long Island Jewish Health System, received a comparatively modest $2.4 million but also was able to bank the eternal gratitude of his peers. In addition to his well-paying day job, Dowling took on an unpaid role leading New York's Medicaid Redesign Team created to reduce hospital costs. Among its first acts: quietly shelving proposals to cap executive pay at nonprofit hospitals.[2]

The million-dollar-plus salaries at health-care nonprofits are by no means limited to New York. Reporters in Washington state counted fifteen million-dollar earners, led by the CEO of Providence Health at $2.4 million.[3] Baltimore alone, which has less than 10 percent of the population of Washington state, has eight hospital CEOs earning over $1 million.[4] The largesse extends well below the CEO level: department heads and other senior hospital officials often earn into the seven figures, and these high salaries are certainly not limited to successful hospitals. At St. Vincent's Hospital Manhattan in Greenwich Village, the top ten officers took home a collective $6 million in 2010, a number made particularly notable as the hospital collapsed under a "blizzard of problems" in April of that year.[5] The failures at St. Vincent's were epic: debts exceeding $1 billion and nurses left with $180 million in unfunded pension obligations, but none of those problems noticeably diminished the executive compensation packages.[6] Hospitals are not the only big payers within the health-care field. Leaders of the nonprofit insurance giant Blue Cross and Blue Shield outlets are often highly compensated: the head of Blue Cross of Massachusetts makes $3.5 million per year, the top six executives at Blue Cross of North Carolina all make more than $1 million per year, with the CEO reaping $3 million, and the head of Blue Cross of California receives more than $4.6 million per year.[7]

Health-care organizations and college athletic departments lead in charitable compensation by a good-sized margin,[8] but they are not the only ones offering eye-popping salary packages. Private nonprofit colleges and universities routinely pay their presidents in the range of $1 million, and some prominent cultural organizations are waging a compensation arms race. Deborah Borda, the head of the Los Angeles Philharmonic, made $930,000 in the most recent reporting year. Michael Kaiser, the CEO of the Kennedy Center, brought home $1.1 million, while the head of the Guggenheim Museum tallied $1.7 million. At the top of this list are Glenn Lowry of the Museum of Modern Art in New York City, who made $2.5 million, and Zarin Mehta, the head of the New York Philharmonic, at $2.6 million. It is not surprising that hospitals and major cultural organizations top the salary charts. Charitable hospitals, as we have seen, are virtually indistinguishable from their for-profit counterparts, and their pay practices too are comparable to those of their for-profit peers. And while $2.5 million in pay may seem outlandish to the average person in a country where median household income hovers around $50,000, it is less jolting for leaders of major cultural institutions where one of the primary qualifications for membership on the board of directors is assets running into the hundreds of millions of dollars and beyond.

But occasionally an entirely unexpected organization wanders onto the best-paid list. In 2008, Donald Johnson, the head of the Evans Scholars Foundation, an obscure charity that provides educational scholarships for needy golf caddies, received $2.05 million in compensation.[9] In the same year, Richard Moe, then head of the National Trust for Historic Preservation, made over $850,000, and David Mosena, the president of the Museum of Science and Industry in Chicago, earned over $950,000, more than double the average for science museum CEOs around the country. The Levy brothers, Philip and Joel, became briefly famous in 2011 when *The New York Times* publicized their pay packages at the Young Adult Institute (YAI) Network, the largest provider of Medicaid-supported group homes to the developmentally disabled. The brothers, who jointly ran the nonprofit for almost thirty years, received individual compensation packages of approximately $1 million a year; in addition to their salaries, the organization provided some impressive perks: luxury automobiles for each and reimbursement for the cost of college tuition for their children, which Philip used to buy his daughter a condo in lower Manhattan. In addition, the Levy brothers were paid consulting fees, about $50,000 a year, from an affiliated charity, the New York League for Early Learning.[10]

While disclosures of these salaries are often greeted with public indignation, reporting on the subject only rarely leads to changes in charitable compensation practices. Public attention to the matter is usually too transitory to affect donations and revenues, and charitable boards are often insulated from public pressure. Moreover, in the wake of scandal, charities are typically desperate to retain experienced staff, and sharply reducing salaries is not reasonably calculated to achieve that end. In the case of the Young Adult Institute Network, both Philip and Joel abruptly resigned in the aftermath of the *Times* inquiry, but it is unlikely that even this signals a long-term shift away from high pay practices. Philip and Joel were not the only "Medicaid moguls" at the institute; at least two other executives below them, including the COO, made more than $500,000 a year. In the wake of the Levy brothers' departure, and under pressure from supervisory authorities at the New York State Office for People with Developmental Disabilities, YAI dramatically restructured its board, pledging to replace more than half of its nineteen members over the course of a year. But amid all these changes, the board also announced that it would maintain the salary of Stephen Freeman, who was elevated from COO to CEO in the wake of the Levys' departure.

Perhaps the granddaddy of all nonprofit compensation packages is the approximately $140 million granted in 2003 to the president of the New York Stock Exchange (NYSE), Richard Grasso, a sum equal to 40 percent of the entire net income of the NYSE during his tenure.[11] In announcing the executive compensation plans of the exchange for the first time in its two-hundred-year history in 2003, its board apparently believed that Grasso had built up enough goodwill restoring the exchange in the wake of 9/11 to be insulated from any controversy. The board was wrong. The prevailing view, reflected in dozens of editorials and countless discussions on cable television, was that Grasso and his compliant board members at the exchange operated in an atmosphere of immorality and self-dealing. In truth, the public flap probably had more to do with unease, in the wake of the Enron and WorldCom scandals, with how American business leaders compensated themselves for activities of dubious economic value. Grasso was a convenient target because he insisted on pay parity with Wall Street chieftains, even though the exchange was not itself a moneymaking enterprise.

The complex status of the exchange suggests a problem with labeling in the nonprofit world. Organized as a nonprofit under New York law and serving an important public purpose, the regulation of the financial markets, the stock exchange is at heart a tool to enable profit from the trade in stocks and bonds—a purpose fundamentally unaltered from when it was founded by twenty-four brokers under a buttonwood tree on Wall Street in 1792. The fight over Grasso's compensation package was unusually bitter. After Grasso resigned under pressure, Eliot Spitzer, then the New York attorney general, sued both Grasso and Kenneth Langone, one of the founders of Home Depot and the chairman of the NYSE's compensation committee, for return of the payments. The defense, for its part, took a red-faced, take-no-prisoners approach to the litigation, most colorfully expressed by Langone: "They got the wrong f—— guy. I'm nuts, I'm rich, and, boy, do I love a fight. I'm going to make them s—— in their pants . . . If Grasso gives back a f—— nickel, I'll never talk to him again." Grasso never gave back a f—— nickel. In 2006, the stock exchange acquired a company called Archipelago Holdings and re-formed itself as a for-profit company, which, according to the courts, made the issues of nonprofit compensation moot. In the end, the court's decision turned on rather narrow procedural grounds, and if the Grasso case stands for anything, it stands for the proposition that some organizations have no business being nonprofits in the first place.

While some of the more extreme compensation packages arise when institutions act, think, and operate like for-profit concerns, others flourish in nonprofits that lack adequate institutional controls. In 1985, Gary Bielfeldt, an enormously successful commodities trader, founded the Bielfeldt Foundation to support his hometown of Peoria, Illinois, and endowed it with a $30 million gift. He appointed five trustees: himself, his wife, and his three children. One of his daughters became the foundation's executive director. For a number of years, the foundation made significant gifts to Peoria institutions: Bradley University, the city zoo, a local museum, and other city projects. But in the late 1980s, Bielfeldt's trading business took a substantial down-turn, and for the first time he began to charge the foundation for handling its investment portfolio. From 1990 to 2002, Gary, his wife, and later his son, David, charged the foundation over $21 million in trading commissions and directors' fees.[12] The fees were not for a job well done. Bielfeldt invested the foundation's money in highly vola-tile commodities futures—his alleged forte—and lost about $36 million. From a peak of over $48 million in 1998, the endowment collapsed to just $12 million within four years. The combination of rich compensation to the Bielfeldts, amounting to more than twice the foundation's distributions, and rapid diminishment of the foun-dation's assets spurred the Illinois attorney general, Lisa Madigan, in 2004 to take the unusual step of suing the Bielfeldts. The state asked for $35 million, a number calculated to recoup salary, commissions, and net trading losses. The case from the beginning faced substantial legal hurdles, in particular the broad latitude given charities to define reasonable and fair compensation, and ultimately Madigan settled it for pennies on the dollar: a requirement that the Bielfeldts repay just $250,000 a year for eight years. Nonetheless, this is one of the very few even partially successful charity compensation cases ever brought.

Megachurches have experienced similar compensation scandals due to the same lack of institutional controls, often aggravated by cults of personality that surround some church leaders. While most churches are 501(c)(3) charitable organizations, they are generally exempt from most charitable reporting requirements. In the absence of public accounting, most reports of abuse have come through the efforts of the press, whose attention is drawn by obvious trappings of wealth. Bishop Eddie Long, it has been reported, favors Rolex watches, Gucci sunglasses, and designer clothes.[13] He and his bodyguards cut a wide swath in Lithonia, Georgia, where he is the pastor of New Birth Missionary Baptist Church, the largest congregation in Geor-gia. The church is in fact only the centerpiece of Bishop Eddie Long Ministries Inc.; over the last twenty years, he has established within the ambit of the church some twenty for-profit and not-for-profit companies, including a music company, a transportation service, and Samson's Health and Fitness Center, where Long hones his physique and counsels the young. Much of Long's earnings are sheltered from public disclosure, but it is clear that his compensation is large and varied. One of the charities associated with the church (though not the church itself) has provided him with a compensation package equal to $1 million a year—roughly the same amount that the charity distributes annually. The package includes a six-figure salary, a six-bedroom, nine-bathroom mansion in Lithonia, and the exclusive use of a $350,000 Bentley. While Long draws no formal salary from the church itself, he has been known to accept an annual "love offering"; in 2010, there was $1 million worth of love.[14]

Long has been vocal, if somewhat impolitic, about his seemingly extravagant compensation, telling *The Atlanta Journal-Constitution,* "I pastor a multimillion-dollar congregation. You've got to put me on a different scale than the little black preacher sitting over there that's supposed to be just getting by because the people are suffering."[15] Bishop Long may have regretted his words—he retained a prominent public relations firm shortly after this interview—but there is an underlying truth to his claim. When he took over New Birth, it was a struggling local church with no more than three hundred members. Today, it has over twenty-five thousand members, $20 million in revenues, and a political writ that runs throughout the South. It is no doubt appropriate to question the extravagance of Long's compensation—the cars, the mansions, the payments from multiple interrelated sources—but it is also fair to put it in the context of an entrepreneur who built a successful organization from the ground up.

If the IRS ever decided to pursue Long for excess compensation, he would be able to point to other churches paying their leaders similarly. The World Healing Center Church in Grapevine, Texas, like New Birth, has become a diversified enterprise, with services held around the world, television shows, and an online school of ministry. Oddly for a Texas church, it holds numerous events in Irvine, California, some fourteen hundred miles due west. The location seems to have less to do with the abundance of unsaved souls in Southern California than a convenience for its pastor, Benny Hinn. Despite his south Texas roots, Hinn lives in Irvine, in a parsonage built by the church. No quaint English parsonage either, but rather a $10 million mansion perched on a bluff above the Pacific Ocean. He also flies in a private jet to overseas appointments, and he is by no means the only jet-setting pastor. The wonderfully named Creflo Dollar, the senior pastor at World Changers Church International, drives a Rolls-Royce, lives in a gated, sprawling Atlanta mansion, owns a multimillion-dollar Manhattan apartment, and flies a Gulfstream III, a $37 million jet off the showroom floor.[16]

Church-related organizations are also susceptible to a particular form of brotherhood, the practice of putting entire families on the organizational payroll. The Trinity Broadcasting Network, which describes itself as the world's largest faith network, employs four members of the Crouch family in senior positions with salaries collectively topping $1 million each year. While all these churches' practices have from time to time drawn the unwelcome scrutiny of Congress and the popular press, all to no effect, they by and large retain the support of their congregants, who see the high salaries as fit rewards for building successful enterprises.[17]

Charities are required by federal law to disclose top executive compensation, and some have developed strategies to conceal its full extent by allocating CEO compensation through several separate but affiliated organizations, thus making each appear relatively thrifty. Safe Kids Worldwide's CEO made more than $2 million in 2008, but that can be calculated only by adding up payments coming from multiple related sources such as its domestic affiliate, Safe Kids USA. The Arby's Foundation and the Children's Hospital and Health System Foundation of Wisconsin operate in much the same way, funneling more than $1 million annually to their CEOs through a series of related enterprises.

In a similar vein, for-profit enterprises sometimes reward their executives with high-paying, low-work jobs at an affiliated charity. The Los Angeles Dodgers, for instance, maintain a sister foundation called the Dodgers Dream Foundation. Unlike some corporate foundations that are solely funded from the parent corporation's assets, the Dream Foundation raises money from the public through direct solicitations and a variety of charitable events including an annual silent auction, a charity golf tournament, and a bowling extravaganza, all headlined by various Dodgers players. The foundation is relatively small, with only about $1.6 million in expenditures per year, a full 25 percent of which—some $400,000—went (until the Dodgers' 2012 sale) to cover the salary of its full-time executive director, Howard Sunkin. By itself, Sunkin's salary is extraordinary, given the limited resources of the foundation, but the story does not end there: in addition to the foundation duties that the Dodgers characterized as full-time, Sunkin simultaneously served as the Dodgers' senior vice president of public affairs. His responsibilities included being a key adviser to the Dodgers' owner, Frank McCourt, and the team's lead liaison to the business and political communities.[18] It is difficult to avoid the conclusion that McCourt found the foundation to be a convenient and tax-advantaged tool for funneling money—other people's money—to a key confidant. McCourt, before he was forced by bankruptcy and Major League Baseball to relinquish ownership of the team, engineered other dubious financial practices for the Dodgers, including keeping both of his sons on the corporate payroll for a collective sum of $600,000 per year, even though they were both full-time students, and spending more than $100,000 on a Boston-based faith healer to provide positive energy to the Dodgers—an investment that has had little evident return as the Dodgers have struggled on the field and McCourt suffered both the loss of his team and a nasty public divorce from his wife.

The practice of turning charities into family affairs is a familiar strategy that creates opportunities to conceal all sorts of unsavory practices. In 1979, Larry Jones founded Feed the Children, a Christian relief organization providing food and medicine to impoverished countries and disaster areas. Jones quickly demonstrated an extraordinary ability to tell the story of Feed the Children and the people it served. Fueled by moving television commercials, Feed the Children became a fund-raising powerhouse, with revenues eventually approaching $1 billion a year. While Jones was very good at raising money for Feed the Children, he wasn't that good at feeding the children. The majority of funds were siphoned off by various service providers, especially marketers, long before the money ever went to actual food delivery; in some years, a full 80 percent of revenues went to pay for the cost of advertisements and fund-raising spots—making television stations, ad creators, and advertising buyers the principal beneficiaries of the charity. Despite these warning signs, Feed the Children was able to maintain for much of this period a four-star rating from Charity Navigator and a Charity Seal from the Better Business Bureau's Wise Giving Alliance.

The Jones family was also a big winner, at least for a time. Three Jones family members held senior executive positions, each drawing a high level of compensation—a lawful if somewhat dubious practice. But in 2009, a power struggle broke out between Jones and an internal faction led by his daughter, revealing some very dirty laundry. Each side lobbed charges at the other: Jones publicly claimed that his daughter had purchased a house in Los Angeles on a Feed the Children account; she in turn claimed that Jones had taken hundreds of thousands of dollars in kickbacks from Affiliated Media, the company that placed hundreds of millions of dollars' worth of Feed the Children television spots. Jones did not dispute the claim, describing the payments as "sales commissions." The conflict peaked when it was discovered that Jones was bugging the offices of his daughter and some of her allies; Jones and his wife were forced out by the board of directors. With uproar in the executive suite and a raft of questions surrounding whether funds were misappropriated, Feed the Children was taken into state receivership, and a welter of civil suits and criminal investigations predictably followed. In April 2012, some two years after the scandal first broke, the organization was finally able to hire a new CEO, this time at the comparatively modest salary of $340,000 per year.[19]

Fewer than ten of the roughly two million nonprofits in this country are penalized each year for excessive compensation. This is often chalked up to thin staffing at the IRS, a real problem described elsewhere in this book, but that alone cannot explain the inactivity. While some of the problem is hidden, much of it sits in broad daylight; an afternoon's worth of online research at the database provider GuideStar, on Charity Navigator, and in newspaper archives will easily produce a hundred charitable executive compensation plans that are either well out of proportion to the services and resources of the charity or so large in absolute terms that they defy social expectations of appropriate pay. The problem lies at least in part with the IRS definition of excessive compensation, which permits almost any compensation package as long as it can plausibly be supported by comparable salaries in either the nonprofit or the for-profit marketplace. A CEO in one case justified his compensation package by comparing himself to Oprah Winfrey and Britney Spears.[20] With more and more pay packages escalating into or near the millions, benchmarks for salaries have moved upward. Excessive compensation begets excessive compensation, and IRS enforcement becomes even more difficult.

Take, for example, the Chicago Dwellings Association (CDA), a sixty-year-old nonprofit that manages just four modest-sized buildings for low- and moderate-income families. The total annual revenue of the CDA is only about $7 million, yet it pays its president, Christine Oliver, about $700,000 per year. The compensation has all the indicia of excessiveness: the allocation of a substantial portion of revenues (10 percent in this case) to the CEO; compensation that is more than three times the average for other local Chicago housing and care charities; the provision of additional and unusual benefits such as home loans for Oliver (in this case $500,000 to purchase one of her three homes); portions of compensation funneled through secondary organizations (in this case its building management firm, Community Management Association); and rapidly escalating compensation (Oliver's salary more than doubled in just five years). The compensation arrangement was approved by the CDA's tiny board, which comprised Oliver and two local religious leaders who themselves had created a separate company that was awarded contracts worth more than $200,000 from the CDA.

It is hard to think of a more textbook case of excess compensation. Yet the IRS reviewed Oliver's compensation as part of a three-year audit of the CDA and found no actionable misdeeds.[21] It is hard to know precisely why the IRS did not pursue the case, but it almost certainly had to do with the wide discretion afforded charities in structuring compensation for their employees, even when it involves self-dealing. The regular reporting of eye-popping salaries at charities combined with the virtual absence of effective regulation has generated substantial public mistrust of the charitable sector, a significant problem in any business but one magnified for a sector that relies so heavily on public trust and support.

Over the last decade, stories of charitable excess have turned up in newspapers, and now do so on blogs and Web sites with regularity. The reports are typically filled with outrage and with threats, from donors and government officials alike, to cut off or restrict future funding. These stories, like the ones in this chapter so far, have fueled a widespread perception that compensation and salaries at charities nationwide are excessive and cushy. Almost twenty years after the fact, newspapers still cite the salary scandal that forced William Aramony to resign as head of United Way, not recalling that Aramony's salary of $390,000, even after adjustments for inflation, is fairly routine by the standards of today's top-tier charities. In fact, even taking into account both inflation and other noncash benefits received by Aramony in 1992, his compensation in current dollars is still 25 percent less than the compensation received by Brian Gallagher, the current head of United Way Worldwide, who made $983,000 in 2008.[22] There is an increasing mismatch between top-end salaries in the charitable community and public support for these compensation practices. The public tends to believe that charities should be modest and maybe even a bit puritanical in how they spend contributed dollars. Increasingly, nonprofits and the public talk past each other during the frequent disputes on the subject, with nonprofits pointing to how their pay practices fit in with other nonprofits' and the public not being persuaded that such parity is meaningful in the slightest.

Oddly, despite the damaging perception that many charity CEOs are overpaid, to the point of looting their own organizations, it is in fact not at all the norm. In a 2008 Charity Navigator survey of three thousand leading charities—the most current available survey—the median CEO compensation was a little under $150,000. There are significant regional differences in these numbers: charities in the Northeast pay $185,000 on average, almost twice as much as those in the Mountain West at $108,000. Compensation differs dramatically by the size of the charity as well. The median salary for large charities (those with more than $13.5 million in revenues) was $280,000; for midsized charities (those with revenues between $3.5 and $13.5 million) it was $157,000; and for small charities it was $95,000. At the top of the compensation pyramid are a handful of CEOs for the largest charities, those with revenues in excess of $500 million. Charity Navigator found thirty-eight of those charities, with a median salary of almost $700,000.[23]

The relationship of nonprofit pay to for-profit pay is uneven. At the top end, compensation for charitable executives is certainly less than private sector CEO jobs in organizations of comparable complexity and scope. At the lower end, experts like Quatt will tell you that non-profit CEOs' compensation still tends to lag behind their for-profit counterparts,[24] but the rapid inflation in charitable pay has seemingly closed much of the gap. Recent IRS surveys show that the typical small-business owner makes $100,000 on revenues of $1.5 million, numbers very close to the charitable averages.[25]

But even perfect parity would not address the critical underlying issue. The overwhelming problem with the nonprofit compensation debate is that it is largely unhinged from any real understanding of the purposes of pay and from any sound analytical tools to evaluate its appropriateness. On one side of the debate sits the mass of public opinion that generally feels charitable pay should be low, out of some notion that each dollar in compensation is taking donated money away from services; on the other side are charitable executives and their boards who seek shelter behind the playground reasoning that they are doing the same thing as everyone else. But pay in fact has a purpose, to retain and attract talent and to create effective incentives and rewards for performance. It, along with other measures to train and improve employees, is among the most important investments that a charity can make. We should not begrudge high charitable compensation when it is tied to meeting specific, measurable, and important goals. The debate over compensation tends to treat all charitable executives equally, whether they are successful CEOs or not. But few begrudged Steve Jobs his extraordinary compensation for inventing Apple or Alan Mulally for turning around Ford, and no one should begrudge generous compensation packages for their non-profit equivalents. If the investment in leadership pays off in reduced hunger or homelessness, or better education for our children, it is a wise investment.

One of the unfortunate elements of the pay scandal involving the Levy brothers at the Young Adult Institute is that it obscured their real achievements in serving developmentally disabled children. The

Levy brothers and the Young Adult Institute were pioneers in offering an alternative to warehousing children in large-scale, locked facilities. We now know how their story ended, but it is equally important to understand the beginning of their story, in the aftermath of a terrible scandal at the Willowbrook State School on Staten Island. New York State ran Willowbrook as a warehouse for the developmentally disabled; six thousand children lived in deplorable and fetid conditions, forced into overcrowded, inadequate, and unsanitary facilities and subject to sexual and physical abuse from school staff. Senator Robert Kennedy, after touring the facility in 1965, reported that children were living "in filth and dirt, their clothing in rags, in rooms less comfortable and cheerful than the cages in which we put animals in a zoo," but it was not until 1972, after vivid reporting by a young WABC reporter named Geraldo Rivera, that the matter received national attention. In the wake of the Willowbrook revelations, the Levy brothers, newly in charge of the YAI, opened a series of small group homes that provided individualized treatment and services to their young, vulnerable clients. For the first time, developmentally disabled children in the care of New York State were offered first-rate medical and dental services and ultimately access to schools, job-training programs, medical clinics, and other never-before-provided services. The Levy brothers professionalized the Young Adult Institute, expanding it into an organization with revenues of $170 million a year that provided the broadest set of services and operated the most homes in New York state. In many ways, modern social services for the developmentally disabled in New York were invented by the Levys.

The Levys' success does not exempt them from a debate over fair compensation, a fact that appears to have been lost on them over the years of rapidly escalating pay and benefits. But it makes little sense to treat their case as similar to that, for example, of St. Vincent's Hospital, where executives were paid millions of dollars over its last years to run the hospital into the ground. St. Vincent's was a Greenwich Village icon, 150 years in the making. It was on the front lines of daily health care for lower Manhattan and in the thick of some of the greatest health-care emergencies in New York history, from the cholera epidemic of 1849 to the sinking of the *Titanic* in 1912 to the 9/11 terrorist attacks in 2001. Its rapid decline to extinction in the twenty-first century reflected, in part, the gentrification of Greenwich Village, whose residents no longer wanted or needed a hospital focused on the poor and the underserved. But it also reflected more than a decade of mismanagement, bordering on fraud,[26] which generated almost a billion dollars in debt, through a combination of poor strategy, incoherent control over financial systems, tens of millions of dollars lost to consulting fees, and runaway compensation practices that included millions of dollars each year for both active and departed senior executives.[27] St. Vincent's was a textbook case of mismanagement, while the Young Adult Institute was generally regarded as a highly successful, innovative organization. Yet the public, and regulators in the state of New York, reacted to the compensation practices in both instances in much the same way, despite evidence of entirely different levels of management effectiveness.

Our focus on charitable compensation should be not on the salary itself but on what the organization is buying with its pay. We should be outraged about compensation when it is not tied to making charities more effective, and by and large charitable compensation today, large or small, is not tethered to any real measures of effectiveness. The average modern charity CEO contract now has some tiny component of it tied to success measurements, a very modest 6.25 percent of compensation on average according to a 2008 Quatt survey.[28] These incentives tend to be small, tied to highly subjective evaluations or latched to quantitative measures unrelated to actual effectiveness—if for no other reason than, as we have seen, few charities care to measure their actual impact. The challenge for charitable compensation is learning to evaluate what charities are really getting in return for their investments in leadership. The public's concern about compensation is justified but misdirected. The outrage is not that charities pay high compensation, but that they pay high compensation without insisting on results in return.

SEVEN

Dawn of the New Charity

THE PICTURE I'VE drawn of the charitable world may be bleak, but it is not without light. Even in a haphazard system that dampens excellence, there exist extraordinary organizations. What makes these charities worthy of note is not necessarily the lightning bolt of inspiration but the rigor taken in building the organization and the care in assessing the impact of its services. The people behind these charities are not merely storytellers—though they have stories to tell—but instead leaders whose highest goal is to understand the true extent of their impact. Their organizations are blazing a trail for the charitable sector to follow.

Pat Lawler is one such leader. At age fifty-five, Lawler still has boyish charm. Carefully groomed, casually but neatly dressed, he has the easy manner of a man at home in the boardroom and the country club. His large office has a generic feel, straight from the nonprofit CEO handbook: framed awards for the organization, a handful of pictures from company events, a handwritten note from the chairman of the board tossed across his desk. Then Lawler, searching for some fact or figure, opens up the whiteboard next to his conference table, and there is what sets his organization apart: ten lavishly produced monthly charts that track the key measures of his organization, carefully Scotch-taped to the board. These charts show, both in the results they reveal and in the simple fact of their existence, why Youth Villages, Lawler's organization, is one of the most dynamic and successful charities in America.

Youth Villages is a model for the charitable sector because it has developed tactics that echo successful for-profit businesses but are tailored to its charitable values. It has grown from modest roots by developing innovative service strategies, rigorously testing them, and amending them as the data dictate and customer needs require and by outworking and out-innovating everyone else in the field. From a single failing site in Memphis, Tennessee, it has become a twelve-state giant with revenues well in excess of $150 million a year. Youth Villages' growth strategy has been successful because it has been able to demonstrate in concrete ways to funders, mostly government funders, that it can provide better and more cost-effective results for at-risk children than any of its competitors. It has obtained business well beyond its home marketplace both by winning competitive contracts from states and municipalities and by acquiring and radically improving smaller charities struggling in a difficult field of service.

While Youth Villages and Lawler are now at the pinnacle of their field, their story did not have such an auspicious start. The roots of Youth Villages extend back to 1969, with the launch in Memphis of a "Boys Town" home for troubled youth named Dogwood Village. From virtually its first day, Dogwood Village was doomed: badly underfunded, inadequately staffed, poorly conceived, and riven by internal dissent. The first executive director quit in despair after six months. His successor was fired six months later, and most of the board of directors disappeared with one or the other departed executive. Its brand-new facility, proudly unveiled just the year before, was already "beat to hell" by its energetic residents, and some of its guts, like its sewage treatment processes, were failing in the most unpleasant manner. The State of Tennessee, smelling disaster, was threatening to pull funding. The entire project was a failure, and what little was left of its leadership determined to shut it down. For this task, they settled on Lawler, simply because he was available and willing to close out operations. At twenty-four years of age and with only a few years of experience in the juvenile justice system and none in management, Lawler was a dubious choice to shut down the facility in an orderly fashion, let alone run the place, but it is likely no one qualified would have touched a project as jinxed as Dogwood Village.

This wouldn't be much of a story if Lawler had been the obedient type. Instead of shutting down operations, he threw all his youthful energy into revitalizing Dogwood Village. He revamped program operations, cut the budget, even mowed the grass, and jumped in front of any audience that might contain potential donors. He began to rebuild the board, starting with the only person he knew who had any money, a classmate from high school who was a local insurance agent. And he did what any small-business man in trouble would do: he held off creditors, begged the banks for small-dollar loans to make payroll, and played whatever games it took to keep the organization afloat. His biggest game was with the State of Tennessee, which habitually overpaid the day rate for youth residents, and Lawler grew expert at staving off repayment demands. Slowly and painfully, over a period of years, Lawler stabilized Dogwood Village, dragging it back from the edge of collapse.

While it survived, Dogwood Village was still a precarious operation, frequently needing bridge loans to make payroll, and always one lost state contract away from disaster. Plus, as a relatively new state vendor, Dogwood Village was continually subject to "last in" elimination from the state rolls. Lawler hit on an ingenious, if gut-churning, approach to this problem. In order to make Dogwood Village more indispensable, he aggressively sought and took on the hardest cases, the forty or so youthful "worst of the worst" offenders whom no other similar institution wanted to take. It turned out to be a brilliant move; every time officials would contemplate reducing or eliminating funding for Dogwood Village, they were faced with the unpalatable problem of figuring out what to do with these cases, something no state politician or government bureaucrat wanted to deal with. Through this kind of resourcefulness, Lawler immunized Dogwood Village from significant cutbacks and restored a kind of threadbare stability to the organization. In 1986, Dogwood Village merged with Memphis Boys Town, another struggling youth services organization, and became Youth Villages with Lawler as executive director.

By the late 1980s, Youth Villages had made slow and steady progress—and had even completed a successful $1.6 million capital campaign to refurbish key facilities—but there was little to suggest the growth to come. Then two interesting things happened. In the late 1980s, Lawler and his colleagues began for the very first time to try to find out what happened to their clientele once they left the Youth Villages campus. For fifteen years, Lawler, like most charity CEOs, had traded on stories—in his case, the image of the fully reformed youth confidently striding out the door of a Youth Villages facility, never to return. Lawler had perfected his pitch over the years. But in truth, Youth Villages had no idea of the long-term effectiveness of its service. Of course, it had anecdotal evidence: kids who were sent back to Youth Villages repeatedly; stories of others who had ended up in jail or, worse yet, had committed suicide; and some cherished success stories. But hundreds of kids each year were going through its programs, and the Youth Villages team had no real data on how many "graduates" were able to live at home, stay in school, and stay out of the courts. Lawler decided to find out. Youth Villages began to track its graduates, first somewhat idiosyncratically and then with increasing precision and purpose. What it found was deeply unsettling: well over half of all Youth Villages graduates, no matter how successful they appeared on the surface, snapped back, often within days, to prior self-destructive or socially destructive patterns. It was a huge blow, especially after twenty years of work.

There are lots of ways to respond to findings like this, starting with rationalizing and sweeping them under the rug. After all, no one else was looking. Neither the State of Tennessee nor other funders were demanding or even aware of this research. But Lawler took a different route, reasoning that if his programs were not working, there had to be a better way. He commissioned a young Vanderbilt business school graduate, Lee Rone, to take a broad look at alternatives. Rone was no expert in the field; in fact, Lawler dubbed him "the blank slate" for his lack of knowledge, on the theory and hope that his research would be untainted by the prevailing notion of the day that isolating troubled youth from family and society created the best treatment and rehabilitation environment. Several months later, Rone came back, recommending that Youth Villages look at an approach called multisystemic therapy (MST) being developed out of the University of South Carolina Medical School. Like many breakthrough ideas, MST was at once radical by industry norms and glaringly obvious. Its underlying concept was that it was insufficient just to treat the youth. Effective rehabilitation required addressing the entire family ecosystem; if underlying family problems weren't resolved, youngsters would revert to prior patterns once out of an institutional setting. There was, however, at least one major obstacle for Lawler: while MST made perfect sense given the Youth Villages experience and it had tested well in highly controlled, clinical trials, the system had never been implemented in a real-life setting.

Lawler persuaded the South Carolina researchers that Youth Villages was a good candidate for implementing its in-home family therapy model. It was an enormous risk for Youth Villages, bucking the prevailing wisdom, but it paid off. As Youth Villages began to implement and tweak MST, success rates started to climb dramatically, jumping from about 50 percent to well over 80 percent in each of the organization's key metrics: kids living at home or independently, staying out of trouble with the law, and remaining in school. In addition, MST was far more cost-effective: the cost of in-home family treatment was much lower than the traditional "Boys Town" or "Girls Town" model of isolation in a locked-down 24/7 treatment facility. Lawler's experiment translated into real-life differences for hundreds of kids and families each year and millions of dollars of realizable savings for the public due to greater efficiency of service and the reduction of costly recidivism. In a rational marketplace, this radical success would have been replicated widely and rewarded with a slew of new projects and contracts. Youth Villages did grow somewhat, but even with all its remarkable and provable success, by the turn of the century it was still only a locally focused midsized charity.

The second twist occurred with a proverbial knock on the door. In 2003, Lawler fielded a call from the Edna McConnell Clark Foundation, asking to visit Youth Villages in Memphis. Lawler didn't know the Clark Foundation, but in the charitable world you don't turn away visits, however mysterious, from well-heeled New York foundations. Within weeks, a team from Clark had descended on Memphis and spent days in interviews and document review, surveying the whole operation. The Clark Foundation is well known, and relatively unique, in the charitable world for focusing its investments on just a handful of promising organizations, banking on building them to scale and sustainability before moving on to new issues and new charities. The Clark team must have liked what they saw because they came back with an offer: $1.5 million for Youth Villages, an unheard-of gift for Lawler in those days. But the gift came with an unusual catch. To earn the money, Youth Villages would have to engage in a strategic planning exercise led by a prominent nonprofit consulting firm called the Bridgespan Group. It was a small price to pay, and Lawler headed into the Bridgespan process with a great deal of enthusiasm for $1.5 million and much less for a strategic planning activity. But the deeper the Youth Villages team got into the Bridgespan process, the more they began to realize that the planning results could be far more important than the financial gift. Out of it came a plan to expand the organization beyond western Tennessee and make the investments and commitments to give Youth Villages regional and eventually national reach. It was an audacious concept, mostly because state and local governments that controlled relevant funding tended to be highly parochial and very habitual in awarding contracts. The plan would not be easily accomplished: it required building a business development and marketing team that could succeed in foreign territories, it meant figuring out how to acquire and integrate other charities to give Youth Villages a foothold in new markets, and it required new training and control systems to maintain service thousands of miles from the Memphis home base. In all of that, Youth Villages succeeded spectacularly, growing in short order from one state to twelve states and the District of Columbia, more than tripling revenues to about $160 million a year, and increasing its service field from twelve hundred at-risk youths to over fifty-six hundred in 2010.

Today, Lawler and Youth Villages have come a long way from the very modest roots of Dogwood Village. Youth Villages operates mostly in the Southeast but with outposts in New Hampshire and Oregon as well. It has entered new markets in innovative ways. In Georgia and Oregon, it has merged with—in truth acquired—local operations, and in other states it won new contracts, often following its proven strategy of taking on the hardest cases as a means to get a foothold in places typically predisposed to award contracts to local social service organizations over strangers from Memphis. Youth Villages offers a wide range of services for youth at risk—intensive in-home treatment, residential treatment, foster care, adoption, transitional living, specialized crisis services, emergency shelters, and mentoring. The programs are enormously successful, even in the toughest cases. Over 80 percent of Youth Villages clients present with multiple, often deeply entrenched problems. More than 90 percent show behavioral problems; 70 percent have emotional disorders; more than half have legal problems; and about a third report sexual abuse, substance abuse, or suicidal ideation. Yet more than 80 percent of Youth Villages clients are successfully integrated at home six months after treatment, and in highly unusual fashion the success rates actually rise slightly twelve months and twenty-four months out. Similarly, 82 percent of the youth are free from legal problems at six months, and those numbers remain constant both at twelve months and at twenty-four months. School attendance is high, starting at 92 percent at six months and declining slightly to 85 percent after two years. These figures compare favorably, remarkably so, with national norms that tend to hover around 50 percent, to the extent that reliable data are even available.

Like that of many successful businesses, Youth Villages' success is the result not of a "bolt from the blue" idea but of careful investments, sound and constant business strategies, and taking advantage of the innovations of others. Over the past two decades, Youth Villages has made internal investments that few other charities have dared to make. Lawler has built a seventeen-person research department that tracks and analyzes every child who comes through a Youth Villages program. The research department, by itself larger than the staffs of most charities that offer youth services, provides instant analysis of programs—and staff—that work and those that do not and permits continuous innovation and improvement. Youth Villages invests heavily in staff training, providing on average more than two hundred hours per staff member each year. It runs its own Youth Villages online university and fields a leadership development team. This obsession with training is central to Youth Villages' growth. With twenty-two hundred employees spread out over a dozen states and close to a hundred separate programs, ensuring quality control and uniform service is both difficult and critical to success. Staff training for Youth Villages means more than taking classes; it includes layers of case supervision, auditing the work of staff counselors and clinicians, and offering sufficient development opportunities in order to retain staff—which it does with remarkable success. Even granting that the Memphis market presents relatively few comparable organizations that might compete for talent, it is still impossible not to be impressed by the parade of staff who have come to work at Youth Villages and now find it inconceivable to contemplate working anywhere else.

These investments in non-service, overhead activities like research, training, and technology, and especially its commitment to data-driven results have allowed Youth Villages to distinguish itself so dramatically from the field. There are literally thousands of people (and their families, friends, and employers) who would have had less successful lives but for the good fortune of ending up with Youth Villages. And it is not an exaggeration to say that this is largely because Youth Villages has been willing to act against prevailing sentiment and make necessary internal investments.

But being the best has its frustrations. During an argument in the movie *Broadcast News,* an angry and sarcastic Paul Moore, played by the actor Peter Hackes, says to Jane Craig, played by Holly Hunter, "It must be nice to always believe you know better, to always think you're the smartest person in the room," and she quite seriously replies, "No, it's awful." There is a similar dynamic for the team at Youth Villages, who still all too frequently lose contracts to other charities that have nowhere near its track record or capabilities. State and local governments, the funders for virtually everything that occurs in the youth services field, often favor local incumbents with whom they have settled relationships; they often prefer to spread funding over multiple organizations to reflect their evenhandedness, and they often do so subject to bidding processes that value inputs rather than outcomes—that is, they evaluate proposals on programmatic criteria such as types of services and annual costs rather than the program's proven effectiveness in reducing problems with youth. Governments buy treatment services; they do not buy the reduction of violence or drug abuse or an increase in school attendance, even though that is what we all want. Ironically and maddeningly, the cost effectiveness of Youth Villages' in-home treatment program actually works against it. While contracts are awarded by the states, much of the costs of juvenile treatment programs are reimbursed by the federal government through two separate programs: Medicaid and Social Security Title 4(e). Those programs spend something on the order of $25 billion a year, the lion's share of the cost of youth rehabilitation programs, and these funds can *only* go toward custodial care. States will thus almost inevitably favor residential programs, even though they are far more costly overall, because they are less costly to them. This is a classic "wrong pockets" problem. The Youth Villages programs would save vast amounts of money but not for the state offices awarding the contract that could otherwise off-load expenses to the federal government. It is only in the upside-down world of government contracting, and charitable services, that finding a highly cost-effective solution to a large societal problem can actually work against you.[1] Being the smartest person in the room does not always work in Youth Villages' favor.

Innovative, results-driven, flexible, and strategic, Youth Villages is literally a textbook case, studied at Harvard Business School. Its success is a testament to the possibility of reinvention and the benefits of investment in strategy, research, and infrastructure, and a vote for dramatic expansion despite all the hobbles of the charitable system. And fortunately, it is not the only high-performing charity that has embraced evidence-based research. Many charities start with a need, a desire to help, an urge to make and to build—but not necessarily a proven ability to help. Recall the charities thrown up to help the victims of Katrina; all were driven by a generous impulse to help, and most were functionally out of business within a year. The best charities are built over time and are able to go the distance only with painstaking planning and self-scrutiny—as in the case of the Nurse-Family Partnership (NFP).

The NFP is a story of patience and careful research—meticulous, maddeningly careful research. It begins with David Olds, now a professor of pediatrics, psychology, and preventive medicine at the University of Colorado at Denver. As a young graduate fresh from Johns Hopkins University, Olds landed his first job at the Union Square Day Care Center, three cramped rooms in a West Baltimore church basement. Olds had originally studied international relations but in the context of the domestic upheavals of the late 1960s and early 1970s found the topic too distant from the problems of poverty and inequity at home. He shifted his focus, ending up working closely with an "attachment researcher" at Hopkins named Mary Ainsworth, a now legendary developmental psychologist who was just then proving the link between normal social and emotional development for children and a close bonded relationship with at least one caregiver. For Olds, that first job in an economically depressed, crime-ridden stretch along West Lombard Street was a natural opportunity to take classroom work into real-life, real-need situations.

In that basement full of three- and four-year-olds, Olds witnessed deep developmental and family problems, problems that he, in a role he subsequently described as glorified babysitting, could do little to solve. Many of the children at Union Square were abused and neglected, products of broken and sometimes drug-addled households. Some of the children exhibited deep developmental problems, including one four-year-old boy who had been abused and abandoned and couldn't even communicate. Olds tried to invite parents into the day-care environment, holding group conversation sessions during nap time, but the only parents who showed up were the parents of the most well-adjusted children. From these experiences, Olds gradually began to realize that only much earlier intervention in the children's lives could prevent these substantial developmental problems. He eventually left Baltimore to pursue a Ph.D. in developmental psychology at Cornell, and it was there that he began to outline a nurse home visitation program for pregnant first-time mothers, with the hope that such a program would lead to more aware and engaged mothers, better prenatal care, and healthier births. The ultimate goals would be to not only improve child development through effective maternal counseling but also help mothers improve their own lives by developing a vision for their future—with the intended results a reduction in unwanted pregnancies, an increase in school attendance for the moms, and an increase in job success. Olds's concept pushed the boundaries of human ecology—the science of family, friends, and support networks—extending social services into the lives and homes of first-time mothers in new and radical ways. Olds chose nurses to administer the program's services in the belief that first-time mothers would be more likely to listen to nurses and that there would be less stigma attached to working with a credentialed medical professional.

In 1975, Olds submitted a proposal to the U.S. Department of Health, Education, and Welfare (HEW), the forerunner of the current Department of Health and Human Services. Rather extraordinarily for a grant submitted by an untested, newly minted Ph.D., HEW offered to fully fund a five-year, $1.5 million test project. Equally extraordinarily, upon hearing the news of the unprecedented grant, Olds, with a caution that has proven to be his hallmark, reconsidered the project. He concluded that he was not ready to run such an extensive study and that he was unsure that his concept was sufficiently developed to warrant fieldwork. Much to the surprise of HEW and his colleagues, Olds turned the grant down. He later submitted a smaller test proposal to the U.S. Public Health Service, which funded a project that ultimately became the first five-year study of the Nurse-Family Partnership (NFP) in Elmira, New York. Elmira, a small town on the Pennsylvania border, had peaked as a manufacturing center of fifty thousand people in the 1950s. By the late 1970s, the town was in full retreat: much of the manufacturing had fled, population had dipped to thirty thousand, and the poverty of the town was reflected in a distressingly high incidence of premature birth, infant mortality, and child abuse. In short, it was the perfect test case for Olds's model.

The Elmira study was a controlled, random assignment study of four hundred first-time mothers, with half assigned to the NFP and half to a control group that would receive transportation to prenatal and child-care services but no nurse visitations. Women in the study group received weekly home visits in the first trimester. After an initial trust-building period, visits were dialed back to once every two weeks and then to varying frequencies through the baby's second birthday. The nurses provided a wide range of counseling, all from a detailed and prescribed NFP playbook. Elements of the service included counseling at-risk mothers (and fathers, if possible) on prenatal care, on healthy eating and living practices, and on reducing the use of cigarettes, alcohol, and illegal drugs; teaching responsible and competent child care; and counseling families on long-term planning, avoiding future unwanted pregnancies, continuing schooling, and finding work. From the first years of the Elmira study, the results were highly encouraging: incidents of child abuse and neglect were dramatically lower for the nurse group, and preterm deliveries were substantially reduced. Eventually, Olds received funding to extend the test to track the groups for fifteen years. Over the entire fifteen years, the treatment group of children had fully half the incidents of child abuse and neglect and 59 percent fewer arrests and convictions. The women also benefited: 20 percent less time on welfare, 19 percent fewer subsequent births, 61 percent fewer arrests, and 72 percent fewer convictions.

For most people, more than a decade of work with such results would have seemed sufficient to justify a move toward national implementation. Not for Olds. While he found the results of Elmira encouraging, he wanted to make sure they were not only long-term but also replicable and operationally correct. In particular, Olds was not confident that the results from a largely white rural area like Elmira would be transferable to big cities or more diverse populations. This was frustrating to some of his colleagues who wanted to "get on with it" and move toward national implementation. Meanwhile, other home visitation programs, mostly using paraprofessionals trained for the program rather than nurses, began to sprout up around the country.

In the mid-1980s, Olds began to look for his next test site, finally settling on Memphis and recruiting over seven hundred mostly young, poor African American women for the study group. By 1991, the study was fully under way, and once again the results were highly positive; over the nine years of the study, the treatment children showed lower mortality rates and better educational performance; treatment mothers presented with less time on welfare and fewer subsequent births, and fewer reported problems with substance abuse. At the same time, Olds began to see "sobering" research results from other home visitation paraprofessional programs, results that tended to show only modest, statistically insignificant, short-term gains and little to no long-term gains—all reflective of the fact that seemingly superficial changes in concept and implementation could have dramatic negative impacts on program effectiveness.

Next, Olds wanted to test his concept with Hispanic populations. In 1995, now some twenty years after he had first proposed the concept, Olds launched a large-scale study in Denver with first-time Hispanic mothers. This time, the study subjects were randomly divided into three groups: a control group, the nurse-visited group, and a final group with home visits made by paraprofessionals—to test the validity of the type of lower-cost home visit program that had popped up in emulation of the NFP. Again, the data for the nurse visits, published in *Pediatrics* in 2002, were remarkably positive. By age four, the treatment children had made significant gains in language development, behavioral adaptation (impulse control, attention, and sociability), and executive function (capacity for sustained attention, fine and gross motor skills). Nurse-visited mothers were more likely to reenter the workforce and far more likely to avoid unwanted second pregnancies. The paraprofessional group did not materially differ from the control group.

Finally, after more than twenty years of study, Olds was ready to formally launch the Nurse-Family Partnership, first with pilot programs in Dayton, Ohio, and in several Wyoming communities. The Department of Justice eventually funded its expansion to seven more sites, and with this jump start NFP began to grow in a significant way. In 2003, Olds and colleagues launched the Nurse-Family Partnership National Service Office to clone the program through local agencies and to provide ongoing support in nurse education and practice, quality assurance, and marketing. Today, the NFP operates in thirty-two states and stands as a model for the development of an effective charity, built on evidence-based research and a deliberate and effective growth strategy.

There are many other home visit charities, with methodologies that seem at least superficially similar to NFP's. But many of those services have also been the subject of randomized controlled tests similar to NFP and have been found wanting. The Parents as Teachers program, which provides home visits by trained parent educators, has been the subject of three separate controlled tests and found to have no statistically significant effect on children and few statistically significant effects on parental knowledge, attitudes, and behaviors. Healthy Families America (HFA) is one of the better-known and better-funded home visit programs in the country, with program sites in virtually every state and forty-one in the state of Illinois alone. The HFA model involves home visits by trained paraprofessionals starting during pregnancy and extending until the child reaches age five. HFA describes itself as an evidence-based organization and prominently touts supporting research, but a careful review of independent studies shows a much more equivocal result. A very large (a test group of 1,250 women) study of Healthy Families New York found significant positive results in year one, but the vast majority of positive markers disappeared by years two and three. Similar studies were conducted with Healthy Families Alaska and with an enhanced version of the program at Healthy Families San Diego. In each case, the studies found only modest, sometimes ephemeral indicators of effectiveness.[2] All this reflects the fact that people and the human ecosystem are complex and desperately hard to affect in meaningful ways and that even trivial-sounding changes to the best programs may vitiate their positive potential.

Yet despite the radically different results reported for the Nurse-Family Partnership and other home visit organizations, it is very difficult for a potential funder to tell them apart. All provide similarly organized services for the same target population. All claim to be evidence-based organizations and tout supporting research of some hard-to-fathom lineage. Research, done poorly, can obscure as much as reveal. Some research projects test outcomes across dozens of factors, and random chance may drive a couple of positive results. Other studies can show positive short-term effects, with little or no positive long-term benefits. Other "pre-post" studies—like those for the

Chess-in-the-Schools program—lack randomly assigned control groups, which makes it difficult to attribute positive results to the tested program rather than to unrelated and untested factors.[3] Charities can cherry-pick research and tout less than compelling evidence to unsophisticated funders. Among home visit programs, mounting evidence challenges the claims of effectiveness of many, yet all soldier on, secure in the knowledge that the funding marketplace does not really differentiate between more effective and less effective organizations.

This problem extends to, and is especially troubling in, the federal government. In 2009, the Obama administration, which had shown some early enthusiasm for evidence-based policy and funding, forwarded to Congress as part of its 2010 budget blueprint a proposal for substantial funding for a "Nurse Home Visitation" project—$9 billion that would have brought the program to every low-income, first-time mother in the country. This reflected a commitment made by Obama on the campaign trail, when he had spoken out for the need to spread the NFP nationwide. While the budget plan did not make specific mention of the Nurse-Family Partnership, the context, including references to evidence-based models and requirements for financial return on investments, made clear that the funds were intended for the NFP. The proposal was a major statement on behalf of charitable effectiveness, but the gesture did not survive the political process. The focus on the NFP was met with concern by other home visitation organizations such as Healthy Families America and the Parent-Child Home Program, both of which felt slighted by the singling out of a rival charity and saw a funding opportunity not to be missed. These organizations had long ties to Capitol Hill through their membership in various well-connected Washington-based public policy groups. They launched a vigorous campaign to broaden the eligibility language and to water down the evidence requirements.[4] Within weeks, the language of the Obama budget proposal had been substantially diluted, describing home visit funding programs more generally; a last-minute compromise salvaged a requirement that the funds be allocated first to organizations able to demonstrate "significant positive effects." But with the final bill lacking the crisp original language describing how to measure positive effects, it portended future disputes over eligibility. Thus, an effort to reward and differentiate the most effective organization ended up compromised and likely to reflect the typical tendency of government to spread its largesse over multiple competing organizations. For all of its extraordinary success, the NFP remains difficult to distinguish and hard to fund to maximum scale. Even success stories can be cautionary tales in the charitable sector.

While Youth Villages and the Nurse-Family Partnership focus on domestic issues, the last two decades have also seen dramatic growth in U.S. charities dedicated to solving problems beyond our shores. Through these organizations and other transnational bodies, huge investments have been made in confronting global health challenges. But while research and development have yielded substantial insights into improving global health, major roadblocks to implementation exist on the ground due to poor delivery systems, weak infrastructure, and inadequate local training. This is known as the innovation pileup, and it is the largest single impediment to ameliorating many of the critical health issues in the world. As we saw with the water charities in chapter 1, many charities, because of institutional and funding limitations, are not well suited to take on such complex challenges, but a few organizations, like the medical supplies charity Village-Reach, have been unusually successful.

VillageReach's origins are found in the ashes of one of the greatest technology company meltdowns in history. In the early 1990s, Craig McCaw, a cellular technology magnate, launched Teledesic, a vast effort to bring mobile telephone service around the world. McCaw's proposal was cosmically ambitious: launch 840 refrigerator-sized, low-orbit satellites to blanket the globe, at a price tag of $9 billion. This communications network would, McCaw envisioned, leapfrog a missing generation of landline technology and bring mobile telephone and Internet service to billions of people lacking fixed-line access. Today, the idea seems interesting if infrastructure heavy, but twenty years ago, when Internet service was bound up in "you've got mail" dial-up access available to only a fraction of the public, the idea was almost Jetson-ian in sweep. McCaw's big idea attracted a rock star group of funders and partners, ranging from the Microsoft founders, Bill Gates and Paul Allen, to the Saudi prince Alwaleed Bin Talal, a man once described by *Time* magazine as the Saudi Warren Buffett. McCaw was able to attract a high-flying management team from around the world, including a young, hard-driving AT&T executive from Gambia named Blaise Judja-Sato, who became Teledesic's director of business development, focusing on Africa and the Middle East. Teledesic was a dream team, a favorite of the investment community, and, within a few years of its 1995 launch, a cautionary tale. Despite McCaw's sweeping ambition, it soon became clear that other, less costly alternatives would be substantially more efficient than filling space with a fleet of flying appliances. McCaw and his team quickly began to strip back their plans, first reducing their satellite array to thirty and ultimately in 2002 abandoning their first two partially constructed satellites in their Italian factory. In its final years, the Teledesic team was radically downsized, leaving each departing member to pursue more earthbound activities.

When Judja-Sato walked out the door of the Seattle offices of Teledesic, he kept on walking, all the way to Mozambique to help coordinate relief for victims of the February 2000 floods that devastated much of the country and demolished large swaths of its agricultural sector. Relief work in an underdeveloped country such as Mozambique is always hampered by inadequate roads, absent transportation systems, and failed infrastructure, and they were all made tragically worse when Cyclone Leon-Eline washed away much of the country. Judja-Sato struggled to get desperately needed medical supplies to remote communities, and on his return to Seattle he founded, along with another former Teledesic colleague, VillageReach, a charity dedicated to improving the distribution of medical supplies in sub-Saharan Africa.

At inception, there was much not to like about the chances of VillageReach's success. Its founders had little direct expertise in the field, its headquarters were some eight thousand miles removed from its target audience, it lacked a clear fund-raising profile, and it had little to recommend it in terms of long-term sustainability. But it did have a new model of distribution for medical supplies and a desire to test, evaluate, and improve it. At the core of the VillageReach plan was the idea of converting medical distribution from a "pull" system, in which each clinic was responsible for collecting and maintaining its own vaccine and drug supply, to a "push" system, in which a central depot run by VillageReach would store and deliver the medicines directly to the clinics.

This may sound like a minor advancement, but on the broken-down byways of rural Mozambique just-in-time delivery to clinics was potentially a breakthrough innovation. The "pull" system was plagued with numerous practical problems. The vast majority of clinics only had access to one car, which sometimes had to be diverted from critical tasks or was simply not available. Clinic vehicles were often out of commission due to lack of spare parts or access to car repair facilities or due to damage from lumbering across deeply rutted, sometimes flooded rural roads. With a limited labor force, clinics usually had to close while staff made the journey to the central depot, which was less than desirable during times of crisis and disease outbreak. And to top it all off, even when the clinic team arrived to transport the supplies back home, they had to do so in vehicles not properly equipped to transfer highly perishable medicines and vaccines. Shrinkage of supply due to the perishing of medicines happened not every day but frequently enough to frustrate medical personnel and sabotage treatment.

To overcome this practical obstacle to effective care, VillageReach developed a hub-and-spoke system that recognized that delivery of medicines was no casual affair in rural Mozambique. Specialized services and skills, and trained staff with the proper equipment, were required to ensure safe delivery to the doorsteps of each clinic. The system started with diversifying available transportation ranging from Land Cruisers to bicycles to account for variations in travel conditions, with each mode of transportation, including the bikes, capable of carrying perishable materials. It included a real-time satellite tracking process for trucks and supplies, perhaps not a wholly surprising innovation given the backstories of the founders. VillageReach introduced low-cost and durable refrigeration systems to the clinics and set up a for-profit propane subsidiary, VidaGas, to provide reliable energy supplies not just to the clinics but also to homes and businesses across rural Mozambique. And finally, it instituted a comprehensive training plan for community representatives to ensure that valuable medical supplies were efficiently used. In many ways, VillageReach is the exact opposite in spirit of the water charities described earlier in this book. There are no inspiring moments of gushing water for VillageReach; it is all mechanics, infrastructure, maintenance, and repair—unglamorous to the core but holding the potential to make a transformative difference in a life-or-death situation.

In 2002, VillageReach launched a five-year demonstration project in Cabo Delgado, Mozambique. The results from the first few years appeared highly favorable: immunization rates were up; dropout rates of children who fail to complete a full course of vaccination were down. As we have seen, for the vast majority of charities these data would have been enough; they would have declared victory and festooned their Web sites, marketing materials, and annual reports with success stories. VillageReach was different. From the very beginning, the team established precise vaccination goals and committed to finding out whether any advances were the product of the new delivery system or were influenced by other health or educational efforts. To that end, they determined to use comparable neighboring provinces as control groups.

The results over five years were gratifying. The VillageReach staff delivered more than 2.1 million vaccine doses across Cabo Delgado Province, and their increased availability had a clear effect on the course of treatment. With the expanded and reliable flow of vaccines, the percentage of clinics with "stock outs" of at least one vaccine tumbled precipitously from over 80 percent at the beginning of the period to virtually zero by the end. The number of children receiving vaccines grew from forty thousand per year to more than seventy thousand by 2007. The dropout rate for children in the multi-dose vaccine course for DPT (diphtheria, pertussis, tetanus) fell by half, from over 12 percent to 6 percent. Most important, the advances made in Cabo Delgado Province were not mirrored in the neighboring control province of Niassa. While vaccine coverage rates in the two provinces were roughly equal at the beginning of the VillageReach pilot project, by 2007 vaccination rates in Cabo Delgado approached 95 percent, a full 25 percent higher than Niassa Province. The evidence over five years demonstrated that the VillageReach delivery system transformed the vaccine culture in central Mozambique.

Today, VillageReach has extended its reach geographically to India and seven countries in sub-Saharan Africa and also programmatically— though always focusing on last-mile challenges of health care. Its services now include developing and supporting communications technology systems for health-care workers in its service areas. And, significantly, it has moved into the role of a funder, providing start-up capital to socially conscious businesses in the health-care fields. In doing so, the VillageReach team has implicitly recognized that it achieves more if it creates a multiplier effect. Instead of doing everything itself, it leverages its start-up expertise and its resource base to spur innovation. In doing so, it in some ways mirrors the investment-and-support model pioneered at New Profit and in a Denver-based nonprofit called Invest in Kids (IIK).

In 1999, a group of Denver professionals—mostly lawyers—banded together around a common concern over the expanding gaps in achievement between children from lower-income and higher-income families and what they perceived as a growing crime problem among lower-income at-risk kids. Their concern stemmed in part from their individual experiences doing pro bono work on behalf of families in need in Colorado. The group, like so many others before and since, filled out the forms (they were lawyers after all) and ponied up the few bucks necessary to start their own charity, which they named Invest in Kids. If they had followed the well-worn path, they would have decided on services and launched their own programming. But IIK decided that its role would be different; instead, it would identify the best and most proven programs from around the country and help provide the infrastructure, training, and some of the resources to implement them in Colorado.

IIK undertook a nationwide review, searching for proven programs, a process that took months. It is a hard search—I've attempted it myself—as there is little in the way of a guide. There are some databases of purportedly effective charities, and of course there are the rating services, but mostly there are just endless claims of effectiveness from the charities themselves. The team at IIK looked at charities from all around the United States until they found what they wanted, ironically only two miles away, at the University of Colorado at Denver, with Dr. David Olds and the Nurse-Family Partnership. The NFP had just finished its third successful clinical trial, and as we have seen, after twenty years Olds was finally ready to grow. And this is where their stories merge. IIK came to NFP at that critical moment and offered to bring in resources and help secure funding (including a rather remarkable twenty-year funding commitment from the State of Colorado, mostly from tobacco settlement funds) necessary to expand the program throughout Colorado. After several years of growth within the state, in 2004 one of the co-founders of IIK, Robert Hill, founded with Olds the NFP National Service Office to facilitate franchising the NFP programs across the country.

In 2002, with NFP already on its way toward success, IIK sought its next opportunity. After determining that Colorado needed early childhood mental health and school readiness programs, it retained a Ph.D. candidate at the University of Denver to conduct an exhaustive six-month search to identify proven programs. With results in hand, IIK settled on one program called Incredible Years—a training program for parents, teachers, and students that aims to reduce childhood aggression and behavior problems and increase social competence at home and at school. The parenting component targets parents of children from birth to age twelve and uses role-playing, brainstorming, and values exercises to teach positive discipline and monitoring, build confidence, and promote parents' involvement in their children's educational experiences. Incredible Years has two programs for teachers: the Teacher Classroom Management Program and the Dina Dinosaur Child Training Series. Roughly speaking, the management program is a six-day skills workshop teaching pro-social behavior, classroom management, and parent partnering skills. Dina Dinosaur prepares teachers to teach the Dinosaur Curriculum, which targets children aged three to eight and trains them in skills such as empathy, friendship, and anger management; variations of the Dinosaur Curriculum have been developed for both problem students and general youth populations.

Incredible Years is the brainchild of Dr. Carolyn Webster-Stratton, a professor and director of the Parenting Clinic at the University of Washington. She developed it over twenty years and has subjected it to an extraordinary run, Olds-ian in scope, of randomized controlled tests, at least twenty over the last decade. Virtually every study shows significant reductions in behavioral problems both at home and at school.[5] But despite a nearly unrivaled testing history, Incredible Years has gained very little traction in the school marketplace. It is plagued by the limitations of many small organizations; while the underlying idea is demonstrably sound, the organization lacks both marketing infrastructure and the financial and implementation resources to expand. Unlike some school programs supported by sophisticated companies like Scholastic, Incredible Years is propped up only by a couple of part-time staff associated with the University of Washington and generally comes only as prepackaged materials without any training or monitoring support. For most of its existence, its reach was largely limited to schools near its home base in Seattle.

IIK plucked the program from relative obscurity and brought it to Colorado. Since Webster-Stratton and her small Washington-based team had little capacity to deliver the program to Colorado in a meaningful way, IIK provided additional support services, supplying initial training and ongoing counseling to local school districts, parents, and teachers and performing research into the program's effectiveness. For three years, the Incredible Years program has been fully monitored and evaluated by IIK, each time showing significant progress in the tested groups. Based on available evidence, it appears that the training and support provided by IIK have made Incredible Years even more successful in Colorado than in Washington state.

IIK continues to search for high-quality programs to bring to Colorado. In 2009, it tested a program called the Good Behavior Game (GBG), a classroom management system for discouraging disruptive behavior that had shown promising results in earlier trials. It is built on a competitive framework, playing on a common instinct of both children and adults to want to compete, win, and get rewards. In each GBG classroom, students are divided into three teams, which receive a check mark whenever a team member engages in disruptive behavior such as fighting or talking out of turn; teams that have four or fewer check marks over a preset period receive tangible rewards like stickers and activity books. The competition is supplemented by weekly teacher-led class sessions designed to enhance social problem-solving skills. The Colorado implementation of the Good Behavior Game was the largest ever. Along with IIK's commitment to promote new and promising ideas comes a commitment to fund only ones that are proved successful. While the research results from the first year of the Good Behavior Game were positive, they were not statistically significant, and IIK has made plans to shift its resources to different projects.

IIK has made it possible for highly effective charities to grow. It is not itself an innovator, it owns no ideas, and it represents no viewpoint other than a demand for excellence. It identifies the best, most relevant, most quantitatively valid ideas and gives them a big boost in Colorado, sometimes big enough to make them visible on the national stage. In this way, IIK shares a mission with several other organizations profiled throughout this book. New Profit, the Cambridge-based investment fund that we met in chapter 5; the Clark Foundation, the organization that helped jump-start Youth Villages; and IIK are all structured to help the best-operating charities succeed. The three organizations share a belief that out of the mass of charities in America, a few highly effective ones can make a real difference in people's lives and need to be nurtured toward maximum scale. They are the critical middlemen to the growth and maturation of an effective charitable sector.

EIGHT

Creating an Effective
Charitable Marketplace

A S I WRITE this concluding chapter, the United States, and much of the developed world, are at the beginning of at least a short-term shift in views on the role and size of government. In the United States, there is rarely agreement between the political parties, and indeed the political parties struggle to be in opposition to each other. Yet they seem to have found common cause on one idea: that the federal budget needs to be cut and that "domestic discretionary spending" should bear a disproportionate share of the cutting. "Domestic discretionary spending" is a cold phrase, one that has lost much of its resonance with repetition, but in real life it is anything but abstract. It is our children's education, housing and job-training programs for the unemployed and the working poor, protection of our natural resources, medical research into life-threatening diseases, childhood development programs, and disaster relief for the victims of earthquakes, floods, tornadoes, and hurricanes. All will likely suffer the budget ax in the years to come.

Reductions in government spending in these areas are always a major challenge to the social sector, which suffers the twin disabilities of decreased funding and greater responsibilities. In these times, we depend all the more on private initiatives executed by charities to address major social problems—problems that require large investments and big solutions. It is never easy for anyone to "do more with less," and as this book has demonstrated, the charitable world is uniquely ill prepared for the challenge. This has less to do with skills and dedication and more to do with a system that promotes inefficiency, inhibits scalable solutions, and does not reward, and sometimes punishes, results-driven management. Without fundamental changes in how we define and build charities, the charitable sector will struggle not only to fulfill its current mission but also to cover the new ground exposed by the retreat of government from social spending.

It does not have to be this way. There are real opportunities to remake the charitable sector to maximize its impact. Some of that change is regulatory, some of it is about creating new market-based institutions and incentives, but both must start with a fundamental change in the attitudes and behavior of the giving and taxpaying public. The public must begin to see donations as investments—investments with social rather than individual returns—and people must take charitable giving as seriously as they do investing in the stock market. This is the critical first step toward creating a new market discipline, a new culture of effectiveness, and efficient, results-oriented service.

The challenge facing us is captured in the story of two conference rooms. The first conference room sits in a colorless office park in uptown Memphis. Gathered in the room are the people principally responsible for decades of remarkable growth and results at Youth Villages: Pat Lawler, his head of operations, the director of research, the company's technology lead, its director of strategy, the VP for development, the chief financial officer, and so forth. This team, largely still intact after almost thirty years, turned Youth Villages from a struggling reform school to one of the most effective charities in the country. Without them and the investments in research, technology, training, and strategy that each represents, the story of Youth Villages would have been a very short, unremarkable one, similar to that of hundreds of thousands of charities around this country. The irony of this conference room is that every last dollar represented in that room—from salaries to technology to research to the company training program—is properly classified as overhead and every last dollar represented in that room has been critical to the success of Youth Villages. Charitable effectiveness, in this case, is the product of making the right investments in knowledge and people and of building a results-driven culture. That, far more than any overhead or administrative ratio, is the key to charitable success.

The second conference room is located in a far more enviable spot, at a resort hotel steps from the Pacific Ocean near the charming town of San Luis Obispo, California. The windowless room, by contrast, is bleak, a common combination in public radio where meeting planners typically fly their colleagues to lovely locations and lock them in highly unappealing quarters. These public radio conclaves are often tense, due less to poor ventilation and more to the currents of conflict that run through the public broadcasting system.

The conversation in the San Luis Obispo conference room, indeed, is strained. The key actors in the room are managers of West Coast public radio stations and the head of radio for the Corporation for Public Broadcasting (CPB), which is principally responsible for distributing federal funding each year to public radio and television stations. For the most part, CPB's disbursement of funds is mechanical, allocated to stations based upon long-standing formulas tied to station size and revenue. But for the first time, CPB is proposing to allocate some of its funds based on measures of station performance, through a reward and incentive program for effective public service. The proposal involves only a tiny fraction of CPB's $500 million appropriation, but it makes a bold statement that market incentives can help build better stations. It would put less effective radio stations on notice that CPB would not fund them forever, at least not at current levels. In putting forth this plan, CPB was daring to touch the third rail of the charitable world: the belief that it is impossible to measure much of what charities do and inappropriate to evaluate people and organizations dedicated to the public weal. That belief, inherently about fairness to the charities rather than to the beneficiaries of the service, is strongly held by many in the charitable world, and sure enough the CPB proposal met the unanimous, implacable, and even angry response of those present on that day.

After receiving identical unpleasant reactions in meetings around the country, CPB quietly shelved its incentive plan, along with its tentative aspirations to a new evidence-based culture. It was a shame, but resistance to measures of effectiveness either in public radio or elsewhere in the charitable sector is not hard to understand. In part, effectiveness research is resisted because it can be: there is little reward and some real risk to what it reveals, and charities can easily skate by with a good story and a "happy sheet," if pressed that far. Research is also resisted because it is believed to be expensive and time-consuming. And that can be true, though not every organization has to take it to the David Olds extreme described in chapter 7, and there are now proven, cost-effective methods for conducting even controlled trials.[1]

There is some truth, too, to the idea that charitable activity does not lend itself to empirical measurement: it is certainly difficult to measure souls saved at church. But the concern is vastly overstated; the large majority of charities fall into the human services category—education, social services, health care, for example—and can be measured, benchmarked, and fairly evaluated. The Robin Hood Foundation, dedicated to fighting poverty in New York City, has not only published the metrics it uses to evaluate its grantee organizations; it has also developed methods of analysis that allow it to compare social impact across disciplines. It can thus benchmark its grantees, regardless of program focus, against one another and direct its funds only to the most effective programs and organizations. Such metrics, widely used, would transform the charitable marketplace by permitting donors to make rational social investments.

The two conference rooms show both the opportunity within the charitable field—the potential for a whole generation of successful organizations like Youth Villages—and the challenge posed by entrenched resistance to change. In large part, the obliviousness of donors to the need for change has created the current stalemate. (CPB is unusual in having broached the issue at all.) But the flip side of the coin is that when donors, large and small, wake up to the need, they can effect enormous change in the charitable system simply by altering their own giving behavior. Here is what they—and we all—need to do.

Resist the old ways. Giving to maximize social impact means shedding old habits. Social investors focus solely on impact, renouncing the numerous unrelated reasons why people give. They ignore overhead and administrative ratios. They focus on the end customer, rather than targeting contributions to smaller charities so they can make a difference to the organization. They base their contributions not upon personal connections and relationships but on objective evidence. That is easy to write, less easy to do. Charitable appeals are often personal, from friends, from professional fund-raisers, and even from the head of the charity itself. Charity fund-raisers often say that donors give to people, not to organizations, and for that reason charitable executives are chosen in large part for their ability to raise money, not to lead an effective company. Social investors must look past charismatic front men and clever marketing. As Warren Buffett has said, "I try to buy stock in businesses that are so wonderful that an idiot can run them. Because sooner or later, one will."

Look for indicia of quality. The key task of the social investor, identifying the top-performing charities, is made difficult by conflicting claims and lack of objective analysis. But the social impact investor can look for certain qualities that mark a high-performing charity. Top-flight organizations are clear about their targets and willing to make their goals and results known internally and externally. Seek out charities that post specific goals and research results on their Web sites and that are willing to be transparent and accountable to their stakeholders. High-performing charities often show real growth year over year in terms of revenues and markets; such growth may reflect careful strategies and effective execution. Conversely, beware of the warning signs. Avoid charities that boast of exceptionally low over-head expenditures; they may be managing their books for public dis-play or shortchanging their potential, or both.

Do the work. Great charities do exist. I have mentioned a handful in this book, and there are many others. But in the absence of good market information, they are not easy to find, and Americans, by and large, are not working very hard to find them. Average Americans spend more time watching television in a single day than they do on their charitable contributions in an entire year. Like financial invest-ing, social investing takes work: researching charities, reviewing Web sites and published reports, and sharing information among friends, peers, and other like-minded givers.

Follow the leaders. But, to be realistic, many people will not want to do the work. That means that in this sprawling and confusing chari-table marketplace, the role of signalers—people and organizations who do invest the time to review and analyze charities—is critical. Historically, that role has been played on a local level by the socially prominent. More recently, the mantle has been assumed by very dif-ferent players, organizations like Charity Navigator, that evaluate and publicize reviews of thousands of charities every year. There are a number of such intermediary organizations—the Better Business Bureau is another—but Charity Navigator is the best known.[2] Yet with virtually no capacity to seriously investigate and analyze chari-ties, Charity Navigator has been forced to rely on the proxy measures of overhead and salary to construct its much-followed four-star rat-ings guide. These ratings have the benefit of simplicity to recommend them but little else; as this book has amply discussed, those data have little to do with charitable effectiveness.

Fortunately, as we have seen, there are other, better signalers in the marketplace, like GiveWell and New Profit and the Gates and Robin Hood Foundations, which are committed to careful research and analysis. Of the organizations profiled in this book, only GiveWell specifically positions itself as a public signaler and publishes its analy-ses for all to see, but it is a simple enough matter to Google a list of grantees of the other donor organizations to find more charities individual donors can reasonably trust.

Following the signalers is a good strategy for individuals to follow, but it is unlikely to lead to wholesale change. The organizations mentioned above, and a handful of similar ones, only cover a tiny piece of the charitable waterfront. GiveWell, an organization that I have touted for its investment grade reporting, has only recently climbed to seven total employees. In its six years in operation, it has rated some five hundred charities, a drop in the bucket for a sector that births five hundred new charities every three working days. More ambitious ideas are needed to bring positive change to the charitable world.

Pool donations. Ultimately, charitable investments may be best left to professionals. Consider the way Americans invest in the stock market. In many ways, it is far easier to invest for profit than to make socially sound donations. There are, after all, only some fifteen thousand publicly traded companies in the United States, and by law each company is required to divulge detailed financial and risk information to the investing public. Financial institutions, tip sheets, Web sites, books, and television shows provide endless advice to would-be investors. The mutual fund industry alone employs over 150,000 people. Yet despite the wealth of data on individual stocks, most Americans still choose to invest in companies only indirectly, through retirement plans, mutual funds, and other professionally directed vehicles. Contrast that with the direct, ad hoc, and amateur nature of most philanthropic activity in this country.

Clearly, an intermediate layer of charity experts who monitor, evaluate, and publish results on nonprofits could transform financing in the charitable world. Charitable mutual funds, for instance, would allow individuals to pool their funds and give under professional guidance. It is a sensible thing to do, even for the most sophisticated and well-heeled of donors. When Warren Buffett decided to give away his billions, he concluded that others, in his case the professional staff at the Gates Foundation, were better suited to manage his money for social purposes. Currently, a handful of organizations such as GiveWell pool donor dollars and channel funds to worthy charities. The choices for the average donor are currently limited, but so for the moment is the demand for such services. With hundreds of billions of dollars at stake, the options will no doubt dramatically expand if the donating public begins to seek such services.

Reinvent government. Despite the huge amount of individual giving in the United States, the federal government remains by far the largest bankroller of the charitable sector. Each year the federal government makes hundreds of billions of dollars in direct grants to charities and provides an equal amount more in indirect support via the tax code, the vast majority without a rigorous evaluation of organizational effectiveness. As Clayton Christensen of the Harvard Business School once noted, "Government currently spends billions of dollars per year in education, workforce and economic development, public health, and related areas. But allocation of these resources rarely happens through a process that would enable us to identify and grow the most powerful innovations."[3] Billions are spent without clear guidance as to who and what works and who and what does not.

The immense size of federal investment in the charitable world—in 2009, government distributed more than $100 billion to human services nonprofits alone[4]—presents an opportunity for fundamental change, not only in how government spends money, but in how we all interact with the charitable sector. This opportunity has two parts. The first is by changing the government's grant practices, which, as we have seen, do not reward and encourage the most effective charities.

It is not a simple matter to change long-standing operational habits of any organization, let alone a slow-footed leviathan like the federal government. Deeply entrenched procurement processes, bureaucratic inertia, and the politics of favoritism all inhibit change, but there are already openings for reform. In May 2012, the White House issued a new budget instruction, to go into effect in 2014, requiring grant-making agencies to increase the use of evidence in grant formulas. The new directive requires agencies to prioritize funding for programs with greater levels of evidence, to create competitive preferences for organizations (for-profits and nonprofits alike) that can prove outcomes, and to pay for success—increasing or decreasing reimbursements depending on results. On one level, these are stunningly obvious edicts—a requirement that agencies make sure they get what they pay for. But in government, this is the stuff of radical reform. If fully successful, it would reinvent government and decisively shift the charitable economy, at least the substantial part of it that is dependent on government funding.[5] It is not at all clear that even a White House order can overcome entrenched political interests and a budget that is ultimately the work of Congress, but it strikes a heartening blow for the evidence economy.

More radical even than changing grant formulas, the federal government could choose to spend its money through professional intermediary organizations that are better prepared than government agencies to evaluate and support charities. There have been small-scale efforts to funnel federal funds in this fashion, through the White House's Social Innovation Fund and the Department of Education efforts described in chapter 5. Local jurisdictions have also created intermediary programs.[6] Creating a new layer of organizations with expertise in evaluating charitable effectiveness and assisting in the development of well-run charities would require substantial resources.[7] But it is not too large a price to pay for far more effective deployment of taxpayer dollars. The ultimate goal of intermediary programs is to channel federal and local funding toward organizations with demonstrated capacity to deliver results. The cost is thus likely to be more than offset by efficiency gains and direct savings within the federal bureaucracy. And the bonus would be that the intermediaries' evaluations could be made available to the public, helping individuals direct the hundreds of billions of dollars in charitable donations they make each year to charities that work.

Both of these innovations would drive substantial change in how government funds the social sector. Change in process comes hard to government, but the time is right—now, when there is widespread skepticism about the size and effectiveness of government. It is time to let a new and professional marketplace move government out of the "inputs" business and into a world of buying provable results.

In the last few pages, I have laid out some things both individuals and government can do to help foster charitable effectiveness. But we should also step back and consider the larger picture. The American charitable system is the most open, most freewheeling, and in many ways the most democratic in the world. As we have seen, a small filing fee, a modest ability to follow directions, and the patience to wait a brief period are the only prerequisites to starting a charity. Once charitable status is gained, it is only lost through the most unusual and unfortunate events. Many charities are abandoned and a few are consolidated, but by and large once a charity, always a charity.[8] There are benefits to an open charitable system: it allows for new ideas, new blood, new causes, and new hope. But it also extracts a significant cost: the torrent of new and old charities creates confusion in the marketplace and stretches limited funding over too many different organizations. This has inhibited the ability of top-tier charities to grow their services and tackle large-scale social problems with large-scale resources.

The absence of clear rules and marketplace data, and terrific opportunities for brand confusion, mean that many charities live in a quasi-lawful zone, distributing some minimal amount of funds to recipients but directing a far greater share of the proceeds to management and the expenses of fund-raising. It has not escaped my attention over the past eighteen months that it can be far more lucrative to start a charity than it is to write a book about charities. Start a small group of charities, put a few key words in the names—"veterans," "policemen," "firefighters," "children," "hope," "support," "beneficial," "cancer," "widows and orphans"—write a compelling, cleverly worded script, and start phone banking. Pay yourself handsomely for the phone-banking operation, and dribble out a modest amount to relevant beneficiaries. You might be a poorly rated charity, but potential donors, especially the elderly, who will be getting calls at dinnertime, won't know the difference, since the name and purpose of your charity will be indistinguishable from thousands of other, more legitimate causes. None of this is illegal, or at least not clearly so.

Given the unchecked sprawl of the charitable sector, lawful and quasi-lawful, it is inevitable that serious charitable reform must include some element of regulatory change. Government's current ability to regulate charitable activity is limited not just by unclear law but by lack of resources at both the federal and the local levels. The Tax Exempt and Government Entities Division at the IRS is chronically short staffed and barely capable of keeping up with the daily influx of new charity applications. Over the last three decades, its volume of responsibility has grown, a function not only of ever more applicants and charities but of increased (though still inadequate) reporting and informational requirements that the federal government has imposed on the charitable sector via IRS Form 990. The IRS is pressed just to keep up and can hardly contemplate a meaningful number of reviews and investigations. But simply by the IRS's existence, the federal government is advantaged compared with the states. Only a handful of states can boast active charity offices, and even those tend to be short staffed and largely inert. As Professor Harvey Dale of NYU, one of the nation's leading authorities on charity regulation, has described it: "In most states, the Charity Bureau of the Attorney General's office is inactive, ineffective, understaffed, overwhelmed, or some combination of these."[9] Only more resources and tighter, more rigorous application of the law will help alleviate the problems of feckless or fraudulent charities.

These failures of regulation reverberate across the entire charitable sector. The public's faith in charities has declined precipitously in the last decade. Only one in ten Americans strongly believe that charities are honest and ethical, and more than one in three believe they "have pretty seriously gone off in the wrong direction."[10] These concerns are not idle. They reflect real stories, real facts, real examples, and there are real consequences for the charitable sector to the public's growing mistrust. Declining trust will ultimately mean declining revenues.

The mistrust sown by scandal is compounded by a frustrating lack of transparency and a reluctance to challenge the myths that dominate the charitable world. When stories of fraud, mismanagement, and waste hit the popular press, as they do with uncomfortable frequency, the scandals seem to implicate the entire sector, as it is difficult to distinguish between honest and successful charities and those that bring the sector into disrepute. Almost any regulatory scheme—whether self-regulatory via voluntary disclosure or one imposed by government—that would help the public distinguish between different parts of a complicated industry would aid in regenerating trust.[11]

Still, deeper scrutiny of the charitable wilderness is not enough. Simply put, it is time to reconsider what constitutes a charity. Businesses that look, act, and feel like for-profit operations—like hospitals and bowl games, to hark back to chapter 3—should be treated as for-profit businesses, both out of notions of competitive fairness and out of the belief that such operations neither need nor deserve public support. More broadly, it may be time to question the vast array of causes that receive privileged tax status. Tax exemptions are just a hidden form of government spending and deserve the same deliberation as the federal budget. The Princeton philosopher Peter Singer remarked on the implied value judgments in public spending when he commented on a painting acquired by the Metropolitan Museum of Art: "If the museum was on fire, would anyone think it right to save the Duccio from the flames, rather than a child?"[12] In effect, we do just that by allocating resources to cultural organizations rather than to any one of a myriad of health and relief programs. When such judgments are made—along with practical judgments about which programs can continue without government support—they should be made in the open, not behind the skirt of the tax code.

The "open gate" approach of the IRS has also facilitated the confusing charitable world we live with. After 9/11, for example, the IRS granted charitable status to hundreds of charities to assist ill and dying first responders, to support the families of victims, to help survivors, and to honor the memories of the dead. The vast majority of them were founded with perfectly good intentions but no expertise and no clear plan—and some lacked even the good intentions. "In virtually every category of 9/11 nonprofit, an . . . analysis . . . uncovered schemes beset with shady dealings, questionable expenses and dubious intentions." Charities were established to build gardens or sew memorial quilts the size of football fields, but ten years on dozens of charities have raised tens of millions of dollars and not broken ground, literally in some cases, figuratively in others. The American Quilt Memorial, founded by an Arizona handyman named Kevin Held, raised more than $713,000 in donations, mostly from school groups, but most of the money went to compensation for Held and his relatives, travel, and fund-raising expenses. There is no quilt. Remarkably, a number of these failed organizations continue to raise money more than a decade after the event.[13]

It may be tempting, as it was for John William Wright Patman, to think about shutting the gate, at least for a while, on new charities. From 2007 to 2009, for example, during the biggest American recession in fifty years, the nationwide ranks of arts organizations swelled by more than three thousand—at a time when public participation in the arts was dropping and existing arts organizations had to fight for their piece of declining public support.[14] But shutting the doors is not the right answer. Any dynamic system requires new ideas and new competition, even if that risks the creation of more Quilt Memorials. It would be more logical to increase the filing fee ($5,000 is a commonly proposed figure) to assure that the charity has some solidity, some support, and a commitment beyond the preparation of legal papers, rather than closing the gates.[15]

Front-end entry requirements have considerable appeal, but the real opportunity for positive change rests with giving charities an expiration date and an opportunity to renew. Charitable status does not have to be a lifetime grant. A dynamic system requires not only new entrants but new exits—organizations that go out of business when they can no longer keep up, generate new ideas, or prove the effectiveness of their efforts. Charitable status should be renewable, after a period of sufficient length (say, ten years) to prove the value of the organization. A renewal requirement would create numerous benefits: the practical prospect of weeding out ineffective and under-performing charities, the opportunity to evaluate charitable effectiveness in a thoughtful way, and the chance to encourage a culture of creative destruction that will make for a more vigorous charitable marketplace. While such a process may, at first blush, seem cumbersome, in fact it is a logical extension of practices that already exist in the nonprofit world. Accreditation is common in the educational and health-care sectors; the Council on Accreditation alone reviews more than eighteen hundred organizations in the human services field every year. With that head start, it is not difficult to envision peer review extending more generally across charitable fields. As the culture of evaluation and testing spreads, the task will become that much easier. At its best, such a system could provide essential peer feedback to charities as they grow.

In the end, a system that distinguishes among charities can only emerge in a marketplace that values measurement. In the short term, such a concept may be deeply unwelcome within the charitable sector. It promises many things that incumbent businesses wish to avoid: more competition, more accountability, and a system that will produce winners and losers. All these things are contrary to the prevailing norms within the charitable sector and unlikely to be warmly embraced. But in the long term, reform will produce better results for the users of charitable services, reward performance, promote scaled solutions, and craft a new compact with donors. It promises a system that works for the innovators, the builders, and society as a whole.

ACKNOWLEDGMENTS

If I had known how much work would go into writing this book, I am not sure I would have ever started. The fact that I made it this far is in large part due to the help and patience of friends, family, and colleagues.

My agent, Gillian MacKenzie, was remarkable from the beginning, helping me understand the publishing business and guiding me through the proposal process. I am grateful for her faith in a first-time author.

Kris Puopolo, my editor at Doubleday, invested hundreds of hours in helping me revise, restructure, and rethink critical parts of the book. Her help in making this book better was extraordinary. I don't know many agents or editors, but out of pure good luck it seems certain to me that I have blundered into two of the best in the business.

My research assistant, Julie Tate, provided many helpful suggestions and insights.

I am particularly thankful to the people who helped guide me through the charitable sector. Kim Syman at New Profit in Boston, Holden Karnofsky and Elie Hassenfeld at GiveWell, and Jon Baron at the Coalition for Evidence-Based Policy were particularly helpful in sharing their knowledge and their time. I also had the chance to visit some of the organizations mentioned in the book and am indebted to them for their time and openness. I owe particular thanks to Pat Lawler and Echelle Rutschman for their stories and for the Gus's fried chicken.

A number of friends were kind enough to read early drafts, when the book was in disrepair. Wading through it could not have been fun, so I am grateful to friends such as Andi Sporkin for their help, comments, and advice. My friends Kent Morton and John Clutterbuck were great traveling companions for field trips in philanthropy.

And, most important, I owe a debt of gratitude to my family. To my parents, Tom and Vivian, for their support throughout this process. To my five-year-old son, Nate, who wrote dozens of little books while I toiled away at one big one. And to my wife, Beth. I started this book after I left NPR, when I had what one might call some "extra time" on my hands. But by the time I was into serious writing, I had a new company to run and we had a young, rather restless boy in the house. I wrote most of this book in my "free time"—on nights and weekends—but they were only free because Beth was willing to do all the things that I should have been sharing equally with her. Without her support, this book would not have been possible.

Introduction

1. A note on terminology: "Charities" and "nonprofits" are terms typically
    conflated in public life, but charities are in fact just a subset of the non-
    profit world—though the overwhelmingly largest component of it. For
    purposes of this book, I use the term "charities" to mean public service
    organizations organized under section 501(c)(3) of the U.S. tax code.
    Under federal law, these organizations are tax-exempt, and donations to
    them are typically eligible for itemized tax deductions. State law generally
    conforms to federal law on exemptions from income and property taxes.
    The 1.1 million figure does not include all of the estimated 380,000 reli-
    gious organizations that are public charities but not required to register
    with the IRS—though many of them do. Nor does it include the more than
    272,000 small public charities that lost their tax-exempt status in 2011
    because they did not file the new IRS Form 990-N for three years in a row.
    Independent Sector, "Scope of the Nonprofit Sector," July 5, 2012. http://
    www.independentsector.org/scope_of_the_sector. The "non-charitable"
    portion of the nonprofit sector includes trade associations, fraternal and
    social organizations, certain political organizations, some labor orga-
    nizations, and business leagues such as chambers of commerce. A use-
    ful statistical overview of how the nonprofit sector works can be found
    at the Center on Nonprofits and Philanthropy and the National Cen-
    ter for Charitable Statistics at the Urban Institute, "Are There Too

Many Nonprofits?" (2012), http://www.urban.org/events/firsttuesdays
/upload/AreThereTooManyNonprofits.pdf.

2. National Center for Charitable Statistics, "Quick Facts About Nonprofits."
   http://nccs.urban.org/statistics/quickfacts.cfm.

3. In 2010, public charities reported $1.51 trillion in revenues and $1.47 trillion in expenses (from Urban Institute report, "Are There Too Many
   Nonprofits?" cited above), as compared with the gross domestic product
   of the United States of about $15.1 trillion.

4. In 2010, government grants and fees for services accounted for about
   32 percent of charitable revenue, or about $486 billion a year of the
   $1.51 trillion in total revenues. Urban Institute, "The Nonprofit Sector
   in Brief: Public Charities, Giving, and Volunteering, 2012," http://www
   .urban.org/UploadedPDF/412674-The-Nonprofit-Sector-in-Brief.pdf.

5. The travails of the Red Cross during Katrina have been widely chronicled
   in internal reports, in congressional investigations, and in newspaper
   reports. See, for instance, Jacqueline Salmon, "Counterparts Excoriate
   Red Cross Katrina Effort," *Washington Post,* April 5, 2006.

6. James Pethokoukis, "Once-Rare Response Is Now Routine and Over-
   used," *New York Times*, October 30, 2012.

7. American Red Cross, "Haiti Earthquake Response: Two-Year
   Update" (January 2012), http://www.redcross.org/images/MEDIA
   _CustomProductCatalog/m3640089_HaitiEarthquake_TwoYearReport
   .pdf.

8. See Keith Epstein, "Triage," Contribute (2008), http://www
   .contributemedia.com/trends_details.php?id=107. Also O. C. Ferrell,
   John Fraedrich, Linda Ferrell, "Business Ethics 2009: Ethical Decision
   Making and Cases" (South-western, Cengage Learning, 2009), at p. 330;
   and Deborah Sontag, "Who Brought Bernadine Healy Down?" *New York
   Times*, December 23, 2001.

Chapter 1: Big Promises, Small Outcomes

1. *Sick Water? The Central Role of Wastewater Management in Sustainable Development* (report of the United Nations Environment Programme, 2010).

2. The Romans, as advanced as they were, had no knowledge of pathogens
   and microbes, but they at least intuitively understood the relationship
   between clean water and public health. The Romans diligently identified
   safe sources of water for their cities and carefully transported water via
   aqueduct to city reservoirs. From there, water was transported by pipes to

fountains for public consumption. While the public drinking water was not "treated" in the modern sense of the word, great care was taken to avoid mixing drinking water with wastewater. Roman water supplies were not much to brag about by the modern standards of the developed world, but they exceeded anything seen in Europe until the late 1880s and sadly exceed what is available in large swaths of the developing world even today.

3. Bill Bryson, *At Home* (New York: Doubleday, 2010), 359–69.

4. For such a closely watched and endlessly discussed measure, consumer spending on Christmas is surprisingly hard to pin down, mostly because of differences over what constitutes Christmas spending. The number provided here, from the market analysis firm IBISWorld, is inclusive of food, gifts, and parties, with gifts being the largest component of that figure. IBISWorld, "How Much Do Americans Spend on Major National Holidays? Holiday Spending Sized Up" (2010), http://www.ibisworld.com/Common/MediaCenter/Holiday%20Spending.pdf.

5. Amy Belasco, *The Cost of Iraq, Afghanistan, and Other Global War on Terror Operations Since 9/11* (Congressional Research Service report, 2010), http://www.fas.org/sgp/crs/natsec/RL33110.pdf.

6. See www.watermissions.org/kenya.

7. Dean Jamison et al., *Disease Control Priorities in Developing Countries,* 2nd ed. (New York: Oxford University Press, 2006), http://files.dcp2.org/pdf/DCP/DCPFM.pdf.

8. Edward Breslin, *Rethinking Hydro-philanthropy: Smart Money for Transformative Impact* (2010), http://www.waterforpeople.org/assets/pdfs/rethinking-hydrophilantropy.pdf.

9. Michael Kremer and Alix Peterson Zwane, "Cost Effective Presentation of Diarrheal Diseases: A Critical Review" (Center for Global Development, Working Paper 117, Washington, D.C., 2006), http://www.cgdev.org/files/13495_file_Kremer_Diarrheal_Prevention.pdf.

10. Jamison et al., *Disease Control Priorities in Developing Countries,* 777–78.

11. Nicholas Kristof, "Nicholas Kristof's Advice for Saving the World," *Outside,* December 2009, http://www.outsideonline.com/outdoor-adventure/Nicholas-Kristof-s-Advice-for-Saving-the-World.html?page=all.

12. Breslin, *Rethinking Hydro-philanthropy,* 6.

13. There is an enormous, and sad, economic codicil to the water problem. Governments, foundations, and individual donors pour billions of dollars into water and sanitation projects each year, but poor people around the world, particularly in urban settings, are forced to pay much of their own money to obtain water—clean or not. Data from Transparency International show that the urban poor spend more money on water and sanitation

than their wealthier counterparts in the same city, and poor households in places such as Jakarta, Lima, Nairobi, and Manila spend more money on water than residents in New York, London, or Rome. Ibid., 3.

14. http://www.state.il.us/court/opinions/supremecourt/2010/march /107328.pdf http://www.state.il.us/court/opinions/supremecourt/2010 /march/107328.pdf http://thoughtsfrommalawi.blogspot.com/2009/10 /playpump-ii.html.

15. Jean Case, "The Painful Acknowledgement of Coming Up Short," Case Foundation website, May 4, 2010. http://www.casefoundation.org/blog/ painful-acknowledgement-coming-short.

16. SWAT was originally short for Special Weapons Assault Team, but the word "Assault" was deemed too provocative. Ever the lover of catchy acronyms, Gates simply changed the name to Special Weapons and Tactics.

17. Jesse Katz, "Gates Battles to Restore His and the LAPD's Image: Law Enforcement: Chief Goes on Offensive to Defuse Beating Furor and Its Impact on the Entire Department." Quotes from Chief Gates compiled by Cecilia Rasmussen, *Los Angeles Times,* March 17, 1991.

18. Dennis Cauchon, "Studies Find Drug Program Not Effective," *USA Today,* October 11, 1993.

19. Donald Lynam et al., "Project DARE: No Effects at 10-Year Follow-Up," *Journal of Consulting and Clinical Psychology* 64, no. 7 (1999): 590–93. The Lynam study was a ten-year follow-up to an earlier study that found no short-term benefits of the D.A.R.E. program. Results were no better a decade later. The Lynam group anticipated the attack from D.A.R.E. and pre-butted one of the key arguments: "Advocates of DARE may argue against our findings. First, they may argue that we have evaluated an out-of-date version of the program and that a newer version would have fared better. Admittedly, we evaluated the original DARE curriculum, which was created 3 years before the beginning of this study. This is an unavoidable difficulty in any long-term follow-up study; the important question becomes, How much change has there been? To the best of our knowledge, the goals (i.e., 'to keep kids off drugs') and foci of DARE (e.g., resisting peer pressure) have remained the same across time as has the method of delivery (e.g., police officers). We believe that any changes in DARE have been more cosmetic than substantive."

20. D. P. Rosenbaum and G. S. Hanson, "Assessing the Effects of School-based Drug Education: A Six-Year Multi-Level Analysis of Project D.A.R.E.," *Journal of Research in Crime and Delinquency* 35, no. 4 (1998): 381–412.

21. Quoted in Gene Tenelli, "Reconsidering DARE, A Report for School

Superintendents," Fall 1997. http://www.reconsider.org/issues/education/dare.htm.

22. U.S. Public Health Service, Office of the Surgeon General, *Youth Violence: A Report of the Surgeon General* (Rockville, Md., 2001), http://www.ncbi.nlm.nih.gov/books/NBK44294/.

23. Edward Shepard III, "The Economic Costs of D.A.R.E." (Institute of Industrial Relations, Research Paper 22, Le Moyne College, 2001).

24. Khadija Swims, "D.A.R.E.: Drug Abuse Resistance Education Is Ineffective at Preventing Future Drug Use in Adolescents," *Journal of Urban Youth Culture* 6, no. 1 (2008), http://juyc.info/pdf/kSwims.pdf. The National Registry of Evidence-Based Programs and Practices, maintained by the Department of Health and Human Services, lists thirty drug prevention programs with solid evidence of effectiveness, many of which have relatively low penetration in the school marketplace. To be fair, one of these programs, Keepin' It REAL, is a D.A.R.E.-organized middle school program that has a peer-to-peer methodology, and it is thus the only D.A.R.E. program not primarily based upon the original vision of police officers leading children. While different in approach, Keepin' It REAL (Refuse, Explain, Avoid, Leave) does at least honor Gates's fondness for acronyms.

25. Robert Kaplan and Allan Grossman, "The Emerging Capital Market for Nonprofits," *Harvard Business Review,* October 2010, http://hbr.org/2010/10/the-emerging-capital-market-for-nonprofits/ar/1.

26. Jennifer Gonnerman, "Truth or D.A.R.E.: The Dubious Drug-Education Program Takes New York," *Village Voice,* April 7, 1999.

27. Ibid.

28. Robert Halpern, "A Different Kind of Child Development Institution: The History of After-School Programs for Low-Income Children," *Teachers College Record* 104, no. 2 (March 2002): 178–211.

29. Ibid., 204.

30. Julie Pederson et al., *Safe and Smart: Making the After-School Hours Work for Kids* (Department of Justice, unpublished report, 1999), https://www.ncjrs.gov/pdffiles1/nij/grants/179991.pdf.

31. Susanne James-Burdumy, Mark Dynarski, Mary Moore, John Deke, Wendy Mansfield, and Carol Pistorini, *When Schools Stay Open Late: The National Evaluation of the 21st Century Community Learning Centers Program: Final Report* (U.S. Department of Education, Institute of Education Sciences, National Center for Education Evaluation and Regional Assistance, 2005), http://www.mathematica-mpr.com/publications/pdfs/21stfinal.pdf.

32. Thomas J. Dishion, Joan McCord, and Francois Poulin, "When Interventions Harm: Peer Groups and Problem Behavior," *American Psychologist* 54 (1999): 755–764, http://www.jdaihelpdesk.org/Research%20and%20 Resources/When%20Interventions%20Harm%20-%20Peer%20 Groups%20and%20Problem%20Behavior.pdf.

33. Rod Paige, "We Must Spend Our Education Dollars Wisely," *Washington Post,* April 1, 2003.

34. Leigh Linden, Carla Herrera, and Jean Grossman, "Achieving Academic Success After School: A Randomized Evaluation of the Higher Achievement Program" (unpublished paper, September 2011), http:// www.povertyactionlab.org/evaluation/achieving-academic-success-after -school-randomized-evaluation-higher-achievement-program.

35. In 1965, the Johnson administration launched Upward Bound, a program designed to provide a pathway to college for low-income students and students whose parents did not attend college. The Department of Education administers grants to local Upward Bound programs, which are mostly affiliated with colleges and universities. The local programs provide many services ranging from test tutoring and mentoring, assistance with the college application process, and summer camps at local colleges to ensure comfort and ease with the college experience. For two generations, Upward Bound has been a cornerstone of the federal government's efforts to provide postsecondary opportunities to disadvantaged students, and it is a robust example of the thriving partnership between the federal government and the charitable sector.

    Despite Upward Bound's iconic role, it is an open question whether it achieves its stated objectives. In 2007, the Department of Education commissioned the first-ever comprehensive study of Upward Bound, a randomized controlled test that would compare the progress of program participants with that of a control group of otherwise similarly situated disadvantaged youth not participating in the program. The carefully planned test was a state-of-the-art study, but it caused considerable fears among the program's supporters around the country. Raising questions about the test's methodology—which was without doubt reasonable from a research perspective—program advocates convinced Congress to bar the Department of Education from conducting a test. In effect, Congress by law declared that it had no interest in finding out whether Upward Bound actually moves disadvantaged children through college or not.

36. Workshop on Science, Evidence, and Inference in Education, National Research Council of the National Academy of Sciences, March 7–8, 2001.

37. Rob Reich, Lacey Dorn, and Stefanie Sutton, "Anything Goes: Approval

of Nonprofit Status by the IRS," Stanford University Center on Philanthropy and Civil Society, October 2009. The 99.5 percent approval rate applies to the public charities that are the principal subject of this book. Applications for designations as a private foundation (a small subgroup of 501(c)(3) organizations) tend to draw closer scrutiny than public charities. When private foundations are added in to the calculation, the overall IRS approval rate declines, but only to a still very high 98.6 percent.

38. Cited on the Chess-in-the-Schools Web site, http://www.chessintheschools .org/s/index.cfm?SSID=3.

39. Heather Haddon and Candice Giove, "Chess Program 'Rooks' Schools: Big Salaries, Big Council Funding," *New York Post,* July 31, 2011.

40. "Chess in the Schools," The GiveWell blog, November 13, 2009, http:// blog.givewell.org/2009/11/13/chess-in-the-schools/.

41. Erik Robelen, "Gates High Schools Get Mixed Reviews in Study," *Education Week,* November 16, 2005.

42. Giving USA Foundation, *Annual Report on Philanthropy* (2009).

Chapter 2: The Charitable Universe

1. Total charitable revenues have grown from approximately $555 billion in 1989 to $1.4 trillion as of 2009, a growth of 155 percent. Comparative data between the charitable sector and the economy as a whole show the relative rise of the sector. From 1985 to 2004, charitable expenditures in real terms grew 107 percent, almost twice the real domestic GDP growth of 58 percent. Paul Arnsberger, Melissa Ludlum, Margaret Riley, and Mike Stanton, "A History of the Tax Exempt State: An SOI Perspective," *IRS Statistics of Income Bulletin,* Winter 2008, http://www.irs.gov/pub/irs -soi/tehistory.pdf.

2. In percentage terms, the charitable sector in the Netherlands is slightly larger than in the United States, due almost exclusively to the fact that the Dutch equivalent of Social Security is administered by an independent charitable organization. In most countries, the services covered by the American charitable world are either government provided or not provided at all.

3. Alexis de Tocqueville, *Democracy in America* (1835), translated by George Lawrence (New York: Anchor Books, 1969), 513.

4. For the history of charities in America in this chapter, I am greatly indebted to Peter Dobkin Hall's *Inventing the Nonprofit Sector* (Baltimore: Johns Hopkins University Press, 1992).

5. Opinion of Henry St. George Tucker in *Gallegos Executor* v. *the Attorney General,* 3 Leigh 450 (1832) at 462, quoted in Peter Dobkin Hall, *Inventing the Nonprofit Sector* (Baltimore: Johns Hopkins University Press, 1992), 23.

6. Edwin Burrows and Mike Wallace, *Gotham: A History of New York City to 1898* (New York: Oxford University Press, 1999), 494.

7. *Vidal* v. *Girard's Executors,* 2 How 27 (1844).

8. The *Vidal* case did not, however, end Girard's relationship with the Supreme Court. One hundred and twenty years later, the Girard will was back in front of the highest court in the land. In the wake of the desegregation decision of *Brown* v. *Board of Education,* civil rights advocates undertook a fourteen-year effort, highlighted with a rally led by Martin Luther King Jr. on the steps of Girard College in 1965, to desegregate the school. The campaign culminated in a return to the Supreme Court and a decision that upheld the principle that the Fourteenth Amendment to the Constitution superseded the restrictive terms of Stephen Girard's will. The first black students were admitted to Girard the next year, and the first black girl student gained admission in 1984. Today, the school is 80 percent African American and since 2009 has been led by its first African American female president. The one thing that has not changed is that the school remains free to all qualified students, and the vast bulk of its operating expenses is still provided by the Girard Estate.

9. Of the seventy-five wealthiest persons in recorded history, a remarkable fourteen of them were born in the United States between 1832 and 1840. It is simply astonishing that in the more than two thousand years since Cleopatra (No. 21) amassed a fortune estimated to be worth nearly $100 billion in today's dollars, fully 20 percent of the richest people in history, including No. 1 (Rockefeller) and No. 2 (Carnegie), were born in one country within one decade. None of these men (and they were all men) had the advantage of royalty (as did about ten people on the list), but they did have the singular advantage of coming of age at the beginning of the greatest industrial and business transformation of the modern age. Malcolm Gladwell, *Outliers* (New York: Little, Brown, 2008), 56–63.

10. Kevin Phillips, *Wealth and Democracy: A Political History of the American Rich* (New York: Random House, 2002), 38. The rapid rise of millionaires was not matched with economic growth for the average American. Girard's fortune was about 17,000 times larger than the average household. For John D. Rockefeller, that multiple was 1.25 million. Structural changes in the economy, the creation of the graduated income tax, and the redistributive policies of the New Deal created a far more level social

system for much of the twentieth century. America's richest man in 1982, Daniel Ludwig, was worth only 60,000 times the average household. But the combination of the technology revolution and substantial changes in governmental tax and economic policies has now created a new Gilded Age, one in which the multibillion-dollar fortune of Bill Gates is more than 1.4 million times the average family wealth.

11. Patricia Beard, *After the Ball: Gilded Age Secrets, Boardroom Betrayals, and the Party That Ignited the Great Wall Street Scandal of 1905* (New York: HarperCollins, 2003), 62–66.

12. The parties of the Gilded Age were grand not only in size but in the sense of entitlement. When Mrs. Hermann Oelrichs, the wife of the shipping magnate, planned her "White Ball" at her seaside mansion Rosecliff in Newport, she asked the U.S. Navy to parade past the estate to enhance the view. When the navy, in a burst of good sense, declined the request, Mrs. Oelrichs commissioned a dozen white-hulled faux ships to be built and anchored within easy eyesight of her balconies, creating the illusion that the navy had deployed in her honor. Ibid., 159.

13. Before the Great Depression, federal spending accounted for only about 3 percent of gross domestic product. By World War II, that had more than tripled to about 10 percent. Today, it accounts for approximately 20 percent of GDP.

14. Peter Dobkin Hall, "A Historical Overview of Philanthropy, Voluntary Associations, and Nonprofit Organizations in the United States, 1600–2000," in *The Nonprofit Sector: A Research Handbook,* 2nd ed., edited by Walter Powell and Richard Steinberg (New Haven, Conn.: Yale University Press, 2006), 53.

15. Hall, *Inventing the Nonprofit Sector,* 63.

16. Ibid.

17. Lester Salamon, "Government and the Voluntary Sector in an Age of Retrenchment: The American Experience," *Journal of Public Policy* 6, no. 1 (1986): 1–19.

18. Lester Salamon, "Nonprofits: The Results Are Coming In," *Nonprofit and Voluntary Sector Quarterly* 16, no. 1 (1987): 45–54.

19. A series of studies in the 1980s showed that certain segments of the social sector were highly dependent on government funding programs—up to 75 percent of revenues in some industries. Hall, "Historical Overview of Philanthropy," 54.

20. Ibid., 52.

21. Hall, *Inventing the Nonprofit Sector,* 7.

22. Hall, "Historical Overview of Philanthropy," 55–56.

23. Hall, *Inventing the Nonprofit Sector,* 13.

24. Stephanie Strom, "The Man Museums Love to Hate," *New York Times,* December 10, 2006.

25. Senator Albert Gore, testifying before the Senate Finance Committee on the Tax Reform Act of 1969, October 22, 1969, pt. 6, 6057.

26. Hall, *Inventing the Nonprofit Sector,* 71. Patman's proposal received considerable support, but it was ultimately at odds with the expansionist tempo dictated by President Johnson, who needed a growing nonprofit sector to execute his war on poverty.

27. John Ensor Harr and Peter Johnson, *The Rockefeller Conscience* (New York: Macmillan, 1992), 10.

28. The story, as it has been told by his biographers, is that the men's room was the accidental meeting place for John and Lewis Strauss, a retired admiral, former member of the Atomic Energy Commission, and new member of the family office staff. Strauss lobbied John to convene a gathering of leading scientists to discuss population matters. Ibid., 33.

29. Eleanor Brilliant, *Private Charity and Public Inquiry* (Bloomington: Indiana University Press, 2000), 43.

30. The Commission on Foundations and Private Philanthropy (called the Peterson Commission in honor of its chairman, Pete Peterson, the then president of Bell and Howell) was established to influence the congressional deliberations that culminated in the Tax Reform Act of 1969. It failed in that goal, in part because the commission report was not issued until 1970.

31. Ibid., 120.

32. Hall, *Inventing the Nonprofit Sector,* 78.

Chapter 3: The Spaghetti Factory

1. *Commissioners* v. *Pemsel* [1891], A.C. 531, 583. For a more general overview, see Peter Elson, *High Ideals and Noble Intentions: Voluntary Sector–Government Relations in Canada* (Toronto: University of Toronto Press, 2011).

2. *Bob Jones University* v. *United States,* 461 U.S. 574 (1983).

3. The public comments about Stroger on Web sites such as Yelp provide a fascinating window into the health-care situation in America. Virtually everyone on Yelp, for instance, agrees that the hospital is badly overtaxed, with degraded infrastructure and substandard sanitary conditions; everyone agrees that the lines are long and the medical and administrative staff

short on customer service skills. But the comments are evenly divided between those who find those conditions unacceptable and enraging and those who accept those conditions as reasonable trade-offs for free medical care.

4. Jason Grotto and Bruce Japsen, "Are Hospitals Passing Off Their Low-Profit Patients?," *Chicago Tribune,* April 10, 2009.

5. Lucette Lagnado, "Twenty Years and Still Paying—Jeanette White Is Long Dead but Her Hospital Bill Lives On; Interest Charges, Legal Fees," *Wall Street Journal,* March 13, 2003.

6. Lucette Lagnado, "Hospitals Try Extreme Measures to Collect Their Overdue Debts," *Wall Street Journal,* October 30, 2003.

7. http://www.state.il.us/court/opinions/supremecourt/2010/march /107328.pdf. Perhaps the Provena case will prove to be a landmark decision: one of the first to strip a hospital of tax privileges in decades. The Illinois Supreme Court was clearly unimpressed by the charitable undertakings of Provena. It took note of the parsimonious nature of the charity care policy: financial support was offered only as a last resort, it was poorly publicized, and applicants had the burden to apply and prove need. The decision also did not give credit to Provena for its other claimed charitable activities, noting that many of these activities, such as its emergency room services, were compelled by law. But read carefully, the Provena decision seems far less consequential. As only a plurality decision in one state, its impact on other jurisdictions may be limited, and as the Illinois Supreme Court itself noted, its decision only applied to the disputed state property tax exemption for 2002. It thus did nothing to alter the hospital's exemptions under all federal laws and its exemption from a myriad of state and local taxes such as the retailer's occupation tax, the service occupation tax, the use tax, and the service use tax.

8. Leef Smith, "Inova Chain Is Accused of Gouging Uninsured," *Washington Post,* September 24, 2004.

9. Lucette Lagnado, "Full Price: A Young Woman, an Appendectomy, and a $19,000 Debt," *Wall Street Journal,* March 17, 2003.

10. Jessica Silver-Greenberg, "Debt Collector Is Faulted for Tough Tactics in Hospitals," *New York Times,* April 24, 2012.

11. Jonathan Cohn, "Uncharitable," *New York Times Magazine,* December 19, 2004.

12. Community Service Society, "Incentivizing Patient Financial Assistance: How to Fix New York's Hospital Indigent Care Program" (February 2012), http://www.cssny.org/publications/entry/incentivizing-patient-financial -assistanceFeb2012.

13. Nina Bernstein, "Hospitals Flout Charity Aid Law," *New York Times,* February 12, 2012.

14. Melanie Evans and Joe Carlson, "Out in the Open," ModernHealthcare .com, December 19, 2011, http://www.modernhealthcare.com/article/20111219/MAGAZINE/312199972.

15. Nina Bernstein, "Chefs, Butlers, Marble Baths: Hospitals Vie for the Affluent," *New York Times,* January 22, 2012.

16. John Carreyrou and Barbara Martinez, "Nonprofit Hospitals, Once for the Poor, Strike It Rich," *Wall Street Journal,* April 7, 2008.

17. Gilbert Gaul, "Growing Size and Wealth of Children's Hospitals Fueling Questions About Spending," *Kaiser Health News,* September 25, 2011.

18. Ibid.

19. Cohn, "Uncharitable." The checkered ownership history of Westlake Hospital effectively highlights the overlaps between the for-profit and nonprofit hospital sectors. Originally opened as a charitable hospital in 1927, Westlake has undergone at least six ownership changes. It was three times organized as a charitable hospital, twice as a for-profit hospital and once as a U.S. Army surgical center. At the time of Dr. Rosenberg's statement in 2004, Westlake was a charitable hospital owned by Resurrection Health Care, a large Chicago-based medical system originally founded by the Sisters of the Holy Family of Nazareth and the Sisters of the Resurrection. In 2010, it was sold to Vanguard Health Systems, a Nashville-based for-profit hospital system with annual revenues of approximately $6 billion.

20. Congressional Budget Office, "Nonprofit Hospitals and the Provision of Community Benefits" (working paper, December 2006), http://www.cbo .gov/publication/18256.

21. For purposes of the study, the CBO defined charitable services as a combination of services provided free of charge to indigent or otherwise needy patients and paid services written off by the hospital as bad debt. While failure to collect is typically not considered a charitable activity, data limitations ultimately forced the CBO to include it for analytical purposes.

22. Gary Young, Kemal Desai, and Carol Van Deusen Lukas, "Does the Sale of Nonprofit Hospitals Threaten Health Care for the Poor?," *Health Affairs* 16, no. 1 (January/February 1997); Gary Young and Kemal Desai, "Nonprofit Hospital Conversions and Community Benefits: New Evidence from Three States," *Health Affairs* 18, no. 5 (September/October 1999).

23. Melanie Evans and Joe Carlson, "Out in the Open: Not-for-Profit Hospitals' Charity Spending Revealed, but Finding a Standard Measure May Not Be So Simple," ModernHealthcare.com, December 19, 2011.

24. Billy Reed, "Ben-Hur Played the Rose Bowl," *Sports Illustrated,* December 23, 1968.

25. The Fiesta Bowl's financial relationship with the State of Arizona has its own interesting twist. By law, charities are barred from engaging in political activities and from making political contributions—a rule frequently evaded through the creation of affiliated, non-charitable organizations that have interlocking goals, leadership, and facilities. The Fiesta Bowl and its corporate alter ego, the Arizona Sports Foundation, made substantial payments over a number of years for lobbying services, contributed to the legal defense funds of prominent politicians, and illegally reimbursed employees for tens of thousands of dollars in political donations. An investigation by the Arizona attorney general and by the U.S. attorney in Phoenix ultimately led the Fiesta Bowl's CEO, John Junker, to plead guilty to both state and federal charges for conspiracy to violate campaign contribution laws. Ironically, while he awaits sentencing, Junker and his wife have been hired by a local charity, the Society of St. Vincent de Paul, for management and fund-raising positions, respectively, at a combined salary of $87,000 per year. Craig Harris, "Former Fiesta Bowl CEO Helps Charity While Awaiting Sentence," *USA Today,* June 30, 2012.

26. In 2010, *Yahoo! Sports* audited the most recent tax returns of twenty-three available tax-exempt bowl committees. Collectively, these bowls recognized about $186.3 million in revenues and reported about $2.6 million in charitable contributions. About $1.6 million of this figure was from just two bowl committees, the Orange Bowl and the Chick-fil-A Bowl. Dan Wetzel and Josh Peter, "Congress Seeks Bowl Truth," *Yahoo! Sports,* May 26, 2010, http://rivals.yahoo.com/ncaa/football/news?slug=ys-congressbcs052509.

27. Playoff PAC, "Public Dollars Serving Private Interests: Tax Irregularities of Bowl Championship Organizations," 2010, http://www.playoffpac.com/upload_files/Playoff%20PAC%20Report%20on%20BCS%20Bowl%20Tax%20Irregularities%20(Final%20on%209-23).pdf.

28. One of those college presidents, Gordon Gee of Ohio State, discovered the dangers of wading into the murky and passionate politics of college football. In defending the byzantine rules of the Bowl Championship Series (BCS), a set of rules that entitle the biggest schools and conferences to the most prominent and most lucrative bowl games, Gee denigrated the records of such lesser-known schools as Boise State and Texas Christian as being compiled through easy victories over "the Little Sisters of the Poor." His remarks set off a torrent of criticism and reignited a national contro-

versy over the BCS system. To his credit, within days of his remark, Gee made one of the great step backs in modern sports history, apologizing for his remarks by saying, "What do I know about college football? I look like Orville Redenbacher. I have no business talking about college football." Gee did not get involved in this violent debate out of love of the game. His belittling comments on the so-called mid-majors were intended as a defense of the existing system, which guarantees that the vast majority of bowl revenues will flow to the six power conferences that dominate the Bowl Championship Series. The BCS was abolished in 2012, but whatever replaces it will undoubtedly still be tilted financially toward the power conferences.

29. Stephanie Strom, "University and Pickens Sue over Fund-Raising Plan," *New York Times,* February 16, 2010. In early 2010, Pickens was a party to a suit between Oklahoma State and Lincoln National Life Insurance Company over Lincoln's management of a donor life insurance program. It is difficult to understand Pickens's involvement in the suit, given that he has no official role at the university and that he was not listed as one of the insured donors in the program; it is less hard to understand Lincoln's countercharge that Pickens (whom the *Times* referred to as "the colorful energy investor") had "willfully and intentionally interfered" in the matter.

30. Joe Drape and Thayer Evans, "Financial Straits of Boosters Hit Athletic Programs," *New York Times,* October 20, 2008.

31. The Wealth Report, "T. Boone Pickens: 'Honey, I Shrunk the Charity,'" *Wall Street Journal,* October 29, 2008.

32. Strom, "University and Pickens Sue over Fund-Raising Plan."

33. Ian Fisher, "$1 Million Gift for New Charity Case: The Viagra-Needy," *New York Times*, June 10, 1998. Greenberg made the gift to the Hospital for Special Surgery in Manhattan, a puzzling choice since the hospital, as its name suggests, specializes in surgery. Greenberg explained at the time that he gave the gift because his wife was on the hospital's board. *The New York Times* described administrators as "dizzily baffled" by the gift, in part because the amount far exceeded the likely demand for Viagra. Even before the Viagra donation, Greenberg had earned somewhat of a reputation for eccentric charitable gifts, having once made a gift of new bathrooms to the Israel Museum in Jerusalem and then insisted on commemorative plaques in honor of his brother Maynard.

34. Quoted in Evelyn Brody and Joseph Cordes, "The Unrelated Business Tax: All Bark and No Bite?" (No. 3 in the series "Emerging Issues in Philanthropy," Urban Institute, March 2001), http://www.taxpolicycenter.org/publications/url.cfm?ID=310257.

35. Daniel Wakin, "A Night at the Opera: Boos vs. Cheers for a New Met 'Tosca,'" *New York Times,* September 21, 2009.

Chapter 4: Money for People

1. Scambusters.org, "Hurricane Katrina Scams," http://www.scambusters .org/hurricanekatrinascams.html. The apparent authenticity of these sites is sometimes buttressed by the use of the .org address, which lends credibility and reliability. In fact, .org is an open and unrestricted domain, and anyone—charity, commercial business, individual, scam artist—can purchase available names.

2. There has been one paperwork advancement at least in the oversight of charities in the last decade. In 2006, the IRS promulgated a rule that organizations that failed to file an income tax return for three consecutive years would lose their charitable status. Presumably, the principal effect of this would be to weed out dormant organizations from the charitable rolls, and in that sense the rule has been more than productive, eliminating some 428,000 charities in the last few years. See "Are There Too Many Nonprofits?"

3. Jeff Testerman and John Martin, "Multimillion-Dollar Nonprofit Charity for Navy Veterans Steeped in Secrecy," *St. Petersburg Times,* March 20, 2010.

4. Jeff Testerman and John Martin, "In 2008, IRS Audited Navy Veterans and Gave the Phony Charity a Clean Bill of Health," St. Petersburg Times, November 19, 2010.

5. Thompson, by then going by the name of Anderson Yazzie, was eventually arrested in 2012 by the U.S. Marshal's Service outside Portland, Oregon. A card in his pocket subsequently led authorities to a storage locker facility where they found two suitcases, one containing birth certificates and other papers sufficient to give Thompson twenty different aliases. In the other suitcase, the marshals found $981,650 in cash. To this date, neither the police nor prosecutors have been able to ascertain Thompson's real name. Kris Hundley and John Martin, "Hunting Navy Veterans Fugitive Bobby Thompson, U.S. Marshals Play Name Game—and Win," *Tampa Bay Times,* May 13, 2012.

6. Marcus Owens, "Charity Oversight: An Alternative Approach" (Hauser Center for Nonprofit Organization at Harvard University, Working Paper 33.4, October 2006), http://www.hks.harvard.edu/hauser/PDF_XLS /workingpapers/workingpaper_33.4.pdf.

7.   Peter Swords and Harriet Bograd, "Accountability in the Nonprofit Sector: What Problems Are Addressed by State Regulators?" (Nonprofit Coordinating Committee of New York, working paper, October 1996), http://www.npccny.org/info/Accountability_96draft.pdf.

8.   Lloyd Hitoshi Mayer and Brendan Wilson, "Regulating Charities in the Twenty-First Century: An Institutional Choice Analysis," *Chicago Kent Law Review* 85, (2010) no. 2/:479; Joel Fleishman, *The Foundation: A Great American Secret* (New York: Public Affairs, 2007), 257–58.

9.   D. K. Row, "Senate Bill 40, Intended to Punish Bad Charities, May Die in the Oregon House," *Oregonian,* May 31, 2011.

10. Jeff Testerman and John Martin, "Navy Vets Leader Made an Unchecked Rise into Elite Circles," *St. Petersburg Times,* December 27, 2010.

11. Associated Press, "Two NYers Admit Running Phony Breast Cancer Charity," reprinted in *Wall Street Journal* online, August 16, 2011.

12. "Lowest Scam in Town: United Homeless Organization Fakes Helping the Poor," New York *Daily News,* December 25, 2009.

13. Melissa Klein and Kathianne Boniello, "Jug Band Keeps Your Change, Homeless Aid Just a Beg Lie," *New York Post,* December 7, 2008.

14. A slightly deeper dig reveals a little more about the Human Fund. The fund's revenues come largely from a concert held annually at the Beachland Ballroom, a local concert hall and tavern built on the site of the former Croatian Liberty Home. Revenues in 2010 amounted to roughly $120,000, and once organizational and event expenses were deducted, only $50,000 remained to be distributed to local arts programs. In the commercial world, economists have labeled businesses principally organized to provide their owners with a particular level of income as "lifestyle businesses." The Human Fund is what we might call a "lifestyle charity," an organization that maintains a certain level of activity with no real pretense of scalability and broad social impact. In such cases, the fund-raising activities of the charity (its concerts, dinners, and galas, for example) may be the primary focus of the organization and provide much of the social benefit of volunteerism. Without any broader studies of the sector, it is difficult to make any useful statements about the numbers of lifestyle charities in this country, but it is clear from my research that there are a *considerable number.*

15. Matthew Stannard, "Friends See Saint, Cops See Schemer / Why Ex-Goodwill Exec Was Accused of Bilking Charity," *San Francisco Chronicle,* June 7, 2003.

16. Liersch ultimately pleaded guilty only to tax evasion as part of a deal in

which federal prosecutors dropped embezzlement charges. He served no prison time but agreed to pay $540,000 in restitution.

17. The Gray case was naturally an Internet sensation for a couple days during July 2010, playing as it did into multiple narratives around the Catholic Church. When Gray was arrested at his apartment, he admitted all his crimes and claimed they were undertaken out of anger at the Church for assigning him to a parish inconvenient to the hospital where his mother lay dying. John Christoffersen, "Kevin Gray, Waterbury Priest, Stole $1.3 Million to Pay for Male Escorts, Say Police," *Huffington Post,* July 6, 2010.

18. Robert West and Charles Zech, "Internal Financial Controls in the U.S. Catholic Church" (Villanova University, unpublished paper, 2007), http:// npoadvisors.com/wordpress/wp-content/uploads/guide-internal -financial-controls-us-catholic-church.pdf.

19. Laurie Goodstein and Stephanie Strom, "Embezzlement Is Found in Many Catholic Dioceses," *New York Times,* January 5, 2007. After the Villanova report was issued, the leadership of the American Catholic Church pledged to institute new internal financial controls across the country. While it is hard to extrapolate from one case, the Gray case at least gives reason to question whether those new controls have been adequately designed and implemented.

20. Alison Leigh Cowan, "Rabbi's Followers Blame Aide for Missing Millions," *New York Times,* December 20, 2011.

21. Lopez was censured and stripped of his committee chairmanship in August 2012 after an internal investigation found that he had harassed and groped two female staff members. He was also barred from hiring interns or employing any person under the age of twenty-one. Danny Hakim, "Lawmaker Is Censored over Sexual Harassment," *New York Times,* August 24, 2012.

22. Nicole Maxwell, *Bargaining for Brooklyn: Community Organizations in the Entrepreneurial City* (Chicago: University of Chicago Press, 2007).

23. William Rashbaum, "Brooklyn Democrat Is Said to Be Investigated," *New York Times,* September 22, 2010.

24. Robert Gearty, "Developers, Architects, Accountants, and Security Firms Cash In After Writing Checks to Vito Lopez," New York *Daily News,* September 29, 2010. The *Daily News* traced $51,000 in contributions to Ridgewood Bushwick vendors over a three-year period.

25. Erin Durkin and Adam Lisberg, "Probe Finds Brooklyn Dem Vito Lopez's Non-Profit Empire Riddled with Fraud," New York *Daily News,* September 15, 2010.

26. Rashbaum, "Brooklyn Democrat Is Said to Be Investigated."

27. David Seifman, "Vito's Golden Girl Gets Booted by City," *New York Post,* January 5, 2012.

28. Fumo also was indicted, and subsequently convicted, of looting another charity, the Independence Seaport Museum. The museum owned two historic yachts that it used for fund-raising purposes and to rent out commercially from time to time. Fumo, a member of the museum's board, annually borrowed one of the two yachts; though he claimed to the museum that it was for fund-raising purposes, the events were always coincident with his summer vacations on Martha's Vineyard, a fact that, along with the complete lack of donations coming from these voyages, seems to have eluded management's attention for Fumo's entire tenure. One year, when both yachts were unavailable, the museum rented another yacht, the wonderfully named *Sweet Distraction,* at a cost of $13,775. Fumo, to be fair, eventually repaid the museum for this rental, but as the U.S. attorney noted, that took three years and an intervening 150-count indictment.

29. The steady flow of charitable fraud discoveries are carefully chronicled on the Web site charitygovernance.com. The site, developed by a charity consultant named Jack Siegel, includes a lovingly compiled and extensive list of the frauds, thefts, and various institutional maladies of the charitable world and makes interesting, if rather depressing, reading. After doing this for many years, Siegel should be forgiven for going a little hyperbolic. His headline for the Father Gray case is avowedly celebratory, "Church Congregation Lost Exactly What It Deserved: Priest Allegedly Stole $1.3 Million to Finance Escapades in New York City," and reflects a view that the charitable world is riddled with badly managed organizations requiring some natural selection. This perspective is reflected in a Siegel blog post tartly titled "Stop Wasting Money: Death Panels for Nonprofits," August 20, 2009.

30. Stephanie Strom, "Report Sketches Crimes Costing Billions: Thefts from Charities," *New York Times,* March 29, 2008.

Chapter 5: The Donors

1. See Peter Hartlaub, "Kroc Bequeaths $200 Million to NPR, Widow of McDonald's Founder Was Avid Listener," SFGate.com, November 7, 2003.

2. René Bekkers and Pamala Wiepking, "A Literature Review of Empirical

Studies of Philanthropy: Eight Mechanisms That Drive Charitable Giving," *Nonprofit and Voluntary Sector Quarterly* 40, no. 5 (2011). Most of the science on philanthropy comes from the United States, but a disproportionate amount comes from the Netherlands as well. This reflects the fact that the United States has the largest voluntary sector in the world, but the Netherlands has the largest on a per capita basis.

3. Robert M. Jiobu and Eric S. Knowles, "Norm Strength and Alms Giving: An Observational Study," *Journal of Social Psychology* 94 (1974): 205–11. Their observation may seem surprising until you begin to think about the actual mechanics of giving to the Salvation Army bell ringers. It is easy to believe that people slogging through slush and frigid temperatures have greater incentives to get inside the mall and less desire to stop, pull off gloves, and root through pockets and purses for change.

4. Dictator games are a form of experimental economics designed to test the rationality of economic activity. While dictator games take many forms, in a typical experiment a single individual (the dictator) will be given a finite resource to keep or apportion as he or she sees fit among the subject population. In pure economic theory the dictator would keep the entire asset for his own use, but in practice dictators often apportion resources to other people—suggesting that other, nonquantitative factors such as self-image, a belief in social goods, and altruism play a part in individual economic behavior.

5. William T. Harbaugh, Ulrich Mayr, and Daniel R. Burghart, "Neural Responses to Taxation and Voluntary Giving Reveal Motives for Charitable Donations," *Science* 316 (2007): 1622–24.

6. James Andreoni, "An Experimental Test of the Public-Goods Crowding-Out Hypothesis," *American Economic Review* 83 (1993): 1317–27.

7. *Commissioner* v. *Duberstein,* 363 U.S. 278 (1960).

8. Kristof, "Nicholas Kristof's Advice for Saving the World."

9. Peter Singer, *The Life You Can Save* (New York: Random House, 2009), 47–48; Tehila Kogut and Ilana Ritov, "The 'Unidentified Victim' Effect: An Identified Group, or Just a Single Individual?," *Journal of Behavioral Decision Making* 18 (2005): 157–67; Tehila Kogut and Ilana Ritov, "The Singularity Effect of Identified Victims in Separate and Joint Evaluations," *Organizational Behavior and Human Decision Processes* 97 (2005): 106–16.

10. Christine Horne, "The Internal Enforcement of Norms," *European Sociological Review* 19, no. 4 (2003): 335–38.

11. Debra Grace and Deborah Griffin, "Exploring Conspicuousness in the Context of Donation Behaviour," *International Journal of Nonprofit and Voluntary Sector Marketing* 11, no. 2 (2006): 147–54.

12. One thing that seems to matter less than is commonly supposed is tax incentives. The effect of marginal rates on giving has been studied repeatedly and remains a subject of some disagreement (Bekkers and Wiepking, "Literature Review," 9–11), but overall it appears that changes in marginal rates have little to do with the total amount of giving, though change may have a significant effect on the timing of giving as donors seek to take advantage of financial benefits either immediately before or immediately after changes in the tax code. While probably contrary to public perception, that finding does make sense. It will almost always be cheaper not to give at all, so the tax code is not really an incentive to give but rather just a reduction in the cost of giving. In that framework, small adjustments in marginal rates are unlikely to encourage or reduce giving materially.

13. One of the ironies of major-donor involvement in charities is that it is the lower-income classes that have been shown to be among the most philanthropic of Americans, by donating a significant percentage of their income to charities. Frank Greve, "America's Poor Are Its Most Generous Givers," McClatchy Newspapers, May 19, 2009 (citing U.S. Bureau of Labor Statistics data), http://www.mcclatchydc.com/2009/05/19/68456/americas-poor-are-its-most-generous.html. Those making less than $19,000 a year, representing the bottom 20 percent of the income pool, on average give 4.3 percent of their income to charities, a number almost twice the average for all Americans. There is a counterintuitive, inverse relationship between wealth and giving, with the two top quintiles giving only 2.1 percent and 2.0 percent of their incomes. The relative generosity of lower-income groups is accentuated by two facts. First, many of the poorest Americans have little discretionary income, and contributing to charity creates trade-offs that higher-income individuals simply do not face. Second, since the vast majority of poor and lower-income taxpayers do not itemize, they cannot take advantage of the financial incentives for their charitable behavior. Only wealthier taxpayers, who itemize on their federal filings, gain economic advantage from the system. No one should be shocked when a tax system favors the wealthier income classes over the middle and lower classes, but when that system is our charitable system—a significant goal of which is to level the playing field for people of lesser means—it is at least an ironic codicil on the policy conversation.

14. Steve Wieberg, "Pickens Understands UConn Donor's Anger," *USA Today,* January 28, 2011.

15. Kris Hundley, "Billionaire's Role in Hiring Decisions at Florida State University Raises Questions," *St. Petersburg Times,* May 10, 2011.

16. Michael Keenan, "CEOs Pushing Ayn Rand Studies Use Money to Over-

come Resistance," Bloomberg, April 11, 2008. By 2008, the BB&T Foundation had given Rand-inspired grants to twenty-seven different colleges, not including a handful of schools such as Meredith College, which first accepted a gift but then returned it after faculty successfully protested the requirement that *Atlas Shrugged* be added to the curriculum. In June 2012, Allison became president of the libertarian Cato Institute in Washington, D.C. His ascension at Cato amicably resolved a control and funding dispute between the organization and its largest donors, the Koch brothers.

17. Stephanie Strom, "Donors Add Watchdog Role to Relations with Charities," *New York Times,* March 29, 2003.

18. Video interview of Adele Smithers-Fornaci by Professor Samuel Bacharach, November 12, 2004, previously available on the Web site of the R. Brinkley Smithers Institute for Alcohol-Related Workplace Studies at the ILR School of Cornell University, http://www.ilr.cornell.edu /smithers/. As of last review, the video was no longer available on the Web site.

19. Brook Hersey, "The Controlled Drinking Debates: A Review of Four Decades of Acrimony" (Rutgers University, working paper, April 2001), http://www.doctordeluca.com/Library/AbstinenceHR/FourDecades Acrimony.htm; Keith Humphreys, "Alcohol and Drug Abuse: A Research-Based Analysis of the Moderation Management Controversy," *Psychiatric Services* 54, no. 5 (2003): 621, http://ps.psychiatryonline.org/article .aspx?articleID=180545.

20. Stephanie Strom, "New Wealth, and Worries, for the Salvation Army," *New York Times,* August 4, 2006.

21. Matthew Bishop and Michael Green, *Philanthrocapitalism: How Giving Can Save the World* (New York: Bloomsbury Press, 2008), 194–213. In addition to "celanthropist" and "philanthrocapitalism," Bishop and Green coined the terms "philanthropreneurship" and "billanthropy." None have yet caught on.

22. Adam Nagourney, "Madonna's Charity Fails in Bid to Finance School," *New York Times,* March 24, 2011.

23. Jo Piazza, "Beware Celebrity Charities: Madonna's Rising Malawi Fiasco Shows Risks of Unproven Charity Organizations," Foxnews.com, March 29, 2011.

24. Hope Consulting, "Money for Good: The U.S. Market for Impact Investments and Charitable Gifts from Individual Donors and Investors" (unpublished survey, May 2010), http://www.hopeconsulting.us/pdf /Money%20for%20Good_Final.pdf. Surveys on this question, however, are not uniform. In one well-known study, researchers in the Netherlands

found "effectiveness" to be only required or preferred by half of respondents. Jos van Iwaarden, Ton van der Wiele, Roger Williams, and Claire Moxham, "Charities: How Important Is Performance to Donors?," *International Journal of Quality and Reliability Management* 26, no. 1 (2009): 5–22. It is hard to know whether to chalk up the differences to cultural norms or to data differences, but the indifference to charitable effectiveness of half the survey group in the van Iwaarden study is a stunning finding regardless of the reason.

25. Hope Consulting, "Money for Good," 20.

26. Ranjani Krishnan, Michelle Yetman, and Robert J. Yetman, "Financial Disclosure Management by Nonprofit Organizations" (University of California at Berkeley, working paper, 2003), cited in van Iwaarden, van der Wiele, Williams, and Moxham, "Charities."

27. Mrs. Astor married Vincent Astor in 1953, the third marriage for each. The marriage was widely perceived in New York society as an arranged one. The novelist Louis Auchincloss, a close friend of Mrs. Astor's, said at the time, "Of course she married Vincent for the money . . . I wouldn't respect her if she hadn't. Only a twisted person would have married him for love." But the marriage apparently had more than financial rewards. She called him Captain; he called her Pookie. When Vincent died in 1959, Brooke took over his philanthropic interests, serving on the board of the Metropolitan Museum of Art and as a major benefactor of the New York Public Library. Liesl Schillinger, "Astor's Place," *New York Times,* June 17, 2007.

28. The gloss on the Monitor Group became a little tarnished in 2011 when it was revealed that it had taken on Libya as a large client. Much of the work provided to Libya and its then leader, Muammar Gaddafi, was in the realm of advice on economic reform and liberalization, seemingly well within the expertise of Monitor and consistent with the general rapprochement then going on between Gaddafi and Western leaders. But the Monitor work eventually slid into other areas, including a campaign to bring American "thought leaders" to see the new Libya, more akin to public relations than management consulting. The association with Gaddafi brought considerable and unwelcome publicity to Monitor, and a subsequent internal investigation by the Washington, D.C., law firm of Covington & Burling concluded that Monitor should have registered with the U.S. Treasury Department as a foreign agent. Coincident with the publication of the report, the CEO, Mark Fuller, stepped down in a move described by Monitor as long planned. Farah Stockman, "Firm Says It Erred on Libya Consulting," *Boston Globe,* May 6, 2011.

29. New Profit also received some unwanted notoriety around its award from the Social Innovation Fund. Paul Light, a prominent nonprofit expert and one of the reviewers of grant proposals for the Social Innovation Fund, complained in his *Washington Post* blog about the incestuous nature of the process, specifically that New Profit had won a major grant after helping create the fund and providing it with its executive director, Paul Carttar (who recused himself from involvement in New Profit's application). Light also complained that New Profit won a role despite the fact that its application was weak and had drawn negative reviews during the evaluation process. Suzanne Perry, "Amid Concerns of Favoritism, Federal Officials Disclose New Details on Selection Process," *Chronicle of Philanthropy*, August 23, 2010.

Chapter 6: Million-Dollar Babies

1. Charity Navigator 2009 CEO Compensation Study, August 2009, http://blog.charitynavigator.org/2009/08/charity-navigators-2009-ceo.html.
2. Jim Dwyer, "Immune to Cuts: Lofty Salaries at Hospitals," *New York Times*, March 15, 2011.
3. Maggie Mahar, "High CEO Salaries at Nonprofit Hospitals Under Scrutiny . . . Once Again," www.healthbeatblog.com, March 24, 2011.
4. Jay Hancock, "For Hospitals, 'Nonprofit' Stops with CEO Paychecks," *Baltimore Sun*, August 29, 2010.
5. Dwyer, "Immune to Cuts."
6. "St. Vincent's Files for Bankruptcy," *New York Times*, April 14, 2010.
7. Blue Cross and Blue Shield Associations are among the mongrels of the charitable world. Blue Cross was originally created early in the twentieth century as a hospitalization plan for teachers, and for most of its history it was treated as a social welfare organization. In the Tax Reform Act of 1986, Blue Cross was reclassified because it sold commercial products, but its status under IRS section 501(m) is still tax advantaged. On the state level, many Blue Cross Associations are classified as public charities, though a number of state plans have transitioned to for-profit status over the years. This has led to an odd mix of status and tax treatments that differ from state to state and plan to plan—even though all the plans operate more or less the same, regardless of classification.
8. That statement is true when it comes to executive compensation, though the highest-paid employees of charitable institutions are probably the basketball and football coaches at private Division I universities. For example,

Lane Kiffin, the football coach at the University of Southern California, makes a reported $4 million a year. Mike Brey, the head basketball coach at Notre Dame, makes a comparatively modest salary of $600,000 (though income from endorsements, camps, and speaking engagements will likely more than double that amount), but Notre Dame did pay $6.6 million in 2009 just to get rid of its head football coach, Charlie Weis.

9. Part of the discontent around pay relates to the opaque manner in which it is reported. Onetime events can radically change how compensation is reported. The Evans Scholars Foundation did not routinely pay its CEO into the millions. Johnson's salary in previous years was on the order of $200,000 a year—not bad pay for doling out dollars to caddies but probably not worthy of national note. Johnson retired in 2008, and his compensation ballooned in that year—likely because of additional payouts related to retirement planning. I experienced some of that myself when I left NPR. When I was promoted from COO to CEO, I knew that my political support from the board was razor thin and that what I needed more than anything else was time to push NPR toward its digital future. I therefore told the board chair that I didn't want a pay raise but I did want a commitment reflected in a multiyear contract. As it turned out, my contract did not in fact buy me that time, but it did mean that NPR owed me the equivalent of three years of compensation when I was pushed out the door in 2008. My annual salary as CEO was a little over $300,000, and under relevant accounting rules NPR had to report compensation for me of an amount just north of $1 million in the year that I was fired. That number hardly reflected the level of compensation that I (and other NPR executives) typically received, but that would have been difficult for any casual reader to divine from NPR's public filings.

10. Russ Buettner, "Reaping Millions in Nonprofit Care for the Disabled," *New York Times,* August 2, 2011.

11. The great majority of Grasso's compensation in 2003 was the payment by the NYSE of deferred compensation and retirement benefits. These payments were in fact part of a larger compensation arrangement that included a plan to pay Grasso an additional $48 million over the next four years. As the controversy unfolded, Grasso agreed to forgo the $48 million, but that concession was not enough to save his job.

12. Tomas Kellner and Robert Lenzner, "One Hand Giveth . . . ," *Forbes,* October 27, 2003.

13. James C. McKinley and Robbie Brown, "Sex Scandal Threatens a Georgia Pastor's Empire," *New York Times,* September 25, 2010.

14. Dale Russell, "Pay Cuts at New Birth Missionary Baptist Church," www

.myfoxatlanta.com, March 2, 2011. Bishop Long and the church drew additional unwanted attention when they were sued by four former parishioners who alleged that Long coerced them into sexual relations. That suit was settled out of court for an undisclosed amount in May 2011.

15. "Bishop Eddie Long Benefits from His Own Church's Charity," *Atlanta Journal-Constitution,* August 28, 2005, reprinted at http://www.ajc.com /news/2005-ajc-report-bishop-619032.html.

16. Jenny Jarvie, "Is Prosperity a Blessing from God, or a Crime?," *Los Angeles Times,* November 12, 2007.

17. Ibid. Jarvie's article contained the following quotations from parishioners:

> "Yes, a minister turns heads when he drives a Bentley," said Democratic state Rep. Randal Mangham, a member of New Birth Missionary Baptist Church in Lithonia, Ga., one of the ministries being investigated. "But that's good. It's important for kids to see you don't have to sell drugs to drive a nice car."
>
> Connie Cotton, 41, a longtime member of World Changers, said, "We give to our pastor because he's a true man of God. He needs a jet to go around the world and preach the Gospel."

18. Katie Thomas and Michael Schmidt, "Questions Arise About Executive's Pay at Dodgers Charity," *New York Times,* July 8, 2010.

19. www.charitywatch.org/articles/feedchildren.html.

20. Ames Alexander, "CEOs Profit from Nonprofits," *Charlotte News Observer,* December 20, 2009.

21. Ellen Gabler, "$685,000 a Year to Run Nonprofit: Executive Receives High Salary to Run Low- and Moderate-Income Housing," *Chicago Tribune,* January 13, 2010.

22. To be fair to Gallagher, he has not been convicted, as Aramony was, of twenty-five federal crimes, including mail fraud, tax fraud, and wire fraud, or embroiled, as Aramony was, in a sex scandal. Aramony was sentenced to eighty-four months in prison and served his time at the federal prison camp at Seymour Johnson Air Force Base near Goldsboro, North Carolina. He was released from prison in September 2001 and died in 2011.

23. It can be assumed from these numbers that the Charity Navigator survey excluded highly compensated industries such as the hospital sector and the college sports world.

24. Brian Vogel and Charles Quatt, *Nonprofit Executive Compensation: Planning Performance and Pay,* 2nd ed. (Washington, D.C.: Board Source, 2010), 6.

25. Scott Shane, "How Much Do Small Business Owners Make?," smallbiztrends.com, November 15, 2010.
26. Brad Hamilton, "D.A. Eyes St. Vinny's 'Go-for-Broke' Plan," *New York Post,* August 21, 2011.
27. Anemona Hartocollis, "The Decline of St. Vincent's Hospital," *New York Times,* February 2, 2010.
28. Vogel and Quatt, *Nonprofit Executive Compensation,* 6.

Chapter 7: Dawn of the New Charity

1. Lawler and his colleagues have been well compensated for their success. In the most recent public filings, Youth Villages reported that it had paid Lawler approximately $570,000 for the year. Other company executives were also well compensated, if not exactly on the same scale as Lawler: the chief marketing officer made almost $360,000, the chief financial officer made $315,000, and three other members of the management team received exactly or just shy of $300,000 in total compensation. Without access to generally confidential salary surveys, it is hard to know whether these salaries are high, low, or average for executives at similarly sized social service organizations, but no doubt the compensation arrangements will strike many as high for an organization that relies entirely on governmental contracts and private donations. But it is not too high a price for building a best-in-class organization that has transformed the youth services sector and has made a measurable difference in the lives of tens of thousands of troubled youths. People might better save their complaints for the compensation practices at the many, many mediocre charities that cannot demonstrate any positive impact for their service groups.
2. Other tested programs, including the wonderfully named HIPPY program (Home Instruction Program for Preschool Youngsters), have not generated results sufficient to draw conclusions about effectiveness.
3. Robert Boruch, Brooke Snyder, and Dorothy DeMoya, "The Importance of Randomized Field Trials," *Crime and Delinquency* 46, no. 2 (April 2000): 156–80.
4. Ron Haskins, Christina Paxson, and Jeanne Brooks-Gunn, "Social Science Rising: A Tale of Evidence Shaping Public Policy" (Princeton-Brookings Future of Children Policy Brief, 2009).
5. While Incredible Years has undoubtedly been more rigorously tested than virtually any other school program of similar size, it has occasionally been

challenged because of the lack of longitudinal studies—studies that show the long-term impact of the program. All existing studies have been limited to one-year assessments.

Chapter 8: Creating an Effective Charitable Marketplace

1. Coalition for Evidence-Based Policy, "Rigorous Program Evaluations on a Budget: How Low-Cost Randomized Controlled Trials Are Possible in Many Areas of Social Policy" (working paper, 2012), http://coalition4evidence.org/wordpress/wp-content/uploads/Rigorous-Program-Evaluations-on-a-Budget-March-2012.pdf. Since early 2012, I have been a board member of the Coalition for Evidence-Based Policy, a Washington, D.C.–based group that advocates for a greater role for empirical evidence in government and funding decisions.

2. The Better Business Bureau's Charity Seal program pledges to "look beyond the numbers" to evaluate a wide range of organizational practices. To qualify for the Charity Seal, a charity must apply to the BBB's Wise Giving Alliance and be prepared to pay up to $15,000 a year for the privilege.

3. Clayton Christensen, "The White House Office on Social Innovation: A New Paradigm for Solving Social Problems," *Huffington Post,* July 1, 2009.

4. Elizabeth Boris, Erwin de Leon, Katie Roeger, and Milena Nikolova, *Human Services Nonprofits and Government Collaboration: Findings from the 2010 National Survey of Nonprofit Government Contracting and Grants* (Urban Institute, 2010), http://www.urban.org/uploadedpdf/412228-nonprofit-government-contracting.pdf.

5. Memorandum to the Heads of Executive Departments and Agencies, "Use of Evidence and Evaluation in the 2014 Budget" (May 18, 2012), http://www.whitehouse.gov/sites/default/files/omb/memoranda/2012/m-12-14_1.pdf.

6. In 1999, for instance, the District of Columbia City Council created the DC Children and Youth Investment Trust Corporation to make independent judgments about which charities would best address problems facing local youths. As a private, nongovernmental organization, it has been able to raise money not only from the city but also from individual donors, local foundations, and major sports teams. In concept, the DC Trust is an example of the broad opportunity to leverage public money to create more effective social investment strategies. In practice, however, the effort has apparently fallen prey to corruption and political influence peddling.

Isaac Arnsdorf, "D.C. Council Uses Trusts to Fund Charities," *Washington Post,* August 12, 2011. According to a *Washington Post* investigation, the independence of the DC Trust was compromised by D.C. council members who repeatedly steered trust grants to pet projects and favored organizations, including organizations run by their major political contributors. Rather than being best-in-class youth charities, some of the recipient organizations were of dubious vintage, including several that the *Post* could not even find. The politicization of the trust's activities came to light during a related controversy involving the council member Harry Thomas, who steered money through the trust to his controlled charity, Team Thomas. Team Thomas in turn used the funds to buy Thomas a luxury vehicle and other non-charitable baubles. Thomas resigned his council seat in 2012 and subsequently pleaded guilty to embezzlement. He is currently serving a thirty-eight-month sentence in federal prison.

7. Dan Pallotta, *Uncharitable: How Restraints on Nonprofits Undermine Their Potential* (Medford, Mass.: Tufts University Press, 2008), 174. To be precise, Pallotta puts the number at $1.03 billion.

8. The one exception to this truism is the 2006 rule "delisting" charities that have not filed federal tax returns for three years running. This has mostly affected smaller charities with revenues under $50,000 that are eligible to file Form 990-N, known as the e-Postcard.

9. Quoted in Marion R. Fremont-Smith, *Governing Nonprofit Organizations: Federal and State Law and Regulation* (Cambridge, Mass.: Belknap Press of Harvard University Press, 2004), 443.

10. Sharon Hoffman, "For U.S. Charities, a Crisis of Trust," *NBC News,* November 21, 2006.

11. René Bekkers, "Trust, Accreditation, and Philanthropy in the Netherlands," *Nonprofit and Voluntary Sector Quarterly* 32, no. 4 (2003): 596–615.

12. Singer, *Life You Can Save,* 150.

13. Associated Press, "9/11 Charities Under Scrutiny for Failing to Raise Money for Victims," *Huffington Post,* August 25, 2011.

14. Peter Marks, "A New NEA Bomb: Too Many Arts Venues," *Washington Post,* February 13, 2011.

15. Rob Reich, Lacey Dorn, and Stefanie Sutton, "Anything Goes: Approval of Nonprofit Status by the IRS" (Stanford University Center on Philanthropy and Civil Society, unpublished paper, 2009), http://www.stanford.edu/group/reichresearch/cgi-bin/site/wp-content/uploads/2009/11/Anything-Goes-PACS-11-09.pdf.

INDEX

Page numbers beginning with 217 refer to notes.

South Carolina, University of,
  Medical School, 179
Southern California, University of,
  240
Specter, Arlen, 45–46
Spitzer, Eliot, 162
Starmann, Dick, 129
Statute of Charitable Uses (1601),
  54–55
Stern, Ken, 14–15, 125–29, 240
Strauss, Lewis, 226
Stroger Hospital, 77–78, 83, 226–27
Sugar Bowl, 89–95
Sullivan, Brendan, 139
Sun Bowl, 91
Sunkin, Howard, 166
Supreme Court, U.S.:
  Brown v. *Board of Education* ruling
    of, 224
  gifts as defined by, 132
  Vidal ruling of, 57, 224
sustainability, 180

Taft, William Howard, 99
Tariff Act of 1894, 76
Task Force on Private Sector
  Initiatives, 64
taxes:
  charitable donations as exempt from,
    3, 60–62, 75, 98, 102–3, 208,
    236
  charities as exempt from, 3, 74–75,
    77, 88–95, 97, 98, 100, 103,
    208, 217
  proposed time limits on exemptions
    from, 213–14
Tax Reform Act (1986), 239
Teacher Classroom Management
  Program, 197
Team Thomas, 122, 244

Teledesic, 191–92
telemarketing firms, 107, 111–12,
  210–11
Testerman, Jeff, 108
Texas Children's Hospital, 86
Thomas, Harry, 122, 244
Thompson, Bobby, 107, 111, 231
Thrower, Randolph, 109
TIAA-CREF, 101
Tocqueville, Alexis de, 54
total patient treatment, 43
Tournament of Roses, 90–91
Transparency International, 219–20
Trinity Broadcasting Network, 165
21st Century Community Learning
  Centers (21st CCLC), 39–45
typhoid, 19

Uganda, water wells in, 18, 25
Union Square Day Care Center,
  184–85
United Homeless Organization
  (UHO), 113–14
United States:
  expanded global role of, 61
  social problems confronted by, 152
United States Golf Association
  (USGA), 98–100
United Way Worldwide, 36, 169–70
Unrelated Business Income Tax
  (UBIT; 1950), 100
Upward Bound, 222
urbanization, water supplies and, 24,
  219–20
U.S. Navy Veterans Association
  (USNVA), 106–9, 111

Vanderbilt, Alva and William, 59
Vanderbilt, Cornelius, 58
Vanderbilt, George, 59

Ken Stern is the CEO of Palisades Media Ventures, a digital media content company, and the former CEO of National Public Radio (1999–2008). He lives in Washington, D.C., with his wife, Beth, and his son, Nate.